D1068855

Dilemmas of Democracy

TOCQUEVILLE and Modernization

Seymour Drescher

Dilemmas *of* Democracy

Tocqueville and Modernization

University of Pittsburgh Press

Library of Congress
Catalog Card Number: 68–12725
Copyright © 1968,
University of Pittsburgh Press
Manufactured in the
United States of America

To George L. Mosse

Preface

This book began innocently enough when I was editing for publication some essays by Alexis de Tocqueville and Gustave de Beaumont on French social problems during the July Monarchy and the Second Republic. After I had begun the initial chapters, it became apparent to me that the only satisfactory way of presenting the material was to show how certain seemingly peripheral concerns affected and ultimately altered central themes of Tocqueville's social thought. And from the tension between center and periphery there emerge, I hope, some novel insights into the entire pattern of his intellectual development. The observer of this intellectual struggle is driven to seek the sources of the man's thought in the social and the intellectual environment he inhabited. In some of its passages, to be sure, the life of the mind bears seemingly little relation to the more obvious and general elements of the environment, and here, where the search becomes most tantalizing, I must confess my own curiosity was more often aroused than satisfied. But the social context from which one views the world is often distinctive enough to account for intellectual options that otherwise would be only logical possibilities. If one imaginatively inspects the baggage of even the most far-ranging intellectual voyage one can form some estimate of its scope and its limitations—perhaps a more accurate one than the voyager himself does. One may also hope to perceive how important are items the traveler never even thought to take along because there seemed to be no need of them. Tocqueville's was such a voyage.

Although some of my indebtedness for this study has previously been acknowledged in *Tocqueville and Beaumont on Social Reform* (Harper & Row, 1968), I did not include a note of thanks for some of the archival resources that are utilized in this book. The Tocqueville and Beaumont manuscript collection at the Beinecke Library of Yale University was, as always, indispensable to my work. The Archives des Affaires Etrangères in Paris, and the Public Records Office and the British Museum in London, the Huntington Library in San Marino, California, and the Houghton Library at Harvard University provided useful materials. The Archives Nationales in Paris, whose *archives privées* were made accessible by Mme. Chantal de Tourtier Bonazzi, proved invaluable, as did those of the Section Outre-Mer. The Library staff of Trinity College, Cambridge, deserves a special note of gratitude for the sheer physical effort required to help haul trunks full of Monckton Milnes' papers into the light of day. Thanks to the invitation of the present Comte de Tocqueville, I also had the opportunity to use the library at the Chateau de Tocqueville, and to enjoy the hospitality of its gracious host. Julius Rubin, Samuel Hays, William Stanton, and Orysia Karapinka, who read greater or lesser portions of the manuscript, all deserve a word of recognition for their involvement, and one of exemption from responsibility for the outcome.

S.D.

Contents

Dilemmas of Democracy

TOCQUEVILLE and Modernization

I

Introduction

OF all the projections of social development written at the juncture of the industrial and democratic revolutions in Western Europe, or, at least at the moment of greatest psychological impact, Alexis de Tocqueville's analysis remains one of the most enduring and remarkable. It takes its place beside the optimistic vision of a scientific-industrial society, forecast by the Saint-Simonians and Positivists, and the specter of total social crisis and transformation prophesied by Marx. All three portraits of the future were derived from an emphasis on a salient characteristic of the present, perceived as its principal tendency. Each saw the importance of the phenomena studied—democracy, science, and capitalism—in terms both of assessments of fundamental social causal relations and of the relative degree of social change wrought by the subject of their investigations.

Tocqueville's vision was the one most rapidly accorded serious recognition by the intellectual and political community of his time. Contrary to the mythology which evolved after his reputation fell into eclipse, he was one of those few prophets who were accorded instant honor in their own countries and abroad by all shades of the reviewing public: "It has been the rare fortune of M. de Tocqueville's book to have achieved an easy triumph," began John Stuart Mill in the most famous of the reviews of *Democracy in America*. It was indeed rare fortune to be immediately dubbed the Montesquieu of the nineteenth century by the elder statesman and Academician Royer-Collard, and to have this metaphor reverberate through the reviews. Within a few years, on the strength of one book, Tocqueville had been elected to two seats in the French Academies, to two legislative bodies, and had rebuilt his chateau with the prizes and royalties from the *Democracy*.

But Tocqueville's star also waned more rapidly than those of Saint-Simon and Marx. Although he had made the most of being well connected at the outset of his career, he was in voluntary isolation, still universally esteemed but without either power or place, when he died in 1859. He left behind no sect, movement, or political party to maintain his authority by means of constant reformulation or ritual invocation. Sustained by its intellectual and emotional power alone, Tocqueville's influence began to decline in the decade following his death, after a brief revival as a hero of liberal democracy. During the last generation, however, after a quiescence of almost half a century, interest in Tocqueville has undergone a remarkable renais-

Introduction

sance.¹ His reputation as a social thinker has never stood
higher, nor has his work ever been so widely read and
analyzed, even eliciting for the first time, to my knowledge,
non-Western scholarly interest.² In our own society his
authority is invoked at all levels of our political culture on

1. This statement applies more to Tocqueville's reputation as a
political philosopher and sociologist than to his standing as an
historian of the French Revolution. His *Ancien Régime* continued
to be reprinted regularly throughout the nineteenth and twentieth
centuries. In France a total of sixteen editions appeared between
1856 and 1934, while in Germany and England republications were
also frequent. See J.-P. Mayer, "Histoire de l'influence de l'Ancien
Régime," in Tocqueville, *Oeuvres complètes*, ed. J.-P. Mayer (Paris,
1951–), II, *L'Ancien Régime et la Révolution*, I, 337; this edition will
hereafter be cited as *Oeuvres* (M). Furthermore, Tocqueville continued to receive steady international recognition as an historian
from the most eminent members of the discipline. Even when the
Ancien Régime, like his other words, was more frequently analyzed
in terms of class identification around the beginning of this century,
it was still praised for its relative independence of class values. The
posthumous publication of his *Souvenirs* (Paris, 1893) and of his
correspondence with Arthur de Gobineau provided material for
French contemporaries which, for a time, seemed to be closer to their
concerns than his observations on America or his speculations on
democratic society. On the reemphasis of Tocqueville's contemporaneity as an historian in France see Marcel Reinhard, "Tocqueville, his-
torien de la Révolution" in *Alexis de Tocqueville: Livre du centenaire, 1859–1959*, Editions du Centre National de la Recherche Scien-
tifique (Paris, 1960), 171–180; George Rudé, *Revolutionary Europe,
1783–1815* (New York, 1964), 68–75; and C. B. A. Behrens, *The Ancien
Régime* (London, New York, 1967), *passim*. The general revival of
interest in France, besides the writers for the *Livre du centenaire*,
has been furthered by René Rémond, Jean-Jacques Chevallier, Ber-
trand de Jouvenal, and especially Raymond Aron.

2. K. Ogawa, "Tocqueville Cho 'America Democracy' Kenkyuno
Genjo [The Study of Tocqueville's *Democracy in America*]," *Nokka
Gakkai Zasschi*, LXXVIII (Jan. 1958), 65–92; Ogawa, "Tocqueville no Taishu Shakei Riron [Tocqueville's Theory of Mass So-
ciety]," *Shiso*, CDV (March 1958), 95–112; and Y. Takagi, "Tocque-

a constantly ascending curve, by presidents as well as scholars and teachers.[3]

The explanation for revival seems to lie roughly in the conjunction of three important phenomena. The first was the sudden and sustained preeminence of the United States on the world scene after the Second World War. There was a renewed interest on both sides of the Atlantic in the classic nineteenth-century European commentary on America. The second factor, related to the first, was the "Americanization" of Western European society to a greater degree than ever before. Relatively rapid institutional democratization was accompanied by the rapid development of mass consumer culture, and by a decline in classical nineteenth- and twentieth-century European ideologies, all against the background of unprecedented economic growth and prosperity. Finally, the dualism of Europe created by the Cold War tended to encourage an emphasis on Tocqueville, with his liberal democratic values, as an alternative to Marxism in its Stalinist incarnation. Tocqueville's explicit contrast of America and Russia as prototypes of the world's future only enhanced this propensity. One of the intellectual fringe assets of *Democracy in America* was its

---

ville's Exposition of Democracy," *Kokka Gakkai Zasschi* [*Journal of the Association of Political and Social Sciences*], LXX (1956), no. 10, 749–767.

3. A striking indication of the contemporaneity or perhaps the timeliness of Tocqueville's writings was given by the *Daedalus* (Journal of the American Academy of Arts and Science) issue on "Mass Culture and Mass Media" (Spring 1960). Not only is Tocqueville listed as the sole posthumous contributor to the issue, but his contribution, excerpted from portions of *Democracy in America*, is printed, like those of the living contributors, without any introductory note.

climactic if marginal prophecy that America and Russia were destined to divide the world between them. At one critical historical moment at least, this prophecy served its author's reputation splendidly.

These phenomena do not, of course, explain all the ways in which Tocqueville's ideas have been interpreted in the last generation, nor do they constitute any sort of historical limit on the creative imagination of scholars, who, for example, have found him suggestive as a comparative sociologist of revolution, as an interpreter of the evolution of modern societies, or as a pioneer of that elusive but compelling sociological concept, national character.[4] I doubt,

---

4. On Tocqueville as an analyst of national character, see, among others, David Riesman, "Tocqueville as Ethnographer" *The American Scholar*, XXX (Spring 1961), 174–184; Riesman with Nathan Glazer and Reuel Denny, *The Lonely Crowd, A Study of the Changing American Character* (Glencoe, Ill., 1961); Seymour Martin Lipset, *The First New Nation: The United States in Historical and Comparative Perspective* (New York, 1963); Louis Hartz, *The Liberal Tradition in America: An Interpretation of American Political Thought Since the Revolution* (New York, 1955); K. D. Naegele, "From De Tocqueville to Myrdal: A Research Memorandum on Selected Studies of American Values," Comparative Study of Values, No. 1 (Oct. 1949), Laboratory of Social Relations, Harvard University. On Tocqueville as an analyst of revolution see, above all, the introduction by G. Lefebvre to *L'Ancien Régime et la Révolution*, II, 1, in *Oeuvres* (M), and Mayer's "Histoire de l'influence de l'Ancien Régime" in the same volume; Lefebvre, "A propos de Tocqueville," *Annales historiques de la Révolution française* (Oct.-Dec. 1955); Richard Herr, *Tocqueville and the Old Regime* (Princeton, 1962); Melvin Richter, "Tocqueville's Contribution to the Theory of Revolution," in C. Friedrich, *Revolution* (New York, 1966) 75–121; Gilbert Shapiro, *Quantitative Studies of the French Revolution*, Second Annual Progress Report, mimeograph, 1965, Part I; Shapiro, "The Implicit Theory of Tocqueville's 'The Old Regime and the French Revolution,' " unpublished paper, delivered April 11, 1959;

however, whether Tocqueville's ideas would appear so relevant to the mature democratic industrial societies of the world without the presence of at least the first two conditions given above. It is only this generation that has made his quest for a new science of politics seem more relevant to our new world.

Tocqueville has reemerged in recent years as the pioneer sociologist and political philosopher of the modern world, and of the age of the democratic revolution. His ideal types of aristocratic and democratic man have been widely accepted as useful points of departure for attempting to understand the historical process called modernization. And his method of emphasizing institutional and psychological tendencies, of working within a framework of a logic of probabilities rather than of determinism, has endeared him to a significant group of contemporary scholars.

There is one aspect of modernization, however, with which Tocqueville's name has only very recently been linked: the transition from a preindustrial to an industrial society. Raymond Aron in Europe, and Reinhard Bendix in America, to name only the most prominent, have made serious attempts to apply the Tocquevillian analysis of modernity to their own analyses of the development and characteristics of modern societies. Both emphasize Tocqueville's characterization of the limited egalitarian ideology which allowed for, and presupposed, certain inequalities and authority-obedience relationships in the organization of society. Both contrast this emphasis on permissible and

---

Sasha Reinhard Wietman, "The Sociological Thesis of Tocqueville's *The Old Regime and the Revolution*," *Social Research*, XXXIII (Autumn 1966), 389–406.

necessary inequalities within general equality, with Marx's insistence on the primary and inflexible inequalities created by the capitalist economic system and industrial technology, which in time would produce ever more intensive social stratification, economic inequality, and, finally, revolutionary social change.[5]

5. Among the works which explicitly contrast Tocquevillian and Marxian analysis or value systems prophets are: Raymond Aron, *Le Developpement de la société industrielle et la stratification sociale,* Cours de Sorbonne (Paris, n.d.), *Essai sur les libertés* (Paris, 1965), and *Main Currents in Sociological Thought* (New York, 1965); Robert A. Nisbet, *The Sociological Tradition* (New York, 1966); Hartz, *The Liberal Tradition in America*; George Probst, *The Happy Republic: A Reader in Tocqueville's America* (New York, 1962); Seymour Martin Lipset, *Political Man* (New York, 1960); Edward T. Gargan, *Alexis de Tocqueville: The Critical Years, 1848–1851* (Washington, D.C., 1955); Kurt Georg Kiesinger, *Die Prognosen des Grafen Alexis de Tocqueville am Beginn des Industrial en Zeitalters* (Karlsruhe, 1961); Imanuel Geiss, "Tocqueville und Karl Marx, Eine vergleichende Analyse," *Die neue Gesellschaft,* Bd. 6/1959, 237–240; Jack Lively, *The Social and Political Thought of Alexis de Tocqueville* (Oxford, 1962); Albert Salomon, *In Praise of Enlightenment* (New York, 1963); J.-P. Mayer, "Alexis de Tocqueville und Karl Marx: Affinitaten und Gegensatze," *Zeitschrift fur Politik* (1966), and his introductions to *Journeys to England and Ireland* (New Haven, 1958) and *The Recollections of Alexis de Tocqueville* (New York, 1959); Max Lerner, Introduction to *Democracy in America,* ed. J.-P. Mayer and Max Lerner, trans. George Lawrence (New York, 1966; subsequent references to the *Democracy* will be from this edition). There has also been a tendency, perhaps already on the decline, to confront Marx with Tocqueville in an intellectual equivalent of the Western showdown. This implies an approach to Tocqueville's thought in terms of "Tocqueville or Marx," or as one writer has put in concisely, "To those who ask, 'What is the importance of Tocqueville in modern world politics?' it is enough to reply that he is the answer to Marx" (Probst, *The Happy Republic,* xiii). This far from unique example can be set off against the Soviet historian M. A. Alpatov's dismissal of Tocqueville's influence as flowing exclusively along class

In the Tocquevillian model, according to these analysts, classes become more ambiguous, economic inequalities less extreme and more acceptable because they are more closely identified with the necessities of economic growth. In the other model, man's behavior is more fundamentally determined by his socio-economic position in society than

---

lines (see "Les idées politiques d'Alexis de Tocqueville" in *Luttes sociales et idéologies politiques en France au XIXᵉ siècle*, 140–168 [Paris, 1954]). This seems to reflect the Cold War atmosphere in the most articulate way. Even where current events are slightly less obtrusive, the vindication of Tocqueville against Marx, either as a realist toward his own age or a prophet of the future, produces counterattacks like James Keeny's "Tocqueville and the New Politics," *New Politics*, I, no. 3 (Spring 1962), 58–65. At a more scholarly level Tocqueville and Marx are placed "at opposite theoretical extremes" and the triumph of the "Tocquevillian over the Marxian image of society and its course of development" is also linked to the context of contemporary revolutions, with parenthetical acknowledgment that the "writ of Marx" may supersede the present ascendency of Tocqueville even in the West (Robert Nisbet, *The Sociological Tradition*, vii). Fundamentally, Nisbet's historical frame of reference is similar to that of Aron and Bendix—and to that of Tocqueville in 1835: that the Western world is in the period of accomplished revolutions, urban, democratic, industrial, etc., which allows us to view revolution as a stage which others must endure but with which we have come to terms, and which we can identify as transitional and temporary. We are at the end of discontinuous historical change with its polarized ideological contortions. In essence, the West finally is where Tocqueville thought France to be exactly a century and a quarter ago—at the end of the era of social revolution. But there is a more subtle form of comparison in the opposite direction that has also tended to distort the analysis of Tocqueville's thought—a felt need to prove that Tocqueville and Marx converged in their analysis of industrial society. J.-P. Mayer, A. Salomon, Kurt Georg Kiesinger, and others have made him a precursor of Engels or even a proto-Marxist on the basis of his observations of Manchester and the factory system, although similar and earlier observations may be found all the way from the liberal economists to the ministers and prefects of Charles X of France. H.

by the generalized value system of his political culture. On the one side is a thinker who supposedly emphasized democracy's thrust toward equality of expectations and obligations, on the other a thinker who underlined the increasing division of labor, new forms of social stratification, and enduring inequalities in the distribution of wealth and power. Following Tocqueville, both Bendix and Aron emphasize the necessity of distinguishing between the political and social processes of democratization, used in the broad sense, and the economic and social processes of industrialization. Both explicitly insist on the relative autonomy of the political process and of value systems from technological and economic variables.[6]

In this light, Tocqueville's thought is of value as a framework for the explanation of the failure of the industrial system, with its division of labor, its inequalities of authority and obedience, to lead to a new hierarchical society, or its subsequent overthrow. Revolutionary and messianic demands for an end to possessor-proletarian and authority-

---

J. Laski almost smuggled him into the socialist camp because Tocqueville considered the possibility, only posthumously published in 1893, that contemporary property relationships were not eternal in Western society. When Marx's conclusions have stood in relatively high esteem with scholars, Tocqueville's work is praised for its concordance with Marx. To those more critical of Marx, Tocqueville is praised for his divergence from Marx. Some, whose scholarly careers are long enough, have taken both tacks. The best recent comparisons, however, use Marx's insights as affirmatively as those of Tocqueville, even though they may emphasize the superiority of Tocqueville's strategy, analysis, or prognosis.

6. On Aron's work see note 5, and his "Idées politiques et vision historique de Tocqueville," *Revue française de science politique,* X (Sept. 1960). On Bendix, see "The Lower Classes in the Age of Democratic Revolution," *Industrial Relations,* I (Oct. 1961), and *Nation Building and Citizenship* (New York, 1964).

obedience relationships everywhere in society are explained as a transitional phenomenon between the breakdown of the old hierarchical social structure and the creation of new functional relationships restricted to clearly delineated segments of life. Bendix, for example, uses Tocqueville's chapter on the attitudes of masters and servants as a paradigm of three stages of modern Western social development.[7] In the first, or aristocratic stage, master and servant regard themselves as two separate species in a hierarchy of beings. Each has separate expectations and permanent status. In the third stage both are regarded, and regard themselves, as essential equals, in a limited contractual and, above all, temporary relationship. Neither master nor servant feels his relation to the world in general, or to each other, to be totally defined by the work relationship. Between these two stages is a critical period when a society legally and ideologically acknowledges that permanent inferiority no longer exists, but the scope of the new relationship has not been clearly delineated.

Symptomatically, most references to Tocqueville in connection with the process of industrialization have been indirect in two senses. They have either used his analysis to show how the democratic political systems, or *moeurs*, generally and perhaps decisively affect the social context in which industrialization occurs. Or, they have used observations which Tocqueville did not apply to industrialization, to show the terminal tendencies of the whole process, at least in Western societies. Most of Tocqueville's own writings on the problem of early industrialization are very rarely quoted and most of them never referred to.

7. Bendix, *Nation Building and Citizenship*, 48–74.

The few widely known passages in *Democracy in America* on the subject are very ambiguous. Scholars have culled it to arrive at his ideas on industrial society and its problems. They make the best of a bad harvest, an isolated paragraph or chapter, but rarely do they point out the sparsity of their sources or the intellectual extrapolation and ingenuity it takes to make a coherent point with them. They have worked them into the general conclusions of the *Democracy* with far more effort toward integration than Tocqueville himself devoted to the task.

Some of what Tocqueville wrote in the *Democracy* on the problem of the brutalization of man in the factory system, for example, seems to imply the existence of a brutalized dependent class as a necessary consequence of the industrial system. Other passages seem to imply the possibility of legislative intervention to alter this situation without specifying what is implied by such intervention. One short passage of the *Democracy* accepts the necessity of increased governmental control over certain effects of large-scale economic enterprise. But the main theme of the same chapter is that every step of increased governmental control opens the door more widely to state despotism. The weight of the argument falls heavily on the side of the overriding danger of despotism by the state, and the consequent erosion of individual and autonomous group initiative. Tocqueville also spoke of the abandonment of the degraded factory workers by the factory owners: "The territorial aristocracy of past ages was obliged by law, or thought itself obliged by custom, to come to the help of its servants and to relieve their distress. But the industrial aristocracy of our day, when it has impoverished and brutalized the men it uses, abandons them in time of crises to public charity to feed them."[8] And what should be the public's reaction to this systematic dumping of human refuse? The *Democracy* does not say, nor did Tocqueville's other classics, the *Recollections* and *The Old Regime and the Revolution*.

It is possible to comb the *Democracy* from one end to the other and discover five or six passages that touch on the social problems produced by industrialization. But it is almost impossible to produce a clear picture by trying to tie together these isolated and ambiguous asides. It is no wonder that this area of Tocqueville's thought has been neglected by the Tocqueville renaissance, and that no study of Tocqueville's economic and social ideas appeared in the edition of essays published on the hundredth anniversary of his death.[9] This lacuna in Tocqueville scholarship has caused lingering uneasiness even in the reception of the most systematic and thorough discussion of Tocqueville's thought. Isaiah Berlin, reviewing Jack Lively's *Social and Political Thought of Alexis de Tocqueville*, parenthetically muses:

The author gives a good if somewhat uncritical account of Tocqueville's view of democracy, in particular of his fear of democratic equality [not of political democracy] as likely to sap originality and pride and liberty. After quoting the celebrated passage in *The Democracy* about industrious sheep, Mr. Lively caps this with Tocqueville's speech in the National Assembly directed against "the right to work," over which the radical left had suffered so crushing a defeat. Mr. Lively's exposition is, as always, just and clear; but he is apt to leave the field too much to his hero. His references to the conditions that led to

8. See Tocqueville, *Democracy in America*, 529–530.
9. *Alexis de Tocqueville: Livre du centenaire, 1859–1959.*

the demands which Tocqueville thought so sinister—the poverty and impotence of the masses, the degrading nature of work in the factories—are too cursory; it is perhaps a little artificial to say so little about these—for us today cardinal and decisive—factors, because they were not conspicuously present in Tocqueville's mind. And can we be so sure that they were not?[10]

Tocqueville's social thought has of course not entirely escaped critical analysis. But most of this analysis has centered around the aristocratic-democratic dichotomy which Tocqueville himself constructed. The questions asked of his vision have been formulated in such terms as "How sympathetic was he to aristocratic social values? How biased was he against democracy?" In this framework, the inter-

10. Isaiah Berlin, "The Thought of de Tocqueville," *History*, L (June, 1965), 203. See also Lively, *Tocqueville*, 100–101.

Marvin Zetterbaum likewise remarks that Tocqueville was conscious of the need to improve the lot of the majority and was "not prepared to accept their misery as an inescapable condition of human existence" (*Tocqueville and the Problem of Democracy* [Stanford, 1967], 30). This would not give the reader any inkling that Tocqueville postulated an "invisible hand" to see to the welfare of the majority and that he was, at one point, prepared not only to accept, but to preach, the necessity of inescapable misery to the industrial minority. Zetterbaum also notes the contradictory nature of some of Tocqueville's economic analysis, however. See his "Alexis de Tocqueville," in Leo Strauss and Joseph Cropsey, *History of Political Philosophy* (Chicago, 1963), 661–668.

The only extended discussion of Tocqueville's confrontation with social problems to date may be found in Gargan's *Alexis de Tocqueville: The Critical Years*, Chapters 3 and 4, which concentrates on Tocqueville's reaction to social change in 1848. Another analysis of Tocqueville that deals briefly with the problem of his social perception is Maxime Leroy, "Alexis de Tocqueville," *Politica*, I (Aug. 1935), 393–424, reprinted in W. Ebenstein, *Political Thought in Perspective* (New York, 1957), 472–500.

preter is led to ask only the extent of Tocqueville's commitment to democracy as opposed to aristocracy, the extent
to which he was a dedicated democrat or ineradicable aristocrat. The crucial question becomes the nature and dangers
of modern political power, and the functions of elite leadership, administrative power, and mass participation.

Granted that Tocqueville was committed, in the abstract, to the idea of the inevitable triumph of the egalitarian principle,[11] how did he envision this principle to be
operative in areas of society which were not yet, or *might
never be*, equal? What were his regulative concepts in deciding how these under-democratic areas were to be related
to the society as a whole? The answers Tocqueville gave to
the serious social problems of his time were less a matter of
aristocratic instincts struggling with democratic commit-

11. Studies of Tocqueville's thought which insist on the crucial
fact of Tocqueville's aristocratic background for understanding his
conception of democracy concede that he never attempted to treat
aristocratic societies as real social alternatives for the future. The
only alternatives were between types of democracy, even when
manipulated for "aristocratic ends" (see Sanford A. Lakoff, *Equality
in Political Philosophy* [Cambridge, Mass., 1964]). Fundamentally
for Tocqueville, the evil tendencies of democracy could only be deflected by the potentials of democracy itself. See Yale Tocqueville
Mss, Beinecke Library, Yale University (hereafter noted as Yale
Mss), C.V. a, paquet 8, p. 1. Tocqueville stated that at least one of his
chief problems was "to live with Democracy while combatting its
vices. To try to attenuate its natural faults while making it produce
some of the assets afforded by Aristocracy, to have government by
the enlightened classes with the control of the people." Only democracy could lessen and meliorate the inevitable evils of a democratic social condition (Yale Mss C.V.k, paq. 7, cahier 2, pp. 52–53).
"Far from wanting to stop the development of the new society," he
wrote, "I seek to produce it" (Yale Mss C.V.k, paq. 7, cahier 1, p. 44,
dated June 22, 1838).

ments than an articulation of the ambiguities inherent in his definition of democracy, his conception of modernity, and his understanding of historical process. In these specific problems the instincts of a proprietor were far more prominent than the memories of an aristocratic heritage, the choices of an active member of a ruling elite far more obvious than the observations of a dispassionate student of American democracy, the ideas of a sophisticated reformer far more prominent than those of a political philosopher of mass society. And, in these practical problems, one can observe the distinctions which had to be made by one who had to help determine, as well as to foresee the future. The logic of possibilities is transformed into a pattern of options.

The main purpose of this study is therefore to bring into focus an important body of neglected or unknown data on what might be called problems of modernization or, perhaps more accurately, the problems created by those whose social condition did not fit well into the nineteenth-century scheme of providential equality as denoted in its classic study of democracy. It also reveals Tocqueville's thought as applied to problems of his age and country, the questions its ruling classes thought they could handle without violence, those it thought it could not, and those it was simply forced to deal with. It should also shed some interesting light on the way in which masters dealt with servants in at least one society in transition.

This work is based on the thought and the active legislative careers of Tocqueville and his intimate friend Gustave de Beaumont.[12] They chose to devote their energies to ques-

12. This study assumes an identity of views between Tocqueville and Beaumont in general political philosophy and social programs. This was a result of their joint travels and of their conscious policy

tions which were not only in the mainstream of contemporary humanitarian reform but were also the residue of a respectable notable tradition going back into the old regime.[13] Social questions, in the parlance of the elite political class before 1848, meant nonpartisan questions by definition. And two legislators who had made their early reputations on the basis of the impartiality of their analysis found satisfaction amidst the frustrations and helplessness of political opposition by turning their attention to the relatively neutral terrain of prison reform, the abolition of slavery, and the amelioration of some of the gross inequalities of nineteenth-century French society. Their joint trip to America, along with the books on American prisons and race relations that resulted from it, also gave Tocqueville and Beaumont a leverage of expertise with which to

---

of mutual reinforcement. Their intellectual coordination is exceptionally clear in their formative intellectual period (1828–1840). Since no two individuals ever issue all their ideas in joint or parallel statements, there are specific points for which one could not produce identical pronouncements from both writers. But the import from their travel notes and correspondence, of their rough drafts and published conclusions, is obvious. In the present study a unity of views, and the absence of contrary attitudes, is implied except where specific reference is made to variations. For further discussions of this question see: George Wilson Pierson, *Tocqueville and Beaumont in America* (New York, 1938); André Jardin's introduction to Tome VIII of the new *Oeuvres* (M): *Correspondence d'Alexis de Tocqueville et de Gustave de Beaumont*, I, 9–42; Seymour Drescher, *Tocqueville and England* (Cambridge, Mass., 1964); and "Tocqueville and Beaumont: A Rationale for Collective Study" in *Tocqueville and Beaumont on Social Reform*, ed. Seymour Drescher (New York, 1968), Appendix.

13. See Shelby T. McCloy, *The Humanitarian Movement in Eighteenth-Century France* (Frankfort, Ky., 1957).

balance their political impotence during the lean years of the July Monarchy.

One must be aware that they shared the general assumption that the social problem of France was the limited and orderly integration of as much of the lower classes as possible into the larger national political and cultural community.[14] They equally shared in the contemporary ideal of a relatively flexible social and economic hierarchy characterized by a good deal of personal mobility within the system. Finally, they accepted along with the majority of their articulate contemporaries the notion that all mature societies contained a very substantial reservoir of poverty, and therefore large numbers of men whose share of the advantages and values of society ranged from meager to almost nonexistent. Social planning could to some extent modify the level and the ecology of the reservoir, but the potentials of such control were severely limited by considerations of changes in the normative areas resulting from tampering with the reservoir, and by a fear of the potential power of the regulating mechanism and of their ability to permanently control it.

Tocqueville and Beaumont therefore began with the premise that the mixing of at least substantial portions of the reservoir into the rest of society was necessary to the stability and values of the society as a whole, but only to the extent that the process of mixing should not radically alter the composition of the optimum sector itself. Their options shifted uneasily between these two poles, balancing, compromising, and reconciling. And, when the old political

14. See Adeline Daumard, *La Bourgeoisie parisienne de 1815 à 1848*, S.E.V.P.E.N. (Paris, 1963), 516–532.

elite was momentarily overpowered in 1848, their attention, without altogether abandoning the idea of a mixture of the poverty reservoir with the bourgeoisie, became more than ever focused on the problem of control, and on the contamination of the optimum sector by an inundation from the reservoir.

II

Models of Democracy

TOCQUEVILLE's perspective on social problems was naturally embedded in his view of society in general and its historical tendencies. Until one grasps the fundamental assumptions of his social thought and his priority of values, many of his questions, answers, and dilemmas cannot be understood. The variations and ambiguities in Tocqueville's thought are minimized here in order to provide a frame of reference. The tableau is necessarily "static" and is not principally concerned with the evolution of Tocqueville's ideas or the difficulties of precise definition. Tocqueville does not aid those who would analyze his thought; this political philosopher was rarely concerned with making all of his ideas logically consistent. And there is a real danger in seeking to systematize all his statements, since they apparently did not all have the same priority in his own mind at all times. His two most fundamental concepts, "democracy" and "liberty," were never defined, nor were clear and fixed denotations assigned to them.[1] I have here attempted to confine my analysis to those conceptions which are both the most general and the most persistently held.

This model of what one might call the major themes of Tocqueville's thought is therefore to be viewed as a foil for the contradictions and ambiguities to follow, rather than as a set of assumptions from which all branches of his thought logically flow and into which they return. I explicitly wish to avoid giving the impression of a metalogic of inner rules which are to be abstracted from his writings, conceived of as a series of propositions, each with an equal and permanent position in an intellectual corpus. My working assumption is rather that, implicitly or explicitly, contradictory ideas may be pure and simple contradictions. These can only be related, if at all, in terms of their author's social and biographical setting. This does not amount to dissolving all ideas into their social or psychological components. But it is one strategy for dealing with that part of them which cannot be made consistent except by resort to a level of abstraction or meaning for which there is no warrant in the original evidence. And I am more

1. For a more extended discussion of "democracy" and "liberty" in Tocqueville's thought the reader is referred to Lively, *The Social and Political Thought of Alexis de Tocqueville*, and Raymond Aron, *Essais sur les libertés*, Chapter I. Lively's discussion is the most extended, and systematic, but is in one sense the most oversystematizing.

prone to use this strategy where scholarly exegesis seems to have led to conclusions that, while logically possible, seem weakened by data which these approaches had not taken into account. Therefore, rather than wishing to synthesize contradictions in Tocqueville, I wish to emphasize the full force of their contradictory and unresolved status in his thought.

Another hypothesis has been offered to explain the ambiguities, paradoxes, and contradictions in Tocqueville's works. Marvin Zetterbaum has suggested that a number of Tocqueville's major ideas be dealt with as salutary myths, which had to be propagated whether the stated conclusions were true, doubtful, or false.[2] This approach allows one to account for the fact that Tocqueville adhered to certain positions despite the intrusion, and often the inclusion, of data which tended to contradict these positions. Tocqueville's choice in the selection of what was to be entered for or against certain conclusions is explained in terms of a desire to persuade rather than to demonstrate. This, Zetterbaum feels, is the only way of rescuing Tocqueville from the charge of hypocrisy where the logic of evidence was clearly against him. Tocqueville's political philosophy is therefore represented as a series of salutary myths, ranging from the inevitability of democracy, through his analysis of religion and patriotism (I would include his argument against racism in this list). Yet, by this rationale, Tocqueville would be rescued from the charge of hypocrisy only by opening him to that of being a bumbling propagandist. A deliberate myth maker would not present evidence to

2. Zetterbaum, *Tocqueville and the Problem of Democracy*, 19–20, 122–123, 147, 155, 157–158.

weaken previous conclusions, which Tocqueville does again and again. The explanatory strategy of the salutory myth, even more than the system of the dialectical resolution of contradictions, emphasizes systematic control of ideas and conscious knowledge of their general implications.

Moreover, why should someone who doubted the prognosis of democracy as the inevitable social condition of the future, have perpetuated his myths in notebooks written for his own benefit and not for public consumption? His notes are often *more* emphatic about the impossibility of operating outside the framework of democracy than his explicit published statements of the same. Nowhere in his published writings did he state as a "principal and fundamental idea" that any attempt to establish a society or institutions other than within a democratic framework was not only imprudent but insane.[3] If the notion of salutary mythologizing in political theory involves a statement that something is certain which the theorist consciously believes to be problematic or doubtful, it becomes more difficult to build a case for this manipulative nexus in Tocqueville regarding democracy on the basis of his intellectual diaries than in the already difficult case of his published work.

Finally, the myth hypothesis ignores Tocqueville's commitment to objectivity and empirical observation, and the extent to which his reputation and the very possibility of maximizing his audience's receptivity, lay in such a strategy. In both the *Democracy* and the *Ancien Régime*, he felt that his work could only be instructive if it did not distort social reality. He worked out his analysis of be-

3. Yale Mss C.V.k, paq. 7, cahier 2, pp. 52–53, Sept. 5, 1837.

havior from given societies rather than human nature. In general, his conclusions were more likely to shift with changes over time in or within his sources of data. Yet this also presents the scholar with the opportunity of discerning both change and continuity in his thought. As Zetterbaum notes in another context, Tocqueville was "rarely content to deal with abstractions, and his analysis of the implementation of a principle is often more enlightening than his exposition of the principle itself."[4]

Tocqueville's approach to the problems of his generation was at once diagnostic and therapeutic. He sought to extract the fundamental social tendencies of his generation and to suggest a logic of probabilities and possibilities for acting on their institutions and values in such a way as to alter some of the tendencies and strengthen others. He simultaneously tried to discover the range and limitations of individual and collective freedom of action.

In the first place, his approach to ideas and institutions, especially public administration and behavior, whether individual or collective, was usually socio-psychological. He would invariably ask of an institution, a doctrine, or a value, how it produced or reinforced a given general habit of mind or behavior. These habitual attitudes or actions were either broken down into a number of related spheres, or compared as totalities with other similar models. Often the two operations were combined. The resulting structure of relations he called the *moeurs* (mores) or the *esprit* (spirit) of the institution or group. These denoted its collective character or social condition. It is important to bear in mind that these models, or *esprits*, were treated as short-

---

4. *Tocqueville and the Problem of Democracy*, 127–128.

hand summaries of social structures, not as causes.[5] Tocqueville was usually too much an anti-determinist even to permit himself to be bound to systematic causal analysis. This provided comfort and flexibility for the political possibilist but inconvenience for the political philosopher.

In sociological style, Tocqueville favored ideal-typology over statistical analysis. Whether he dealt with comparative national communities or social classes, he usually chose to reduce them to psychological rather than statistical units. His descriptions of human relationships were discursive and psychological rather than quantitative.[6] His most acute contrasts of social or national groups are personifications, often presented in polarized contrast for maximum stylistic effect. An unfailing ability, as revealed in his *Recollections*, to draw striking character sketches with flawless concision, is probably related to his sociological style. His analysis of institutions, as of social character, was personified as well. Bureaucracies were presented in terms of the bureaucrat, government in terms of the ruler, slavery in terms of the master and the slave. It is a method which maximizes external contrasts and minimizes internal nuances once the sociological unit has been determined, since a coherent

5. Social condition was an all-embracing term: "the ensemble of facts whose conjunction forms the situation of a people at a given period" (Yale Mss C.V.h, paq. 3, cahier 5, p. 8).

6. Tocqueville and Beaumont were not unaware of the use of statictics in social analysis, and used M. Guerry's *Statistique morale de la France* (Paris, 1832) and documentary reports with skill in detailed accounts of prisons and slavery. But their works tend to emphasize the limits, rather than the usefulness of contemporary statistics. See *On the Penitentiary System in the United States and its Application in France*, trans. Francis Lieber (Carbondale, Ill., 1964), Chapter 3, and *Democracy in America*, 197–202.

personality portrait inevitably tends toward internal integration and indivisibility of will or action.

Secondly, Tocqueville was preeminently a political man. At even the most abstract level of analysis he was vitally concerned with the maintenance of political liberty in France. The quest for political liberty and its psychological and social bases was the starting point of his investigations and the end for which he framed his questions and answers. He was always a politician or potential politician addressing other politicians and citizens. He was interested in the specific political and legislative choices that could be or could have been made in a given situation in order to achieve or to maintain individual and political liberty. His main political question was how one could arrive at a society that would preserve a maximum of individual liberty and collective participation in decision making, a maximum of social activity through nonrevolutionary channels, and a maximum of permissible dissent and creativity within the confines of a plebiscitarian framework. For a French liberal aristocrat standing amid the ruins of his class and its ancient ruling house, his personal problem and that of France seemed to converge on the adjustment of the nation to an egalitarian social condition.

The most fundamental social fact of modern times was an ever-increasing equality of conditions. An attempt to understand the development and future of this centuries-long democratic or egalitarian revolution was Tocqueville's chief contribution to social thought. His method of clarifying the emergent democratic society was to contrast a present model of egalitarian societies, drawn primarily from studies of America and France, with a generalized conception of aristocratic Europe drawn from contemporary England and from the history of France and Germany. Between aristocracy and democracy was an era of "transition," which had come to a climax at the end of the eighteenth century. Tocqueville, at least before 1848, believed himself close enough to social examples at the "democratic" end of the evolutionary development to be able to describe all three stages with reasonable clarity.[7]

The predemocratic or aristocratic era was characterized by permanent inequality.[8] Hierarchy and tradition were the ruling principles of a society based on an infinite variety of reciprocal obligations of obedience and protection. Inferior and superior functions were located in relatively well-defined and durable groups. The stable control of land and territory provided a visible index of status. At the apex of the temporal order was placed the patrimonial ruler, selected by providence and tradition, whose relationship to society was defined by reciprocal relationships of protection and obedience with his direct subjects or vassals. Men were born into a status, participated in the society in relation to that status, and were more or less bound to a set of rights and duties defined by that status. Each member of society conceived of himself not as an in-

7. For the basis of this interpretation of the transformation from aristocracy to democracy, see "Author's Introduction," *Democracy in America*, 3–14.

8. Tocqueville considered aristocracy to be itself an historical stage between an original nomadic egalitarian savagery and an ultimate egalitarian era connoted by the term "civilization" (see *Tocqueville and Beaumont on Social Reform*, ed. Drescher, I, 6–7). The best application of the model of democratization in Tocqueville's practical politics can be observed in his analysis of the process of the abolition of slavery (*ibid.*, 140). The general picture of egalitarian society drawn here relies primarily on pre-1848 materials. The shift in his thought after 1848 will be dealt with in Chapter VII.

dividual or a citizen, but as a member of one or more communities within the hierarchy which both bound and protected him. Status-fixed relations between rulers and ruled were mediated by intermediary individuals or groups, and power was located in claims to land and office, and in those who were born to it. Dependency in reciprocal relationships, and within a fixed hierarchy, was thus the fundamental characteristic of aristocracy.

Tocqueville constantly pointed to the cardinal fact that a durable society was able to exist for centuries despite the fact that a relative handful of individuals monopolized wealth and power. This was due to the fact that both the dependent and the protector felt bound by a shared relationship of community. This idealized portrait of habits of mind, rather than of social relations strictly speaking, was Tocqueville's basic outline of aristocracy. Each member knew his rights and obligations—what was expected of those above as well as those beneath him. In the aristocratic community each felt himself part, not of universalized and equal rights and duties, but only of a shared value system. It was psychologically gratifying as well to the extent that each member of society could vicariously participate in the power and glory of its highest members, who in turn were themselves considered vicars, not incarnations, of divine power.

Conversely, a new social fact, equality of conditions or democracy, had come to symbolize a new social psychology and a new type of political community. Its progressive and inevitable triumph was, for Tocqueville, a "providential fact," placed outside the range of contemporary alternatives and already beyond human control. By his use of the term "providential," Tocqueville wanted to convey a sense of its predetermined historical triumph and of its sanction by divine plan. For the legitimist elite in his French audience, the term potentially provided a justification for accepting democratization. Tocqueville, at the abstract level of aristocracy and democracy, stated that the movement toward democracy was ultimately both inevitable and just. It was beyond men's power to directly attack it and dangerous for them to even make the attempt, since the survival of other nonegalitarian principles depended on democracy's timely acceptance by the old elite.

Quite apart from its moral justification, however, Tocqueville believed that the evidence for its triumph was overwhelming. His point of departure was based on an analysis of historical trends, and not on scriptural authority or general hypotheses about human nature. Beaumont also clearly used "providential fact" in a secular developmental context. "What are called providential laws," he wrote, "are nothing but closely examined, general, logical, durable, perceptible, and intelligible causes. . . . Thus for an individual the impressions of infancy are a general cause that dominates his entire existence; in the same way, the education of a people, its point of departure, influences its whole future."[9] It may be concluded that, whatever the

9. Yale Mss C.XI.b. 3: "Philosophy of History." Tocqueville's conscious reinforcement of "what is" with "what ought to be" has led to the viewing of his use of historical necessity as a social myth, designed more to bend wills than to analyze social reality (see Zetterbaum, *Tocqueville and the Problem of Democracy*, 7–21, 147, 159–160). Marvin Zetterbaum has shown that the "inevitability thesis" in *Democracy in America* was linked to what Tocqueville considered to be his task of political education, long after he was in a position to observe both the moral and empirical difficulties in such an approach (*Tocqueville and the Problem of Democracy*,

philosophical difficulties this term raises about the role of historical determinism and of metahistorical undertones in Tocqueville's thought, it shows at the very least his presentation of democracy as the most unalterable tendency in the evolution of human society. It was "the great, the only entirely new fact in the Modern World."[10] No other process was accorded such distinction, neither liberalization, which he valued more highly, nor centralization, which he feared more completely.

Democracy was essentially the negation of aristocracy or permanent inequality as represented in a legally stratified hierarchy of privileged orders. In democracy distinctions of rank were confused, barriers separating men were lowered, great estates partitioned, education universalized, intellectual powers equalized, and extremes of wealth and poverty were unknown. It was a stage of social evolution

---

Chapter I). But there is no evidence that he ever considered altering his analysis of general historical evolution. He later simply muted the note of fatalism and providentiality in favor of a simple pronouncement on long-range secular trends. Instead of speaking of an irresistible providential fact, he spoke of an "unknown force that one can hope to regulate and retard but not to overcome," and of the destruction of aristocracy rather than the rise of democracy (*Oeuvres* (M): *Ancien Régime*, I, 73). Zetterbaum's view is reinforced by similar analyses of Tocqueville's treatment of religion, which is in fact more susceptible to such an hypothesis. (See, among many others, Zetterbaum, *Tocqueville*, 19, 118–121, 147, and Lively, *The Social and Political Thought of Alexis de Tocqueville*, 37–38, 197–199.) But in the case of religion, Tocqueville was arguing primarily for the maintenance of religious beliefs and institutions in terms of deliberate choices on the part of the legislator and the citizenry. Religion, like liberty, and unlike democracy, was problematic and socially negotiable in Tocqueville's prognosis.

10. Yale Mss C.V.h: notes for the 1835 edition of *Democracy in America*, paq. 3, cahier 4, p. 116.

already achieved by the United States and one in which France was closer to total achievement than any other European nation.

For the young aristocrat who visited America a few months after the July Revolution in France, democracy's image was first and most fully revealed in America. Contrasted with the old aristocratic model, democratic society was essentially classless. The criteria of democracy for Tocqueville were many: equality before the law, equality of political rights, but above all "equality in the relations of social life," the lack of permanent distinctions inscribed by birth, wealth, or vocation. What Tocqueville meant by a classless society, then, was one in which there was no "radical inequality" (i.e., relatively permanent barriers fixed by law, politics, family relationships, profession, or marriage customs). The emphasis on "radical" is important. The criterion was the psychological attitude and acceptance, the "spirit" in which men regarded their social status. Distinctions of habits, education, and wealth would continue to exist, but they were "passing distinctions and by no means form classes properly so called; they give no superiority, even in thought, to one man or another. So that although the two men may never see each other in the same drawing-rooms, if they meet outside, they meet without pride on one side or envy on the other. At bottom they feel themselves to be and they are, equal."[11] Legal equality, political equality, economic equality, the standardization

11. See Alexis de Tocqueville, *Journey to America*, ed. J.-P. Mayer, (New Haven and London, 1962; subsequent references will be to this edition), 258–260. An exhaustive study of the journey is to be found in Pierson, *Tocqueville and Beaumont in America*, abridged by Dudley C. Lunt as *Tocqueville in America* (Garden City, N.Y., 1959). Seven years after his American journey Tocqueville wrote:

of attitudes and behavior, these were the tendencies of equality of conditions and of history.

In relations between man and man, the old mediatory and paternalistic relationship was no longer psychologically compatible with equality of conditions; nor was it any longer the binding and protecting chain it had once been. New ties between men would have to be artificially or consciously built on the basis of a community of equal individuals and the political community on the basis of legally and politically equal citizens. Not only would men again share in a common value system, but in one which was both universal and uniform in its application, first to the entire national community and implicitly to the human race.

Between these two stages of human society came the stage of the democratic revolution. It was a period of instability, of variable length but of definite characteristics which were to be analytically distinguished from the age of stable equality. America had escaped this stage or had suffered it in the mildest possible form. It was a transitional one between two stable forms of society and community, when the values of an individualist-egalitarian value system had not yet achieved full ascendancy over a patrimonial-hierarchical system. During this interim, conflicts would appear at every level of social interaction. Equality "in general" would be the legal and acknowl-

---

"A democratic people, society, epoch does not mean a people, society, time where all men are equal, but a society, people, epoch where there are no longer castes, fixed classes, privileges, exclusive rights, permanent wealth, immobile property in the hands of families; where all men can incessantly rise and fall and involve themselves in everything" (Yale Mss C.V.d: draft of a preface to the second part of *Democracy in America*, Feb. 5, 1838, pp. 50–51).

edged fundamental social value. But all forms of individual authority would be resented by those who had to submit to them, and all assertions of individual equality at the other end of the relationship would be resented by those who had to experience them. If the collision resulted in violent readjustment, the old authorities might temporarily withdraw from the spheres of friction altogether. Above all, the psychological sense of community suffered its most critical strains during this phase, when "the lines between authority and tyranny, liberty and license, and right and might seem to them [masters and servants] so jumbled and confused that no one knows exactly what he is, what he can do, and what he should do."[12] But this revolutionary phase was to be distinguished from the final democratic community. Among other things, Tocqueville had selected America as the best place to observe a stable model of democratic society. That he ultimately allowed for a stable fusion of revolutionary *and* democratic social psychology will be shown below.

Tocqueville's conception of the evolution of class relationships remained relatively stable throughout the formative period of his thought, the gestation of *Democracy in America*. But his conception of the role of the state in modern democratic society and its relation to the individual altered relatively radically, affecting not only his own prognosis of the nature of democratic political society, but opening up a new range of problems for political thought in general.[13]

12. See *Democracy in America*, 554.
13. Compare Tocqueville's Introduction to *Democracy in America* (1835) with his concluding chapter (1840), especially 8–9 and 677–679.

Tocqueville at first considered that the relationship of a country's population to its political institutions roughly followed an analogous three-stage process of development to the general social process. Concerning patriotism, the loyalty of the citizens toward their community as a whole, Tocqueville applied this three-stage process. The first, or traditional, stage was characterized by emotional identification with a locality or a ruling family and was closely bound up with religious sanctions and enthusiasms. It was above all instinctive and passionate. The final democratic stage was a period in which patriotism like society as a whole became rationalized, enlightened, and individualized. Disinterested patriotism gave way to enlightened egoism, less passionate, less selfless but more creative and more lasting, because it was a result of individual participation in deciding the course of action and of knowledge of the cumulative effects of these actions. Between these two stages was, once more, the "revolutionary" period of egoism without enlightenment, when "old customs are changed, *moeurs* destroyed, beliefs shaken, and the prestige of memories has vanished, but when nonetheless enlightenment has remained incomplete and political rights ill-assured or restricted." In this stage men did not recognize *their* community either in the old beliefs or the new laws and lawmakers. They hesitated in confusion between "the instinctive patriotism of a monarchy" and the reflective patriotism of a republic.[14] At this stage a community had to choose between being all free or all slaves, all having equal rights or all being deprived of them, between

14. See Yale Mss C.V.h: notes for Part I of *Democracy in America*, cahier 3, p. 3, and *Democracy in America*, 217–219.

being a society founded on a rational self-interested par-
ticipatory patriotism, or submitting to the unlimited authority of a single man whose powers would equal those of
the harshest Roman emperors. The choice of moving from
the transitional to the final stage was presented and was
both clear and limited. All that was required to move into
the third stage of individual loyalty to the community was
a rational option to allow almost all its members full participation in it. It was a matter of active choices on the
basis of calculated costs.[15]

The three-stage process was applied, at least originally,
not only to the belief system of the political community,
but to its institutions as well, especially in the process of
the centralization and decentralization of power. At about

15. *Ibid.*, 8–9, 219, 289. One should note two things about Tocqueville's characterizations of the relations of the state to society in this
portion of the *Democracy*. They are portrayed as inherently in conflict about power. The state might seize all power and create a despotism or the people might parcel out power and create a self-
governing society. The state may seize power because the governed
temporarily cannot see clearly, and *give up* power in panic and ignor-
ance. But the state had to grasp power, which, given time to think, the
citizens would have wanted to retain in their own hands or in
local bodies. See also the fragment "Accidental Causes" in *Democracy
in America*, 770. Tocqueville's model of rational-participatory patriotism was derived primarily from the American democratic system.
The previous generation had derived the same model from the
English example. The continuity of the liberal framework in both
the empirical examples and the observers is clear. See Pierre Reboul,
Le Mythe anglais dans la littérature française sous la Restauration
(Lille, 1962), 64–65.

On Tocqueville's civic ideals see Doris Goldstein, "Alexis de
Tocqueville's Concept of Citizenship," *Proceedings of the American
Philosophical Society*, CVIII (1964), No. 2, and Zetterbaum, *Tocque-
ville and the Problem of Democracy*, 149–154.

the midway point in the composition of the *Democracy*, Tocqueville merely considered centralization also as part of a three-stage transitional movement toward democracy. From a first stage of primitive decentralization societies moved through a period of centralization to a third stage of balanced enlightened decentralization.[16]

Thus the nations of people whose social condition is becoming democratic almost always begin by centralizing power in the prince alone; later when they have accumulated the necessary strength and energy they break the *instrument,* and transport the same prerogatives in the hands of an authority responsible to themselves; [when they have become] still more powerful, better organized and more enlightened, they make a new effort, and, taking back some portions of administrative power from their general representatives, they confine them to secondary representatives. Such appears to be the natural, instinctive, and one could say compulsory course followed by societies which are pulled towards democracy by their social condition, their ideas and their *moeurs.*[17]

16. Yale Mss C.V.g: note for *Democracy in America*, paq. 9, cahier 2, Baden, Aug. 14, 1836, p. 136.

17. Tocqueville, "Etat social et politique de la France avant et depuis 1789" in *Oeuvres* (M): *Ancien Régime*, I, 57 (Tocqueville's emphasis). This essay was written late in 1835, after the publication of *Democracy in America* and Tocqueville's second journey to England. It was written at the request of John Stuart Mill, whom Tocqueville had met in England. Mill translated it and published it in the *London and Westminster Review*. With certain significant changes it contains many of the ideas of Tocqueville's *Ancien Régime,* published in 1856. Little has been done to assess the impact of Restoration antecedents on Tocqueville's intellectual development. (See Luis Diez Del Corral, "Tocqueville et la pensée politique des Doctrinaires," in *Alexis de Tocqueville, Livre du Centenaire,* 57–70.) Gargan, in *De Tocqueville,* 29–30, correctly shows that before 1830 Tocqueville was already familiar with theories characterizing centralization as a permanent feature of European history and civiliza-

It was precisely this formula of "temporary" centralization as a necessity for revolution or rapid social change that Beaumont used as the model for democratizing Ireland, and Tocqueville suggested for the abolition of slavery in the colonies. Even Robespierre might have approved this reformulation of his revolutionary theory.

In this analysis the state machine was treated as a dependent variable of an inevitable social process. Democratic decentralization, like democratic patriotism, was an option, and here it was presented not only as a rational choice by both the state and its citizens, but as an historical tendency.[18] It was written at the high point in Tocqueville's political optimism. Symptomatically it appeared in the same essay in which Tocqueville gave his lengthiest

---

tion in general. Guizot (and by no means Guizot alone) made this theme one of the principal features of his courses in history, which Tocqueville attended for a time. Tocqueville also derived his ideas on the antiquity of centralization in France from his own forebear Malesherbes. (See Yale Mss C.V.h, paq. 3, cahier 5, p. 3, and *Democracy in America*, 696–697.) But whether Tocqueville permanently adopted this conclusion is doubtful, especially in the light of contrary conclusions based on his experience in America, which during the early 1830's he regarded as the model society of the future. As in so many other things Tocqueville's general conclusions varied over time in direct relation to change in his subject matter. My own conclusion is that he permanently accepted centralization as a general feature of democratization only when he had finally accepted European, and not American, development as the primary basis of prognosis toward the end of the 1830's.

18. Tocqueville, "Etat social et politique de la France avant et depuis 1789," 54–55: "Among democratic peoples local government is often a creation of the central power, which permits some of its powers to be taken away, or which voluntarily divests itself of them" when the science of government was sufficiently perfected.

definition of liberty and one which was more emphatically based on a rationalistic-individualist psychology than in any other of his works.[19] During the composition of the second part of his *Democracy in America* he began to swing both from his rationalist conception of the democratic individual as a politically acquisitive being and his conception of political institutions as instruments of the social process. Rather, he came to view the supreme political institutions as an autonomous mechanism of social change that could, and probably would, operate without regard to the expressed wills or choices of citizens even in democratic societies. With this discovery on Tocqueville's part the three-stage symmetries between social and political development were broken and a new logic of possibilities was revealed.

There are clear indications that Tocqueville perceived withdrawal symptoms in French political life even before 1835. But he tended to discount the symptoms for two reasons. First, the withdrawal seemed to be most characteristic of the legitimists—a symbolic repetition of their previous exodus. Secondly, and more important, all withdrawal could be explained in terms of the loss of orientation produced by frequent changes of regime and abrupt breaks in social traditions. This was simply the political equivalent of the "time of troubles" between masters and servants, when citizens paused in confusion between the older instinctive patriotism and the newer rational consensus. As long as withdrawal was characterized as an aspect of a period of revolutionary transition, as distinct from a stable

19. *Ibid.*, 62.

condition, it did not appear as an integral part of Tocqueville's democratic model. Such was its status in *Democracy in America* in 1835. In the part of the work published in 1840, however, apolitical behavior was detached from the revolutionary-transitional model and explicitly carried over to the stable democratic state. Tocqueville now raised the possibility that elements of the revolutionary phase might be prolonged indefinitely in modern society, although he did not elaborate on the implications of such a thesis. But he already recognized a possibility that revolutionary atomization, properly formalized, could "become permanent, and one may almost say, eternal."[20]

The psychological process by which Tocqueville was led to abandon his original statement of this process is important to his understanding of modernization. The change in his political thought resulted from his perception of the tendencies in French society, superimposed on his impressions of England and Ireland during the period when he wrote Part II of *Democracy in America*. In Part I of the *Democracy*, France had been characterized as a relatively centralized society, the result of a process dating back into the old regime. There was reason for Tocqueville to believe the process was about to be reversed. America was

20. *Democracy in America*, 675. Tocqueville, in his notes for the *Democracy* of 1835, drew a detailed picture of France as a transitional (revolutionary) society, and America as a completed society. He referred to this period in France as a temporary period of individual egoism without strength, and of weak equality without collective power (Yale Mss C.V.h., paq. 3, cahier 3, pp. 106–112). By 1840, apolitical egoism had been redefined as democratic individualism, which was not temporary, nor did it interfere with the existence of a powerful state (Yale Mss C.V.g, paq. 8, p. 29; C.V.c, pp. 31–33; and *Democracy in America*, 674–75).

an administratively decentralized constitutional society.[21] France was already constitutional and almost as democratic as America, more so in some ways. There seemed no logical, nor ideological reason for a large degree of decentralization not to occur there as well. The regime in France after 1830 was in the official custody of the liberals and Doctrinaires of the July Monarchy, who had placed local self-government on the agenda of the libertarian society. Moreover, a local government act in 1833 seemed to be the first step in the process of redistributing administrative functions. Although by 1835 France still remained relatively underdeveloped in her level of associational and local governmental activity, the regime had been conducting a five-year battle for its very existence against assassination conspiracies arising from both the Right and the Left.

21. On Tocqueville's original view of the United States as a fundamentally decentralized society, see Seymour Drescher, "Tocqueville's Two *Démocraties*," *Journal of the History of Ideas*, XXV (April–June 1964), pp. 201–216. The perspective in which Tocqueville viewed the problem of centralization in America before 1835 can be further observed in his classification of notes for the *Democracy*. His entry on "centralization" was followed by the phrase "lack of centralization; what it consists of . . ." (Tocqueville's elision). Another classification read *"public functions*: paid little, desired little, honored little." Finally there was: *"paternal power*. Its weakness in America." Tocqueville was not only thinking of the weakness of centralization in the federal government but of paternalism in American society as a whole (see Yale Mss C.II.c: "Sources manuscrits," a topical summary of notes on America). The centralization-democratization theme was reinforced by Beaumont during his second journey of 1837. See Beaumont to Tocqueville, Dublin, July 27, 1837, Yale Mss C.I. a.1 (copy); *Oeuvres* (M): *Correspondance Tocqueville-Beaumont*, I, 215–216; and Beaumont's notes on centralization in Ireland, Yale Mss C.X.3 and C.X.5: "Irlande-Centralisation-Grand Jury."

France might still be liquidating its "transitional" stage, and decentralization was difficult when authority was continuously challenged. Beginning in 1835, however, three patterns converged to alter Tocqueville's optimistic prognosis in the *Westminster Review*. First, the rate of violent acts against the regime dropped dramatically. Second, the Doctrinaire Ministries showed no inclination to liberalize the regime. The restrictive legislation enacted in the volatile period was not repealed. It was even extended by the famous "September Laws" on the press in 1835. Finally, the Chamber of Deputies made no attempt to press liberalization on the Ministries, and the electorate, the "legal country" of François Guizot, brought forth no movement for a redistribution of decision-making power forecast for the postrevolutionary stage.

Tocqueville at first welcomed the slackening of violence in 1835 as the first stage of the entrenchment of constitutionalism. He was disheartened by the press law, but tried to interpret it as at least a *parliamentary* initiative which might at least presage a shift in political power from the executive to the legislature and lead to the ultimate strengthening of constitutionalism.[22] The Chamber of Deputies made no moves to further the decentralization of

22. See Tocqueville, *Oeuvres* (M): *Correspondance anglaise,* Tocqueville to Mill, Feb. 10, 1836. Tocqueville's optimism had eroded somewhat a year later and had turned his hopes from the Chamber, which he now admitted lacked energy and leadership, to the liberal and democratic instincts of the country (*ibid.,* Tocqueville to Mill, June 24, 1837). Just one year later his "mass society" pessimism descended to the citizenry itself (Tocqueville to Royer-Collard, June 20, 1838, Ms 3992, Bibliothèque de l'Institut). For Tocqueville's influence on Mill's thought, see: Iris Wessel Mueller, *John Stuart Mill and French Thought* (Urbana, Ill., 1956); H. O. Pappe, "Mill and Tocqueville," *Journal of the History of Ideas,* XXV (April–June

administration but Tocqueville was still optimistic for the
spirit of local government because "almost all of the Deputies are at the same time members of the departmental
councils [*conseils-généraux*]; that is indeed a great boon."[23]

But as he continued to observe France's political evolution during the next two years, his optimism eroded and it
began to seem more significant that deputies held offices
in the public administration than that they were members
of the *conseils-généraux*. Attitudes toward the government
seemed more determined by the first correlation than by
the second. Tocqueville became despondent at the ease
with which the liberals and Doctrinaires who rotated
power among themselves became accustomed to the concentrated base of decision making. He became even more
alarmed at the acquiescence with which legislators accepted the necessity for extending the scope of centralized
state action for economic development.

Most serious of all, as the chances for the violent overthrow of the regime ebbed, neither the French electorate

---

1964) 217–234; and Richard Freidman, "A New Exploration of Mill's
Essay *On Liberty*," Political Studies, XIV (Oct. 1966), 287–289, and a
forthcoming study on Mill and Tocqueville.

Tocqueville had not clearly formulated his mass society thesis in
1835, and Mill was totally unconvinced by the fragmentary arguments produced by Tocqueville on democratic centralization, and by
Beaumont on democratic anti-intellectualism during their trip to
England that year. He insisted that, in intellectual life especially,
democracy was diametrically opposed to their fears. See Tocqueville,
Journeys to England and Ireland, ed. J.-P. Mayer (New Haven, 1958),
81–82, and Yale Mss C.X (1): "*Littérature, démocratie*," Conversation
of Beaumont with John Stuart Mill, London, June 18, 1835. Mill
later accepted, and emphasized, Tocqueville's elaboration of the
thesis in the *Democracy* of 1840.

23. Yale Mss C.I. a.2: Tocqueville to Beaumont, Sept. 22, 1836;
Oeuvres (M): *Correspondance Tocqueville-Beaumont*, I, 167.

nor the organs of public opinion clamored for decentralization and the dispersion of political participation at all levels. They seemed more apathetic toward changing the decision-making process precisely at the moment when, according to the earlier conception of political evolution, they should have become more active in asserting their independence.

As he began the final and, to him, most important section of the second volume of *Democracy in America*, Tocqueville's evaluation of the contemporary scene became transformed at an abstract level of analysis into the major "political idea" of the book. The "vague morals" and "low actions" of the government, the rampant quest for "places" among the population, the appeal to "material interests" by the former and the positive response of the latter, became the two symbiotic concepts of Tocqueville's delineation of modern political society, a new variety of centralization, and a new kind of politically disinterested individualism.[24] A new final stage of democracy was conceptualized. Its ultimate danger was not the tyranny of the majority but the apathy of the masses.

24. According to his correspondence with Royer-Collard and Beaumont, Tocqueville's pessimistic estimation of the depoliticization of the July Monarchy had reached its nadir just as he was in the process of writing the last portion of *Democracy in America*. He was at the point where he wrote: "There is truly no Government and it is impossible to see how one will be able to create one" (Tocqueville to Beaumont May 7, 1838, *Oeuvres* (M): *Correspondance Tocqueville-Beaumont*, I, 295–296). See also their letters of June 10 (on the Doctrinaires' support of state subsidies to railroads), June 15, July 1, July 8, 1838, in the same volume; Tocqueville to Royer-Collard, April 6, 1838, Ms 3992, Bibliothèque de l'Institut, and Yale Mss C.V.k: note for the *Democracy*, April 20, 1838, paq. 7, cahier 1, pp. 9–12.

Therefore, amidst the general filling of the "middling" areas of society by its constituent groups, one important polarization occurred. The disappearance of traditional or natural (in the sense that they were not consciously created) mediating classes and institutions left the individual and the state confronting each other directly. It created the conditions Tocqueville summed up in the dual tendency toward social isolation and the concentration of state power. The individual in egalitarian societies believed himself to be the legitimate starting point of all opinions, and the equally legitimate end toward which he should concentrate all his efforts. On the one hand, all feelings were turned toward himself alone; on the other hand he saw in others an endless extension of beings like himself. Less prone than before to accept the authority of any intermediate or traditional source of authority, he was far more prone to accept the authority of himself as reflected in the majority, or endlessly echoed in the mass. "So in democracies public opinion has a strange power of which aristocratic nations can form no conception. It uses no persuasion to forward its beliefs, but by some mighty pressure of the minds of all upon the intelligence of each it imposes its ideas and makes them penetrate men's very souls."[25]

Similarly, the individual in a democracy came to look on the sovereign power first as a means of destroying the hierarchy of privileged orders and classes, and later as a means of supporting the individual in his own weakness amidst the mass of his equals. In times of equality, then, men were most likely to look to their individual needs, and to turn

25. *Democracy in America*, 400.

increasingly to the centralized state to meet them. Tocqueville devoted an impassioned coda to his original plan for *Democracy in America* to highlighting the symbiotic dangers of egoistic apathy on the part of individuals, reinforced by a bureaucratic state inclined to fill in the social vacuum left by the dissolving traditional ties.

The very mechanism used to destroy the aristocratic structure in the stage of the democratic revolution would thereby constitute a permanent feature of the stable democratic period. Europe, not America, constituted the paradigm of this process. This was to him the most durable feature of French history in modern times. Of all the dangers which threatened democratic peoples, centralization was the most continuous and pervasive. By the completion of the *Democracy* in 1840, centralization had become the most important corollary to the providential democratic fact.[26]

Such were the tendencies, providential and probable, of modern society. On the basis of what normative criteria were men to attempt to modify or direct them? For Tocqueville the answer could be summed up in one term, again vaguely defined, but with certain central characteristics: liberty. For Tocqueville, it was the supreme value. Of its sacredness to Tocqueville there is no doubt. His very few approaches to definition seem to indicate that he did not clearly distinguish, or seem to feel the need to distinguish, between the negative sense of individual independence, of freedom from restraint from the state or

26. See Drescher, "Tocqueville's Two *Démocraties*"; *Democracy in America*, Vol. 2, part IV. See also Yale Mss C.V.g: note of March 7, 1838, paq. 9, cahier 2, pp. 78–79.

society, and the positive sense of liberty as participation in the collective decision-making process. His concern seems to have been the creation and strengthening of values and institutions that would preserve both men's sense of their individuality and their sense of being participants in the destiny of the collectivity. His faith in the future was based on the conclusion that democracy possessed within itself certain universal values and potential institutions in which liberty could find expression.

In predemocratic times liberty could be considered the enjoyment of a privilege, simply part of a status: "To want to be free in one's actions or part of one's actions, not because men have a general right to independence, but because one possesses a particular right to remain independent, such was the way in which liberty was understood in the middle ages and as such one has almost always understood it in aristocratic societies."[27] What Tocqueville insisted upon was the preservation of the exalted sense of freedom of action, of control over one's destinies which these liberties had afforded. But "according to the modern notion, and I venture to say the just notion of liberty, each man, being presumed to have received from nature the necessary intelligence to rule himself, is born with an equal and imprescriptible right to live independently of his fellow men, in all that relates only to himself and to control as he sees fit his own destiny."[28] Here the definition is negative in two ways. Liberty is considered only in terms relating it to the individual's power as against external

27. Tocqueville, *Oeuvres* (M): *Ancien Régime*, I, 61.
28. *Ibid*, 62. An excellent discussion of Tocqueville's conception of liberty may be found in Lively, *Tocqueville*, Chapter I.

control and only as it relates to himself. It is also considered a right, a precondition to the actual exercise of these rights. In America, where every man was held to possess the right of self-government, he was also immediately taught to extend his conception of self-government to associational activity. By an extension of his sense of independency, by an extension of self-interest rightly understood, the citizen identified collective activity as an extension of his own creativity. Laws and wealth were created by him through an extension of his own will and power, and the principle of self-government was extended until it encompassed the national community itself. *Association* filled the social vacuum created by the social polarization of society between individuals and the state.[29]

Once again, a three-stage process was operative in the

29. See *Democracy in America*, 55–56, 344. A word on the relation of Tocqueville's personality to his view of the optimum scale of human activity is perhaps suggestive here. It has often been noted that Tocqueville failed to live up to his own expectations and those of others in the large arenas of public life in which he participated, parliaments and academies. His speeches universally struck his contemporaries as clear and intelligent, but lacking in any spontaneity or enthusiasm. His own physical and vocal frailty may have contributed to his mediocre performance, but his inability to produce an emotional impact on large audiences and to get caught up in its responses was certainly more psychological than physical.

On the other hand, if Tocqueville felt uncomfortable and exhausted by large-scale human activities, he was equally unsuited to the role of recluse. He dreaded isolation. "To be happy, even calm," he wrote to an intimate friend, "I have always needed to experience about me a certain interaction, and to count on the sympathy of a certain number of my fellow men. To me, above all, could that saying be applied, 'It is not good to be alone.'" He ultimately learned how to speak before crowds with animation, but he never became reconciled to isolation. A "certain interaction"—the intimacy of friendship or the informal discussion of small groups—seemed to him the optimum human condition.

transformation from aristocratic to democratic liberty, although the outcome seemed more uncertain and the dangers far more potent. In the aristocratic stage all those might be said to be independent and free who possessed the rights belonging to their status, and dependent insofar as they could not affect the destinies of the larger com-

---

His correspondence with close friends reveals a warmth almost totally absent from all but one or two of his parliamentary speeches; moreover, he regarded his marriage and his few lifelong friendships as fortresses of security against a mediocre and insensitive world. Far from being artificial, his conversations with friends, or in small groups, generally were considered models of spontaneous flowing prose in a social milieu where talking was universally cultivated as an art. At informal debates in the Academy he impressed even so unsympathetic an observer as Sainte-Beuve by the emotional effectiveness of his interpellations. The greatest social triumph of his life, his lionization by London high society in 1857, rested as much as anything on his performances at breakfasts and receptions. When Nassau Senior's famous diaries of conversations with the French elite were published, Tocqueville's were the only ones accorded the honor of separate publication.

For anyone who so emphatically envisaged the social future as one of atomized masses facing a monolithic state, small-scale association could hardly have been a more personal choice to fill the social vacuum. Projecting his own experience, Tocqueville could envision local government and small-scale association as the medium in which the artificiality of impersonal activity could be mitigated, in which one could perceive actors in terms of whole personalities rather than impersonal agents, and above all, where the individuality of one's own acts and one's own sense of identity could be heightened. The results of interaction in small groups reinforced the sense of controlling the whole social frame of reference, and of multiple satisfactions incidental to the outcome of the process, so that the process was of central importance and the results secondary. The result of interaction in large or highly formalized groups seemed, on the contrary, a continuous reinforcement of a sense of impersonality—one's own as well as others. This valuation of human interaction is basic to the libertarian outlook.

munity. In the democratic socio-psychological environment all would have to participate directly and equally in
the concerns of the sovereign power. But once the idea of
equality had entered into the minds of the lower classes,
no personal or class mediation would be regarded as legitimate. All aristocracies were thereafter unjust and unnatu-
ral. Above all, it was no longer possible for there to exist
various forms of honorable dependence that were not
actually servile.

There was one way, however, in which societies might
find their way back to a *collective* servitude of a new kind.
They might all participate in the distribution of power or
they might all relinquish it to the state which spoke in
their name but left room for merely a formal recognition
of the supreme authority of the governed. In the name of
equality men might exchange their power, and even their
desire for civic independence, for a mild despotism of a
new kind. This new variety of despotism would entail a
new form of dependence. It would be a dependence of man
on a providential state, not of man on man, and not by the
power of tradition but by a rational calculation of individual security on the one hand and the state on the other.
Here the values of equality ground against those of liberty.
When the desire for independence and participation were
held in low esteem liberty was fragile and just one more
negotiable social commodity.

The related problems of independence and state power
were the framework in which Tocqueville attempted to
grapple with the problems of social reform. In his attempt
to maintain a place for men as free moral agents in the new
society, Tocqueville assumed, as did almost all his liberal
contemporaries, that in one realm equality was irrevocably

Models of Democracy 49

gained for all men: equality as individuals before the law. In a second realm, Tocqueville unlike many of his contemporaries of 1830 believed in the inevitable victory of political equality and suffrage for almost all men.[30] In the

30. The *Journal des débats* of Jan. 14, 1831, considered the restricted electoral law to be a reflection of France's progress in civilization. Capacity and not number was the basis of political rights: "One looks for independent men, and you know that independence is hardly ever found combined with poverty. You look for men who have received a liberal education, and you know that this education comes only in families where there is a certain degree of comfort. Finally you look for men whose own interest is tied to the general interest, who need order and repose, who have more to fear than to hope from revolutions, and you know that property is essentially a friend of order and repose. The sign that you seek is before you—property, represented by taxation, property the measure of independence, the measure of enlightenment, the measure of prudence. What remains to be done? One thing alone: fix the tax figure that represents the measure of wealth necessary to give him who possesses it the characteristics that we have just listed." See also the editorials of Sept. 13 and 14, 1830, of Jan. 8 and 20, and Feb. 28, 1831. It should also be noted that even before the July Revolution, aristocracy was a neutral value word for the liberals. "The Electoral college has no wish to become an aristocracy," said the *Débats* on July 1, 1830. The attitude toward democracy was more ambiguous, but could be used very positively if carefully qualified: "What France really needed by way of democratic institutions were for example to be confined to local affairs '*there* will be truly democratic laws, there will be institutions where the people will have a large voice'" (*ibid.*, Aug. 24, 1830). In his social attitude toward the most democratic political systems of his time Tocqueville retained the elitist values of contemporary French and American notables. His reaction to the changes in the structure of Jacksonian politics conformed to the judgments of the Whig leaders. See Lynn L. Marshall, "The Strange Stillbirth of the Whig Party," *American Historical Review*, LXX, no. 2 (Jan. 1967), 463–464. On notable political values in general, see Max Weber, "Politics as a Vocation" in *From Max Weber*, ed. H. H. Gerth and C. W. Mills (New York, 1946), 77–128.

long run, this was politically and psychologically necessary to form a new community. For Tocqueville it was no longer possible to draw a line between legal and political servitude. Any attempt to do so would be neither durable nor stable. One had to make preparations for the final transition while time allowed. But while Tocqueville busied himself with setting out the pattern of the egalitarian world and attempted to lay the foundations for the acceptance of liberal institutions within the framework of social equality, voices were raised which demanded the extension of the concept of rights into the realm of economic and social life while others demanded that the individualistic independence established by the French Revolution be maintained with the same rigor as the legal independence from mediating groups. Others raised questions, which Tocqueville only slowly came to view as important to his own study. It was these questions that in a manner of speaking impinged on his prognosis and caused him to look more carefully at new dimensions of the egalitarian revolution.

III

Industrialization and Democracy

TOCQUEVILLE'S earliest formulations of the economic development of modern society and its relation to politics were produced in a preindustrial framework.[1] The socioeconomic vision of the *Democracy in America* of 1835 was primarily agricultural, middle-class, and, to a much lesser extent, commercial. The model New England town was rural not urban. Its locus was the town meeting, not the

1. This chapter is devoted principally to the relation between Tocqueville's economic thought and the development of social equality. On the problem of economic behavior and liberty, see Goldstein, "Alexis de Tocqueville's Concept of Citizenship," *Proceedings of the American Philosophical Society*, 52; Zetterbaum, *Tocqueville and the Problem of Democracy*, 101-111; Drescher, *Tocqueville and England*, 126–133.

market place. Tocqueville had passed through every major urban center in the United States, but discussion of the role of the city in America was confined to a single footnote in his work. This it not at all extraordinary in terms of the travelers' own basis of comparison. France, in 1830, was still overwhelmingly agricultural. To *proprietaires*, like Tocqueville and Beaumont, the most important social fact of the democratic revolution, in its French variety, was the creation of a small peasant class that was both a socially democratic and property-owning one. To two young lawyers, the single most important legal fact of the French Revolution was the extension of democratic property by the law of equal partition. To aristocratic liberals the most important political fact of the immediate past was the July Revolution with its rhetoric of the victory of the middle class over the traditional dynasty. Although there was far less shift in power than the term "bourgeois monarchy" implied, to Tocqueville and Beaumont, at least, the pretentions of one political class, the legitimist aristocracy, were severely impaired.[2]

The fact that Tocqueville and Beaumont first chose to visit America, rather than England like many of their liberal mentors, reveals how sharply they shifted their frame of reference toward democracy as the future of mankind after 1830. But a comparison of their itinerary with that of another French contemporary also shows what they were not looking for in America. They made a valiant

2. On the distribution of political and social power in France during the July Monarchy, see J. L'Homme, *La Grande bourgeoisie au pouvoir, 1830–1880* (Paris, 1960), and especially A.-J. Tudesq, *Les Grands notables en France (1840–1849): Etude historique d'une psychologie sociale*, 2 vols. (Paris, 1964).

effort to see every geographical section of America in nine months, to visit every major city, to talk to as many American political leaders as possible. They visited prisons until they felt themselves imprisoned by their own mission. They sacrificed comfort, and almost their lives, to view the American West at first hand. But though they knew of the world famous industrial experiment at Lowell, Massachusetts, they simply passed it by. Their one hour in Pittsburgh, "the first manufacturing town in the Union," was spent in catching up on correspondence. They were deeply impressed by Cincinnati's throbbing industry but spent their extremely rationed time with its lawyers rather than its industrial classes. One need only contrast their itinerary and their notebooks with the travel account of their contemporary, Michel Chevalier, to measure the range of untapped possibilities. To the trained eye of the enthusiastic Saint-Simonian, who visited America two years after Tocqueville and Beaumont, the wedge of industrial feudalism was already insinuating itself beneath the democratic institutions of the American republic.[3] The earlier visitors

3. See Michel Chevalier, *Lettres sur l' Amérique du nord,* 2 vols. (Paris, 1836), I, letters 12, 16, 19, 20, and notes; recently republished as *Society, Manners, and Politics in the United States,* ed. John William Ward, trans. after the T. G. Bradford edition (Garden City, N. Y., 1961). Chevalier was also on mission for the French government (1833–1835) to study American transportation systems. A graduate of the *Ecole Polytechnique,* and a member of the Saint-Simonian sect, Chevalier was most significant politically in the Second Empire. He was an architect of the Anglo-French commercial treaty of 1860. Chevalier's stop at Lowell was not at all unique for French visitors. See René Rémond, *Les Etats-Unis devant l'opinion française,* 2 vols. (Paris, 1962) I, 338–339. Chevalier's journey to America is, after that of Tocqueville and Beaumont, the most noteworthy of their generation. His visit to America lasted from the end of 1833 to Oct. 1834, about the same length of time as his predecessors.

were aware of industrialization but looked past it to the democratic future.

There is another telling contrast between the two itineraries. Chevalier traveled to America by way of England, and his published letters on North America were prefaced by the two on the railroads of England as symbols of industrial pioneering. Tocqueville and Beaumont had intended to visit England on their return voyage from America, a detour which their schedule did not permit in 1832. When he actually visited England in 1833, a few months before Chevalier arrived on his way to America, Tocqueville wrote home that he would have liked to have seen the Liverpool railroad but had decided instead to visit Oxford and its venerable aristocratic institutions. His interest in England, in 1833, was in its castles and landed estates rather than its factories and railroads.[4]

4. Compare letters 1 and 2 of Chevalier with Tocqueville's *Journeys to England and Ireland*, Chapter II. See also Drescher, *Tocqueville and England*, Chapter III. Since Tocqueville visited England after two decades of intense French interest in the English material development, he could hardly have been unaware of the importance of England's industrial growth in 1833. "I very well know in a vague way," he wrote to Beaumont from London in 1833, "that what would be most useful for us to study is the progress of human industry in England; the means taken by the government to favor it; the degree of liberty she enjoys; the way she goes about creating so many marvels for herself. I see all this vaguely. But when I come to examining my ideas I find them so vague that I do not know how to pose the questions I want to put" (Tocqueville to Beaumont, London, Aug. 13, 1833 [Yale Mss C.I.a.2]; *Oeuvres* (M): *Correspondance Tocqueville-Beaumont*, I, 127). Beaumont also felt at a loss in trying to orient his friend where it was a "question of political economy" (Beaumont to Tocqueville, Aug. 24, 1833 [Yale Mss C.I.a.1 (copy)]; *Oeuvres* (M): *Correspondance*, I, 130). The inquiry did not seriously begin until Tocqueville came to England a second time with Beau-

The importance of the distribution of land ownership in the minds of Tocqueville's contemporaries is nowhere more clearly revealed than in *Democracy in America*. Before he arrived in America Tocqueville was already so convinced of the social significance of the French Revolutionary land settlement that he pounced on a passing reference by an American to the importance of land inheritance laws in America.[5] Despite contrary American opinions downgrading its importance, he hailed it four years later as the clue to American and indeed all social structure. Southwest of the Hudson the great social fact of the revolution was the abolition of entail and primogeniture. The parallel with the French Revolution, "overthrowing the walls of our dwellings, and removing the landmarks of our fields," was too compelling. Tocqueville regarded the study of land inheritance as the first concern of social analysis and the chief concern of the legislator who, once having regulated the laws of inheritance, could retire ("the mechanism

---

mont, in 1835. Even then, the total time spent in Birmingham, Manchester, and Liverpool did not equal one sixth the time spent in London, and did not equal the duration of their stay in Dublin. And Tocqueville's generalizations in Lancashire show him as concerned with the problem of administrative centralization as with industrialization. Tocqueville was therefore no less aware than Chevalier of the importance of England's industrial growth. Indeed, he was vaguely aware that it was perhaps the most important aspect of her society in long-range terms. But he found it impossible to establish and duplicate the precision and coherence of his "questionnaires" on democratization to the problem of economic growth. There was not a word on English industrial development in Tocqueville's travel diaries in 1833.

5. Tocqueville, "Conversation with Mr. Livingston," *Journey to America*, 19–20.

works by its own power and apparently spontaneously aims at the goal indicated beforehand").[6]

More than the distribution of wealth was entailed in this landlocked analysis. (While Tocqueville, after 1835, began to discount the causal influence of land inheritance law in itself he remained thoroughly wedded to the idea of a fixed relationship between the landholding structure of society and its social psychology.)[7] Essential political and psychological relationships in a society depended on the existing pattern of landholding. Land alone could create the basis for a permanent aristocracy, rigid and permanent social classes. Tocqueville's first definitions of class were based on the landowning factor, and only from real property could arise a social hierarchy that really maintained distinct and separate *moeurs* for the members of its class. A landowning aristocracy could alone maintain the whole network of stable relationships necessary to permanent "inequality of conditions": continuity of family status, a distinctive code of morality, a hereditary claim on political

6. *Democracy in America*, 44–45. Tocqueville's determinism was even more precise in his American notes: "Give me thirty years of equal division of inheritance and freedom of the press and I will bring you a Republic" (Yale Mss B.II.b, p. 10). Tocqueville's topical summary of his American travel notes shows as many (or more) entries for *lois sur les successions as for égalité, centralisation, moeurs,* or *point de départ* (Yale Mss C.II.c: "Sources manuscrits").

7. See Tocqueville's "Political and Social Condition of France, First Article," *London and Westminster Review*, III (and XXV) (April 1836), 137–169, and in *Oeuvres* (M): *Ancien Régime*, I, 43. In 1835, the structure of land ownership was considered to be the one which would most essentially characterize a society. Increasingly, after his visit to England in 1835, land law yielded pride of place to public administration. From 1840 onward he recommended the study of the mores of public administration as the quickest means of understanding the social psychology of a society.

power, a protective relationship with durable groups of dependents, and a mediatory relationship between these groups and the larger society.

Tocqueville and Beaumont put far greater emphasis on the psychological implications of land ownership than on the productive relationships or economic roles in any society. Land ownership rather than land use were of central importance. And ownership implied an *automatic* set of social relationships. The structure of ownership rather than that of productivity was thus central to their analyses. Large-scale individual ownership could be correlated only with an aristocratic social condition, and small-scale ownership only with a democratic social condition. This was why Tocqueville was so utterly confounded in 1833 by the stability, and even growth, of large-scale agriculture in England. He became aware of the social difference between pre-capitalist and capitalist forms of land use in agriculture only after his portrait of modern society was complete. The primacy of landholding was reflected in his conception of democracy as well as of aristocracy. The existence of a large proprietary class of small holders was the basis of democracy itself, and perfectly fit his picture of the "middling" tendency of equality of conditions. In this case, both France and America conclusively projected the image of the future representing the stage of mature democratic social development. ("All things considered," wrote Tocqueville assuringly in the mid-1840's, "France is the country that holds the fewest poor, but it is also the one where we find the fewest rich.")[8] Men were more equal, land was divided, its possessors were a part of that moving and impalpable

8. Tocqueville, "La Centralisation administrative et le système representatif," *Le Commerce*, Nov. 24, 1844.

cloud of dust into which former classes were disappearing from above and below. This rural landed class promised to combine some of the most advantageous potentials of social democracy. It was individualistic but independent, non-revolutionary but thrifty, above all a popular class whose primary social demands had already been essentially met. Tocqueville's local base of power, a politically moderate and predominantly rural small landholding constituency, gave him no cause to question this projection.[9] It is no wonder that even the French conservative classes in 1830 actually embraced the myth of the great Revolutionary partition. The existence of this massive property-owning class was undoubtedly an important element of Tocqueville's general economic optimism. It certainly helped him to maintain his image of the peasantry as a self-sufficient class.

One should note, however, that Tocqueville's concept of liberty and political participation was less property-oriented than those of many contemporary French notables. Almost all of them formulated a conception of society in terms of legal equality. The franchise was not limited to any precise class nor frozen at a single point, at least in theory. But in the general conception political participation was a privileged sphere which one entered only with

9. See Charles Pouthas, "Le Corps electoral de l'arrondisement de Valognes au temps de Tocqueville," *Mémoires de la Société Nationale académique de Cherbourg*, XXVI (1961), 29–44. Beaumont's constituency was also predominantly landed and proprietary. Between 40 and 50 per cent of the electorate in each of the cantons of Mamers electoral district listed themselves as *proprietaires*—to which one would have to add most of those listed as only in their capacity as unpaid magistrates or retired officers, amounting to 59 per cent of the Mamers *pays légal*. (Compiled from Ms electoral lists in the Beaumont papers at the Archives Nationales, Archives Privées, 42 AP 123.)

credentials of "capacity" to make independent choices and guarantees of loyalty to the social order. The ownership of property was accepted as the best empirical index of both. Tocqueville did not conceive of political participation in terms of an upper sphere of social action reserved for the capable and independent. Political activity was precisely the field of social interaction where the individual became psychologically attached to his society once equality became the fundamental social value. It was the prerequisite to loyalty to the community, not its confirmation. As regards the idea of social independence, Tocqueville's break with his contemporaries is far less clear.

Tocqueville's perspective on the social significance of land ownership, combined with, or perhaps because of, the preponderance of the rural agricultural element in France in 1830, also affected his analysis of political institutions. His all-important model of local government was the rural New England township. Its high degree of social activity, compared with similar institutions in the South, gave weight to the educational and religious factors but none to the economic function of the town in urbanization. The political system as a whole was treated in terms of the relationships between the geographically distinct hierarchy, of local, state, and federal governments. The principal focus of conflict in the Union was thus territorial and sectional.

Against the background of American equality and the French Revolutionary accomplishments, Tocqueville developed his favorable prognosis of the typical democrat as proprietor. Individually owned, constantly enlarged, and divided at death, property became one of the more certain and final effects of the democratic revolution. Perceiving an agricultural proprietary class as the largest and most stable element of a democratic society, it is no accident that Tocqueville conceived of contemporary colonial attempts abroad as extensions of the French agricultural society. Others saw in colonization either a means of ridding Europe of dangerous criminal and political refuse or of creating utopian agricultural communities for landless proletarians. Tocqueville and Beaumont saw in these deportation schemes an expensive adventure almost certain to end in social revolution, as in Haiti, or in foreign seizure. (Fifteen years after his trip to America Tocqueville still considered America as a primarily agricultural community, and its rural population as the great cause for the success of the colonization of America. One of the great French problems in Algeria was that the 100,000 Europeans were all urbanites. Their cities were beautiful but the countryside was empty. American-style rural communities were therefore the ideal settlements.) A stable colonization process, like any stable society, could rest only on "small societies analogous to those of our French villages."[10] The first need of Algeria, echoed Beaumont, was the extension of civil rights, above all individual property rights to Europeans in Algeria. Both proclaimed in their legislative and academic capacities that land surveys in

10. Tocqueville expressed this opinion in the 1842 Parliamentary Commission on Algeria, Jan. 30, 1842 (Archives Nationales, F80 1699). On America as the model for colonization, see the letters of Tocqueville to Francis Lieber, July 22, 1846, and Lieber to Tocqueville, Sept. 25, 1846 (Mss pertaining to Tocqueville and Beaumont, the Huntington Library, San Marino, California). On the dangers of criminal colonization, see Tocqueville's appendix on penal colonies in *Du système pénitentiaire*.

Algeria and systematic studies of Moslem land law were the most important prerequisites of colonization.[11]

Tocqueville and Beaumont were also inclined to look at the land law as the most effective and surest means of social reform. They were convinced that the independent French peasant offered the best model for social change from aristocracy to democracy. And they felt most certain of themselves when they could advise a change in the laws of land ownership as the principal mode of altering the social structure. Tocqueville and Beaumont were at first certain that England could only become democratized through land redistribution. Beaumont's chief solution to the misery of Ireland was to simplify the laws relating to the purchase, inheritance, and division of land—a consciously nonviolent equivalent of the French Revolution. Tocqueville's solution to the problem of orderly abolition of slavery was to follow a similar approach. In its psychological characteristics, proprietorship seemed to provide the greatest certainty of social stability in modern societies.

For all the sense of security and stability that the small farmer class seemed to promise for egalitarian epochs, Tocqueville and his notable contemporaries were by no means agrarian populists and still less agrarian anticapitalists. If the great partition in the French Revolution evoked the nostalgic vision of destroyed dwellings and littered landmarks in *Democracy in America,* there is none

11. This meant of course that Tocqueville's consideration of the natives in Algeria was an afterthought. Melvin Richter has already noted that Tocqueville's liberalism could not be easily reconciled with his colonialism (see "Tocqueville on Algeria," *Review of Politics,* XXV [July 1963], 396). But the compartmentalization of liberalism went further than his views on Algeria and its native population.

of Namier's cry of pain for the lost rootedness of the bucolic eighteenth century. Tocqueville and Beaumont were too close to the *temps perdus*. As avowed French nationalists they realized the modern dependence of national power on economic growth. As liberals they realized that certain aspects of the entrepreneurial spirit were both compatible and complementary with liberty and equality. As students of America and England they found empirical support for both these conclusions.

Once again, their intellectual itinerary reveals certain early options whose import is clear even if their precise cause is obscure. They began their study of political economy with the optimistic works of Jean-Baptiste Say, rather than with the pessimistic and skeptical Sismondi. On board the ship that took them to America they devoted all their energies to "doing political economy with the work of J. B. Say."[12] After their English journey of 1835, they con-

12. Pierson, *Tocqueville and Beaumont*, 22, refers to, "Notes sur l'économie politique" based on Say's writings. In the library at the Chateau de Tocqueville are specimens of the work of Say and of Adophe-Jerome Blanqui (not to be confused with his revolutionary brother), who was the embodiment of the "optimistic" school of economics in France. When Beaumont planned a review of a book on political economy in 1840 he noted that his library was well stocked for such a task with Smith, Ricardo, Malthus, Say, Turgot, Senior, and Blanqui (letter to Tocqueville, Aug. 25, 1840 [Tocqueville, *Oeuvres* (M): *Correspondance Tocqueville-Beaumont*, I, 424]). Tocqueville and Beaumont were very familiar with Senior's popular works such as *An Outline of the Science of Political Economy* (London, 1836), *Letters on the Factory Act* (London, 1837), and *Statement of the Provision for the Poor . . . in America and Europe* (London, 1935), as well as his co-authored report for the English Royal Commission on the poor law. Senior's contacts with Tocqueville were more or less continuous after 1835, and beginning with 1848 he kept a series of diaries in which were incorporated long conversations

tinued their education in English economic thought as interpreted by their close friend Nassau Senior, who was probably the closest thing to the Establishment economists in contemporary England.

No legislator in protectionist France, including Tocqueville or Beaumont, could afford to be blindly obedient to the theoretical recommendations of Say and Senior. On specific problems they might rely on hostile witnesses of industrial development like Villeneuve-Bargemont. In areas such as the economic effects of land division in France they might reach conclusions in direct conflict with the English school as represented by Senior and McCulloch. But they generally accepted its framework as the theoretical norm for evaluating government intervention in the economy. This was of importance in areas where either there were no local economic interest groups to be considered or where their own psychological preferences could have free play. Tocqueville's relationship to classical economics might well be couched in the very terms with which he described the effect of political philosophy on lay politicians. It formed "a kind of intellectual atmosphere in which both governed and governors move, and from which they draw, often without realizing it, the principles of their conduct."[13] One must not make the mistake of oversimplifying either the ideas of the English economists, or the lessons that Tocqueville and Beaumont drew from them.

---

with Tocqueville. These were published as *Correspondence and Conversations of Alexis de Tocqueville with Nassau William Senior* (London, 1872), and will be republished in the *Oeuvres complètes* under the editorship of Hugh Brogan and J.-P. Mayer. A manuscript copy may be found in the Beinecke Library at Yale University.

13. *Oeuvres* IX (Beaumont edition): *Etudes économiques*, 123.

None of them were blind advocates of laissez-faire, and the most intelligent of their mentors, including Senior, made a careful distinction between optimum conditions and legislative possibilities. Certainly Senior would have been the last to sacrifice a people or their security to a principle of political economy. But all had preferences in their attitudes toward government intervention in economic and social development, which were necessarily vulgarized in the political process. Options were always required, and the more revolutionary the crisis the more reflexive were the reactions and the less important the nuances.

What pleased Tocqueville and Beaumont most about a free-market society was that it tended to produce certain habits of mind, or attitudes, that reflected the libertarian ideals of ordered activity, independence, and participation. From his American and English experience Tocqueville concluded that a business ethic fostered the nonrevolutionary, dynamic, and self-reliant attitudes necessary to liberty, while it simultaneously produced "those marvels of industry which astonish the world."[14] Believing that America was the acquisitive society universalized, and comparing her prosperity with Europe's, Tocqueville and

14. Yale Mss C.V.g: copy of rough drafts for Part II of *Democracy in America*, paq. 9, cahier 1, p. 171. Tocqueville privately assured his English friends that he regarded free trade doctrines as optimal aims for French political economy. See *Oeuvres* VI (Beaumont edition): *Correspondance d'Alexis de Tocqueville*, letter to Lord Radnor, Nov. 5, 1843. His private views were well enough disseminated so that as the French Foreign Minister he was regarded as a good channel of appeal against attempts to raise tariffs on English goods. See Public Record Office F.O. 27/858 France. Domestic various, "Instruction to Ld. Normanby (private) July 14, 1849, from Lord Clarendon to Lord Palmerston; and Tocqueville's assurances to Normanby on behalf of the Ministry, Aug. 30, 1849, in F.O. 27/847.

Beaumont could hardly have been more convinced that a market-oriented society maximized productivity and the distribution of wealth according to the mechanisms described by J. B. Say.

Tocqueville never clearly distinguished between the processes of commercialization and democratization in his work. He assumed that in egalitarian epochs "civilization" was increasingly universalized, and with civilization came the gradual conversion of society from a pre-market economy to a market economy. With this change came the gradual incorporation of all members of society into the productive network, accompanied by the exaltation of the work ethic and the legitimization of the acquisitive spirit. When every member of society became civilized and imbued with the notion of economic gain and indefinite improvement, as in America, the novelty of modern society and its contrast with the republics of antiquity were most sharply revealed. Simultaneously there occurred an enlargement of the middle class in modern society. Its values became normative for that society as well. For Tocqueville this universalization of the middle class was the most significant economic fact of modern democracies. By and large, maximum prosperity for the society as a whole, and a maximum acquisitive motivation on the part of each individual in that society were simply assumed as given and self-sustaining facts. Pockets of unproductive cultures, whether of aristocratic leisure or of listless poverty, would be gradually and inevitably eroded by the acquisitive middle class.

Tocqueville's conceptions of the genesis and the causal factors in economic change are also almost exclusively psychological. The brief sketch of economic history given at the beginning of his *Memoir on Pauperism*[15] is the most extensive and revealing one he has left. It clearly shows how exclusively he looked to individual psychology for causes of economic development, as well as for their effects. The investigation of economic mechanisms always was peripheral to Tocqueville's interests. One can find in *Democracy in America* an isolated chapter on American prosperity, one on manufactures in general, plus a few axioms of economics among analyses of slavery, science, art, literature, religion, and centralization. But these scattered passages are never built into anything like a coherent picture of economic behavior. Putting all the passages together only leads to confusion, for one ends up with varying degrees of ambiguity and contradiction. The reason seems to be that Tocqueville never felt it necessary to do more with economic institutions than to draw from them circumstantial evidence for psychological portraits, and only insofar as they impinged on social or political behavior. In one passage capitalist behavior appears libertarian, in another authoritarian, and, in a third, servile and dependent. In an analysis of a given political or social institution the relation may be clear, but it gives no sense of what these various behaviors have in common with each other. Perhaps more in economic behavior than anywhere else psychological typology and portraiture were substituted for an analysis that would take into account technological, productive, and market factors. Thus, for example, the economic superiority of free over slave labor is proved through a psychological portrait of men in the American North as opposed

15. See *Tocqueville and Beaumont on Social Reform*, ed. Drescher, Chapter I.

to those in the slaveholding South. And the productive superiority of small landholding over large landholding is demonstrated through the argument that the small producer is more highly motivated to produce on his own soil. When Tocqueville began a passage with a bona fide "axiom" of economic behavior (e.g., the cost of manufactured goods always varies in inverse proportion to the size of the establishment), he was as likely to be mistaken in his use of single technological constants as when he ignored technology altogether.[16]

This view of economic behavior in the modern world was not only peculiarly psychological in its angle of vision but it emphasized consumer hedonism based on material self-interest as the most important motivation behind economic activity. As a comfortable if not affluent *proprietaire* with very little day-to-day interest in maximizing even his own sources of income, and who left hard bargaining with tenants to his wife, Tocqueville was prone to separate economic activity from spiritual values.[17] His account of the

16. *Democracy in America*, 46 and note, 317–320, 423, 443, 502–503, 508, 524–531, 557–559, 656–658.

17. As Tudesq writes, "The Notable, in the France of 1840, is the proprietor; it is the landed estate which is the primary mark of status which consecrates acquired [accumulated] wealth" *Les Grands notables*, I, 429. M. André Jardin, of the working committee supervising Tocqueville's complete works, writes: "Tocqueville had nothing about him of the great rural proprietor smitten with agronomy; his lands were primarily an intimate bit of space where he loved to take long meditative walks." (See "Tocqueville et la décentralisation" in *La Décentralisation*, VIᵉ colloque des lettres et des sciences humaines, Aix-en-Provence, December, 1961, p. 107). For his analysis of the future prices of farm leases in *Democracy in America*, Tocqueville consulted the renowned botanist and agricultural expert, Augustin de Candolle (Yale Mss C.V.a, p. 31). Tocqueville was never among

economic development of Europe in the *Memoir on Pau-perism* is almost exclusively concerned with the role of the psychological desire for material comforts. The decisive factor was the change from one psychological state to another. The point of departure was an originally hierarchical agricultural society in which all classes, whether rich or poor, felt limited and easily satisfied needs. The poor simply vegetated, the rich led brilliant but physically uncomfortable lives. Both lived without a sense of deprivation. The causal mechanism in the development of the modern economy was the growth of new needs (*besoins*) and new satisfactions (*jouissances*). Thereafter, the process of satisfying these needs is pictured as automatic, self-accelerating, and perpetual, a takeoff into self-sustained insatiability. The demand for material satisfactions as the fundamental psychological mechanism in the economic process is clear.[18] In addition, the entire analysis was luxury-oriented, in that the process depended from the outset more on the endless creation of new and more "artificial" pleasures than on the development of organizations for capital accumulation, on technology to satisfy mass consumer needs through mass production, on the more efficient use of materials, or the more efficient satisfaction of essential economic functions such as the movement of goods and

---

the economic innovators either in parliament or on his estates. He had a penchant for associating trade and industry as ventures more akin to a lottery than to agriculture. Like many French observers he looked on the rapid industrialization of England as a gigantic and dangerous gamble. The English people had simply been carried away by the passion for wealth.

18. See below, 221*n*.

information. In short, the entire productive and marketing structure was omitted from the process of economic modernization. In *Democracy in America,* Tocqueville wrote:

It has often been remarked that industrialists and merchants have an inordinate taste for physical pleasures, and trade and industry have been held responsible for this. I think that is to mistake the effect for the cause. It is not trade and industry that give men the taste for physical pleasures, but rather the taste for them which induces men to go into trade and industry, so as to satisfy this taste more completely and quickly. If trade and industry do increase the desire for well-being, that is because every passion grows stronger the more attention it gets and is swollen by every effort to satisfy it. Every cause which makes love of the things of this world predominate in the human heart also favors trade and industry.[19]

In describing the psychology of the businessman, moreover, Tocqueville never emphasized either the idea of vocation or dedication, or even a rationalism related the productive process or the market. The businessman's distinguishing feature was addiction to physical gratification, an addiction which the aristocrat naturally held in rather low esteem. At times Tocqueville in his notes almost glimpsed the Weber thesis on the relationship between Protestantism and capitalism, but his overriding conception of religion as "spiritual," and economics as "material" realms of human activity kept his focus on the inhibiting potentials of religious values on economic behavior. It is no accident that the *Democracy* speaks constantly of economic psychology in terms of the quest for *material* well-being. Religion, as the embodiment of the realm of the

19. *Democracy in America,* 524.

spirit, was called in to redress the dangers of materialistic excess.[20] Despite the fact that Tocqueville noted that the two most acquisitive societies that he observed in the world, England and America, were simultaneously fervently religious and fervently acquisitive, he apparently missed and certainly did not emphasize the possibility that they might be mutually reinforcing psychological forces rather than countervailing ones. Whatever the relationship between the Protestant ethic and the spirit of capitalism, by Tocqueville's hedonistic business psychology, the brothel or the harem should long before have produced modern commercialization, with Don Juan as its ideal type, rather than Benjamin Franklin or Richard Arkwright.

Even the business cycle was couched in exclusively psychological terms. Because in democracies all were totally absorbed in the pursuit of well-being, at the least difficulty all fortunes were simultaneously shaken and the state itself was endangered: "I believe that the recurrence of these industrial crises is an endemic disease among all democratic nations in our day. It can be made less dangerous but not cured, for it is not due to accident but to the essential *temperament* of these peoples."[21] What Tocqueville meant

20. Cupidity, the source of baseness and bad faith, was one of the basic principles of trading people. In certain cases like America, however, "religion creates a barrier—it is a brake" (Yale Mss B.I.f.6: note entitled "Moralité"). This note also contained the following schema:

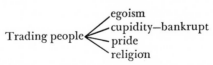

See also *ibid.* C.I.b.3: undated letter on religion and liberalism.
21. *Democracy in America*, 527.

here was quite clear. Economic crises were not tied to a given economic system, which would have made them accidental to democracy, but to a specific psychological factor—the inordinate thirst for well-being fostered by equality of conditions.

The economic system that emerged from the psychological search for well-being was equated, like English political economy, with the sum total of the desires of individuals, each engaged in a private accumulative process. It was an outline of a system which again presupposed a proprietary, acquisitive, individualistic middle class. There were spiritual and political dangers that might arise out of the excesses of the search for well-being. But the continuous and automatic diffusion of individual accumulations of wealth was taken for granted in the final stage of egalitarian societies. However confused the outlines of the new democratic society, this much seemed most ascertainable and certain. The middling man, whether peasant or tradesman, seemed to bear the future within himself. If life among this endless series of lower middle-class elements seemed to portend the flat monotony of a brave new world, it also pointed to the fulfillment of the historical journey from hierarchy to equality, from class to mass, from social dependence to social independence. If all men might fall prey to isolation and the encroachment of the state, they had at least one firm social base for private independence. Private property and economic self-sufficiency remained islands of security on an unchartered voyage.

Tocqueville's almost total lack of attention to industrialization during his journey to America is clearly reflected in his first volume on America in 1835. Manufacturing was subordinated to the discussion of American commerce, and neither was discussed in connection with the process of democratization itself. Tocqueville and Beaumont were aware that the factory system existed in America. They also knew that the process implied a form of economic organization based on large-scale production and the division of labor. More important, from their particular vantage point, they believed that factory organization unequivocally contradicted the principle of equality of conditions as it related to the work situation, to the principle of popular sovereignty, and to the ideal of economic and social independence.

For a number of reasons the industrial process in America seemed to present no major social problem to the process of democratization. The phenomena of social mobility and the supremacy of the masses in America were the decisive facts of American life, and they simply canceled out all hierarchical and inegalitarian tendencies. The manufacturing process implied an increased division of labor, and generally reduced the capacity of labor to transfer from specialized functions. But men changed jobs and positions so quickly in America "that the division of labor might almost be said not to exist," and one met men "who had been in turn lawyers, farmers, merchants, ministers of the Gospel, and doctors."[22] General mobility prevented permanent social stratification as well as psychological degradation and a general condition of dependency.

Industrial organization also seemed to imply relationships of authority and dependence permanently fixed in certain groups and was diametrically opposed to the egali-

22. *Ibid.*, 370, 768.

tarian process as formulated by Tocqueville and Beaumont. In America, however, all power in political society came from below. "The rich make the poor work in factories, but the poor cast their votes for or against the rich in elections." Deference was paid to the poor, not to the rich, since popular election was the road to power: "The voice of the masses is heard, and shatters all these *little* barriers of resistance and hostility against popular power."[23]

Finally, the existence and growth of great industrial fortunes seemed to contradict the concept of equalization of wealth, but once again other "general" tendencies intervened. American inheritance laws, which set the psychological norms for society, had abolished entail and primogeniture and "caused democratic passions to prevail." Consequently, mobility in wealth, as within the labor force, prevented the formation of classes. If the hazards of trade did not destroy accumulations of capital, equal inheritance did.[24]

If industrialization in general was at the fringe of Tocqueville's vision of democracy in 1835, the related question of poverty was simply excluded from the mainstream of his prognosis of democracy in America. There is no more graphic proof of the existence of a conception of two distinct social worlds in the vision of Tocqueville and Beaumont than in the organization of and separation of their American data for publication. All told, they published three studies of America: their joint *Penitentiary System*

23. *Marie, or Slavery in the United States*, trans. Barbara Chapman (Stanford, Cal., 1958), 230.
24. *Democracy in America*, 772.

(1833), Tocqueville's *Democracy* (1835), and Beaumont's *Marie* (1835). The *Democracy* was a study of political institutions, culture, and society. Equality was the designated motive principle of American society, and what was peripheral to that principle was peripheral to his work. The Negroes, for example, were not only systematically excluded from the political and social mainstream of the American polity but they were also treated in the *Democracy* as having no place in white American society. The destiny of North American society was conceived of as the destiny of its white, Anglo-American population. The full treatment of the oppressed races was reserved for Beaumont's dramatic but equally fatalistic novel, *Marie*.

The place of the poor in Tocqueville and Beaumont's America is therefore indicative of a general principle of selection. Tocqueville and Beaumont knew that there was poverty, and institutions primarily created for the poor in America. Their *Penitentiary System* included substantial notes on American poor laws, poorhouses, relief systems, penal laws against debtors, the inequalities of the bail system, and public education. Beaumont's *Marie* included a chapter on pauperism in America, and particularly on the Baltimore Almshouse, where the poor, the sick, and insane were thrown together. Institutionalized poverty was American enough but not quite democratic. The existence of pauperism was acknowledged in the book devoted to the treatment of marginal men, the *Penitentiary System*.

We find other evidence for this process of elimination at work in Tocqueville's thought between his visit and the appearance of *Democracy in America.* In this book, the United States was cited as the one nation where, along with universal suffrage, the principle of popular sovereignty had been "adopted" in practice in every way the imagination could suggest.[25] The suffrage for free Negroes at that point was of little significance for Europe proper. But Tocqueville was also explicit about the poor in general. In his notes for the *Democracy* he wrote: "Even in the United States the poor who pay no taxes obey laws to which they have neither directly nor indirectly consented. How could this come about if the right to participate in the affairs of government is a right inherent in the nature of man?"[26] From the final version of the *Democracy* Tocqueville dropped both the poor and the fact of their political exclusion. They were put beyond consideration. In the *Democracy* of 1835, the poor were not only ignored but sometimes denied existence. When Tocqueville alluded to the poorer classes in America at one point he emphasized that he was implying only relatively low income, not impoverishment. Compared to those of Europe, the poor of America might often seem well-to-do. The rich were less rich in America, the poor were less poor. At one point the *Democracy* went even further. There were no poor in America, no disinherited proletarians, and no dehuman-

25. *Ibid.,* 53.
26. Yale Mss C.V.h: copy of notes for first part of the *Democracy,* paq. 3, cahier 5, p. 6. Although Tocqueville was an advocate of popular sovereignty in general, he drew an early distinction between "the right of a people to choose its government, and the right of each individual to take part in it" (*ibid.,* p. 4).

ized industrial serfs.[27] From the *Democracy* alone there was no way for a reader to determine what proportion of the population was pauperized in America, or whether poor laws were even necessary in that prosperous land. The effect of the methodological segregation of subject matter on poverty leads to the likely conclusion that, like the criminals, the poor were located in a separate analytical world for Tocqueville. It was a world in which their mutual exclusion from the normal social relationships was so complete that they were acknowledged only in works on crime and slavery in America.

Thus in the formative period of their intellectual development Tocqueville and Beaumont had come to some conclusions that were reflected in their belief about the general relationship of industrialization to democratization. Popular sovereignty and economic mobility would be overriding characteristics of all democratic and commercial societies. With political and economic democratization exclusively on one side of the social ledger, the specter of industrial feudalism, feared by so many contemporaries as the central social fact of modernity, was accepted as an endemic and confined social disease. Wherever Tocqueville and Beaumont mentioned it through 1835, they figuratively drowned it in democracy.[28] Although Tocqueville accepted as axiomatic the inherent inequality of the industrial process, along with its radical and degrad-

27. *Democracy in America*, 194n., 220, 163. As far as I can determine, the first part of the *Democracy* made three references to the existence of state aid to the poor, on pp. 58, 197n, and 201. Significantly, neither the Lerner and Mayer, nor the Bradley indices of *Democracy in America* notes *any* reference to poverty in the first volume of the work.

28. *Ibid.*, 772, and Beaumont, *Marie*, 100–101, 230.

ing dependency, he discounted industrialization in relation to general social development. Power, dignity, and independence were to be found outside the factory system. Tocqueville's second trip to England, in 1835, reinforced his picture of the contradictions of industrialism. His panorama of the horrors of industrial Manchester is as vivid as any before or after it. But he remained as convinced as ever of the exceptionality of the industrial town in the democratic societies of the future. In the *Democracy* of 1840, a slow and gradual rise of wages was one of the "general laws of democratic communities." It is significant that Tocqueville made it a general law of democratic and not industrial or modern communities.

The extent to which Tocqueville discounted industrialization as fundamental to the modernizing process may also be seen from the example he chose as his paradigm of wage-bargaining relationships. In his chapter on wages in 1840 he wrote, "I take as my example that occupation which in our day is still the most commonly followed among us, as among almost all other nations, the cultivation of the land. In France most agricultural wage earners themselves own some little plot of land which, at a pinch, will keep them alive without working for another man. When such as these offer to work for a great landlord or for a neighboring tenant farmer and are refused a certain wage they go back to their little domain and wait for another opportunity."[29] This was the economic structure which was to ensure the congruence of wage relationships with general equality of conditions in modern societies. The example, if the point may be underlined, was an ideal type who was a rural

29. *Democracy in America*, 558–559.

agricultural proprietor. He knew nothing of the division of labor; he himself was, in fact, its virtual antithesis. He lived on a guaranteed subsistence outside the realm of wage labor. Organizational discipline was utterly alien to him within his work system. He worked intermittently and discontinuously for others, and he could never literally experience unemployment. He was marginal to the market economy. He was the very antithesis of industrial man. Yet this was the *only* example of the normal wage earner projected into the normal future by Tocqueville.

The topical structure of *Democracy in America* reinforces the same conclusion. The discussion of wages in democracies was raised in the context of what one might call dominance-subordinance relationships (Part III: "The Influence of Democracy on Mores Properly So Called"). It is the last chapter of a trio that begins with the relations of masters and servants, moves to the relations between tenants and landlords, and concludes with masters and workers. Why almost four times as much space is devoted to the first chapter as to the second and third is understandable when one observes that the last two chapters start with the declaration that what is true of masters and servants applies generally to landlords and tenants or masters and workers.[30] Tocqueville's chapters on the relation between masters and workers, and masters and servants were in fact originally projected as a single chapter covering both topics, and they remained essentially subtopics of a generic

30. Note also that Tocqueville felt called upon to coin new words for new things or at least to proclaim the insufficiency of the old. But "masters" did not seem too alloyed to use for employers and managers.

model. The structural differences between domestic, peasant, and industrial labor systems are minimized under such an approach. At the very least, the secular displacement of domestic and agricultural labor by industrial labor was not reflected in a framework where the industrial population was severed from "normal" wage labor, and the emergence of a white-collar labor force was unrecognized.

Even if one accepts the dubious assertion that Tocqueville was writing here only about mental climates and socio-psychological relationships and not really about wages, leases, and economic organization, the implication of his approach was the assumption that while human relationships were essentially changed by the shift from aristocracy to democracy, they were essentially unchanged by the shift from domestic service and precapitalist rural agriculture to an urban industrial economy.

This is not to say Tocqueville was blind to all the implications of industrialization. Indeed, he was haunted by them, but not insofar as the relationships between labor and capital were concerned. To choose the isolated semi-independent peasant as the typical worker meant that Tocqueville excluded contemporary technological, organizational, and economic novelties from his equation. The result was a socio-psychological sketch of personalized contacts against a placid background of cultural homogeneity (traditional-rural), psychological equality (independent proprietary), and personal relationships. In a sense the whole wage-bargaining process for the ordinary worker involved the sale of a surplus item which could readily be detached from his means of subsistence and was psychologically detached from his conception of his own condition. With this model, economic independence was a given and not problematic tendency of modernization.

Scholars have asserted that Tocqueville rightly prophesied a general pattern of incomes clustered around the middle rather than the extremes. But they have falsified his reasoning by claiming that he based his prognosis solely on something as vague as the inevitable effect of democracy on wealth; that somehow or other the "general" spirit of equality would overcome any discordant tendencies. Tocqueville was explicit about what factors would maintain economic eqaulity: small-scale industry, small-scale possessions, equal-share inheritance laws, and a nation of "independent" tradesmen and farmers. For an industrial society—a society dominated, and not simply infiltrated, by large-scale production—Tocqueville could neither predict nor even hope for the maintenance of equal conditions.

Nevertheless, even in 1840 he was no longer able to dismiss completely two possibilities tied up with the growth of industrialization. First, viewed in the European context, the social stratification produced by the factory system seemed to open the door to a new aristocracy and a new serfdom, a more or less permanent inequality of conditions. The problem worried him throughout the gestation of the second part of *Democracy in America*. At one point he decided that, like every social process, manufacturing began as an "aristocratic" system but would follow the general evolution toward deconcentration. Here it would appear that the social process of land division in France operated as a model. But Tocqueville finally accepted it as axiomatic that the cost of production was inversely proportional to the scale of production, and that this would make the factory a permanent feature of all modern societies. From this conclusion came his famous chapter on the possibility of an industrial aristocracy where the paradox of the factory system was stated in all its force. Amid the enormous increase of productivity and at the highest stage of civilization loomed the contradictions of industrial power in the hands of a minority on one side and a mass of helpless psychological cripples and social dependents on the other. As a matter of historical observation, Tocqueville's chapter on manufactures was no more than commonplace, and was intended to be no more than a summary statement of well-known facts. Even the generally optimistic Nassau Senior concluded his outline of political economy with a note on gross inequalities of income occasioned by the excessive division of labor. But Senior, probably Tocqueville's source of economic analysis on the subject, regarded the evil as both inevitable and limited. Tocqueville looked at the problem in a similar way. The chapter on manufactures was placed, without any attempt at introduction or integration, at the end of a subdivision concerning the influence of democracy on the feelings of Americans. The chapter itself does not mention America and has only the remotest relation to democratic feelings. Like the aristocracy of manufactures itself, the chapter that surveyed it was an epiphenomenon in relation to the whole. Moreover, although the chapter complained of the worker's dependence on the manufacturer and his degradation by him, it addressed itself primarily to the potential danger of the manufacturing aristocracy to the society as a whole. The essential question concerned the industrialists' social power and their possible emergence as a dangerous new class. Tocqueville's answer was a cautious optimism. It was optimistic precisely *because* of the total alienation of the factory operatives as well as social mobility and lack of class consciousness among the manufacturers.[31]

More important to Tocqueville than the relation of those in the manufacturing classes to each other was their relation to the state, and thus to his fundamental problem of centralization. By the late 1830's, all industrial trends seemed to point to increased administrative centralization. The chief danger was that this form of dependency might spread even to the hitherto healthy and energetic agricultural classes and convert the entire nation into a mass of placemen and solicitors. Industrialization reinforced the new kind of authority-dependency relationship within the bosom of democratic societies. All industrial classes were socially more organized and economically more insecure. They were even more likely to demand new kinds of social action from the state. As he observed the increasing role of

31. If his general prognosis of greater equality of conditions has struck later readers as prophetic, it is despite his prognosis based on extrapolations from a proprietary present on the one hand, and from an inflexible vision of industrialization on the other. History perhaps canceled out two prophecies.

Luis Diez Del Corral, in "Tocqueville et la pensée politique des Doctrinaires" in *Alexis de Tocqueville, Livre du Centenaire*, 66–67, also notes the failure of Tocqueville's static social model to explain important aspects of the industrial revolution. He ascribes it to Tocqueville's "aristocratic schema" rather than to his proprietary outlook in the sense indicated above. But it would be difficult to assert that Guizot, whom Diez Del Corral describes as having a bourgeois and Calvinist mentality, understood the implications of industrialism any better than Tocqueville. See Douglas Johnson, *Guizot: Aspects of French History, 1787–1874* (London and Toronto, 1963), 85.

the government in French economic life and social welfare toward 1840, his emphasis on industrialism shifted to industry's special liability to state control. From the worker, to the entrepreneur, to the great publicly owned or supported enterprises, from incorporation laws to factory inspection, all phases of industrial activity were more prone to state regulation than were nonindustrial enterprises. At the end of *Democracy in America* virtually all innovations that emanated from, or depended on, the state for *any* part of their operation were portrayed as being agencies fostering the concentration of sovereign power. "Industry leads us along, and they [rulers] lead industry," was the conclusion. While the factory system might only be a sport in the totality of social relations, industrial relations as a whole affected all aspects of society, and the industrial class, after having been an exceptional class, threatened to become the only class.[32] In addition, Continental capital and labor, bound by traditional habits of dependency on the monarch, and looking to the state for initiative and security, threatened to drag all society into a condition of administrative semi-dependency.

One might well ask how it came about that the "exceptional" industrial aristocracy of Part II of the *Democracy* of 1840, and the "exceptional" industrial labor force of Part III dramatically threatened to become "the chief, and one might say the only" class in Part IV.[33] The explana-

32. *Democracy in America*, 660–663. About half of Tocqueville's chapter on "How the Sovereign Power is Increasing Among the European Nations of Our Time" (655–664) was devoted to industry as a special cause of centralization.

33. Compare *Democracy in America*, 529–531 and 559 with 660–661.

tion of this ambiguity is not readily apparent. It would seem that Tocqueville might have realized certain implications of industrialization at only a very late stage in the composition of the work. It is clear, for example, that he and Beaumont had regarded land ownership as the primary source of democratic values from their first wanderings in America until far into the composition of the second part of the *Democracy*. They had vigorously defended this view against the arguments of Nassau Senior that land should be regarded as simply one form of fixed capital. Yet, just as he was launching into the final part of the *Democracy* in 1838 Tocqueville began to refer in his notes to industrial property as the "democratic property par excellence"[34] and to indicate the ways in which agriculture was being assimilated into the economic nexus of industrial society. We also know that Part IV caused him a long intellectual crisis. After he wrote it he reordered his thinking to such an extent that it took the better part of a year for him to revise the earlier parts. One might be tempted here to apply to Part IV Sainte-Beuve's general criticism of Tocqueville, that he pretended to know from all eternity what he had learned only yesterday. It was certainly a case of poorly or incompletely incorporated insight. But this is really too simple an explanation. Tocqueville did spend a year in revision, yet he chose to emphisize

34. Yale Mss C.V.g, paq. 9, cahier 2, p. 123. This was his comment on a discussion of mining legislation in the Chamber of Deputies (Aug. 8, 1838). Beginning with 1838, Tocqueville's annotations of French legislative debates tend to emphasize any data that could be used to link economic growth and centralization. See also Yale Mss C.V.g: comment on the *Journal des débats*, March 6, 1838, paq. 9, cahier 2, p. 42.

the exceptionality of industrialization in Parts II and III, and the centrality of industrialization in Part IV.[35] In a sense his argument was empirically based in both cases. The population of France was not urbanized and certainly not industrialized in 1840. But the secular movement by 1840 was statistically obvious and psychologically unnerving. The argument in Parts II and III for exceptionality was as myopic in its use of the part-time peasant-worker as Part IV was in its portrait of the omnivorous industrial explosion.

Permitting the ambiguity to stand without resolution may have been conscious or unconscious on Tocqueville's part. What is certain is that industrialization seemed more serious and alarming to him in relation to political centralization and less alarming insofar as it merely affected social democratization or economic equalization or cultural homogenization. What Tocqueville feared most was not the threat to equality but the threat to liberty. What most vitally concerned him was neither industrial serfdom nor an industrial aristocracy, but industrial centralization. In

35. It is also important to note in this context that Tocqueville's shifts of emphasis were more often a reconsideration of old data in the light of additional information than conversions. Tocqueville did not suddenly realize in 1837–1838 that governments could be large-scale entrepreneurs. He had commented on a similar phenomenon in America in 1831. But despite the great public projects launched and completed by American states, he discovered no propensity in American democracy to systematically absorb all economic activity into the state. Far from stressing even a potential danger to society, the *Democracy* of 1835 came close of ignoring the role of government in American economic development altogether. His shift in perception came as a result of legislative developments in France. See the letter of Tocqueville to Royer-Collard, April 4, 1838, Bibliothèque de l'Institut.

relation to the dynamics of administrative concentration it represented the ideal type of a new variety of social dependency. Industrialization heightened the opportunity to reintroduce *political* paternalism into the democratic social process at the very moment when the great middle section of humanity was throwing off aristocratic tutelage. Lulled by the hum of industrialization, society contentedly curled up at the feet of its beneficent patron.

The dangers of centralization, to which all Tocqueville's discussions turned sooner or later, were considered against the background of an individualistic, middle-class society. Citizens would be legally equal, literate, and economically independent, even if politically unambitious and insignificant. Governments, no matter how powerful, would conceive of their own power in terms of that social base. They would be bureaucratically dependable, not arbitrary and rapacious. Above all they would be moderate, respectful of life, industry, property, family, and privacy. It was the subtle dangers of the state to this propertied, self-sustaining, and middling class to which Tocqueville's thought continually returned. In relation to this social group the chief danger was in allowing the state to encroach on the available social activity of modern society.[36]

36. From the above analysis it would be impossible to accept without crippling reservations Raymond Aron's conclusions (1) that "Modern democracy, as seen by Tocqueville is fundamentally a commercial and industrial society," (2) that Tocqueville implied that democratic society "is the society of the universal wage earner," (3) that Tocqueville "had a tendency to combine commercial and industrial activity," (4) that "the inequality of fortunes implied by commercial and industrial activity did not seem to him to contradict the equalitarian tendency of modern societies," or (5) that "Tocqueville, as early as 1835, was fashioning that half-enthusiastic, half-

From the libertarian point of view it was *more* significant that France contained the lowest proportion of wealthy individuals in Europe than that its proportion of poor individuals was also the lowest. Representative institutions, the press, and voluntary associations were the chief means by which its potential collective initiative could be nurtured. Psychologically, Tocqueville's ideas were formulated in terms of his selective Anglo-American experience and expounded in the individualistic and proprietary milieu of French liberalism. When he came to view the problems of classes who did not fulfill the social preconditions of independence and self-sufficiency, he found that the costs of any social action to the *normative* classes and his own libertarian values weighted his options, intellectual as well as political.

---

resigned—perhaps more resigned than enthusiastic—theory of what is known today as the welfare state—or universal *embourgeoisement"* (*Main Currents in Sociological Thought*, I, 191–192, 201, 223). The difficulty in accepting the first sentence can be observed from the fact that Tocqueville's social "point of departure" in *Democracy in America* is land structure and change; the second sentence is contradicted by Tocqueville's chapter on wages in *Democracy in America*, Part II; the third and fourth are contradicted by his specific isolation of manufacturing in his notes and in the chapter on the manufacturing of aristocracy (in turn partially contradicted by statements in a later chapter); the fifth is unwarranted in its dating of any conception of a welfare state, as well as in anachronistically equating the welfare state with *embourgeoisement*. This will be elaborated in the discussion of the right to work debate in Chapter VII.

IV

The Residue of Dependency
and the Notables

THE positions of Tocqueville and Beaumont in relation to the reform movement in France has never been adequately explained or even broached. Was their investigation of the penitentiary system in America simply a pretext?[1] Why then did they choose this pretext? And why, after fulfilling their obligations to the government with their classic report, did they continue to take part in the movement to the extent that they were among the most

1. On Tocqueville's and Beaumont's motives for their visit to America and their choice of subject, see Pierson, *Tocqueville and Beaumont*, Chapter III.

prominent, if not the actual authors of the prison system that France was about to adopt on the eve of the Revolution of 1848? It was they who defended a specific version of the penitentiary system in parliament, the Academy, and the press, and it was their conclusions that were quoted and counterquoted, even against their originators.[2] If their interest in prison reform was only a pretext in 1830, it was a cause after 1833, and by 1843 it was in Tocqueville's own words a more important question for themselves than for the government. An understanding of the historical background of their concern can at least suggest the reasons for both the cause and continuity of their interest in social reform as a whole in the decades before 1848.

Neither democracy nor America was virgin territory to French social analysts when *Democracy in America* appeared in 1835. Yet *Democracy in America* had an unmistakable ring of both novelty and comprehensiveness that captured the admiration and respect of almost all contemporaries, whatever their political affiliation. The underlying aim was novel and the execution was exhaustive. There was no dearth of contemporary literature on America for Tocqueville to draw on, but until the *Democracy* the general image of America was dominated by exotic pictures of the American wilderness and of the antique republic of the founding fathers, or by equally mundane descriptions of American manners and political constitutions.[3] Tocqueville's work seriously treated America as a possible guide for France in its major social trend, and he

2. See *Tocqueville and Beaumont on Social Reform*, ed. Drescher, Part II.
3. See Rémond, *Les Etats-Unis*, II, part 3.

wrote his work in the comparative mood. It claimed recognition not primarily for its insights about an alien society, but for its attempt to glimpse the possible and probable tendencies of France's future. The selected model for the future was the significant break with the Anglocentrism of his notable liberal contemporaries.[4] Tocqueville was so determined that the chain of ideas should be as free as possible from all extraneous influence that he refused to look at all other contemporary accounts of the United States, including Michel Chevalier's letters. Judging from his own intellectual exclusiveness and his readers' acknowledgments, Tocqueville's work on America was relatively freer from obligations to contemporary French opinion than most works of its genre. The same thing, *mutatis mutandis*, can be said of Beaumont's *Marie*.

With the exception of their work on comparative prison reform, however, the same cannot be said of Tocqueville's and Beaumont's views on poverty and public welfare. They made no systematic attempt, for example, to get an independent perspective on poverty in America as they did with democracy, As noted before, the evidence would seem to indicate that they regarded American industrialization, poverty, and public welfare as irrevelant both to democracy in America and French problems. At best, poverty in America was something qualitatively different from poverty in Europe, and American welfare institutions were more anachronistic imitations of the English than harbingers of the future.

4. See Margery E. Elkington, *Les Relations de société entre l'Angleterre et la France sous la Restauration (1814–1830)* (Paris, 1929), and Reboul, *Le Mythe anglais dans la littérature française sous la Restauration.*

However, even as regards poverty in Europe, Tocqueville and Beaumont were willing to rely on a vision of the problem as refracted through contemporary analysis. It was enough to try to fathom the sociological implications of the central transition from aristocracy to democracy without having to take on the formidable task of an independent study of the industrial development of Europe. As he neared the end of his book on democracy Tocqueville noted that the economic problems to which he was devoting a few brief pages were at least worthy of a whole book in themselves. But the very process of writing had already cost him so many years of labor and anxiety that he resolved never to write another major work.[5] His attitude might be summed up in his own words on the general need for reliance on authority:

If a man had to prove for himself all the truths of which he makes use every day, he would never come to an end of it. He would wear himself out proving preliminary points and make no progress. Since life is too short for such a course and human faculties are too limited, man has to accept as certain a whole heap of facts and opinions which he has neither leisure nor power to examine and verify for himself, things which cleverer men than he have discovered and which the crowd accepts. On that foundation he then builds the house of his own thoughts. He does not act so from any conscious choice, for the inflexible laws of his existence compel him to behave like that.

No philosopher in the world, however great, can help believing a million things on trust from others or assuming the truth of many things besides those he has proved. Such behavior is desirable as well as necessary. Anyone who undertook to go into everything himself could give but little time or attention to each question. . . . His intelligence would be in-

5. See Tocqueville to Beaumont, July 8, 1838, (Yale Mss C.I.a.2); *Oeuvres* (M): *Correspondence Tocqueville-Beaumont*, I, 310.

dependent but weak. So a choice must be made among all the things about which men have opinions, and some beliefs must be accepted without discussion so that it is possible to go deeply into a few selected ones for examination. . . . So somewhere and somehow authority is always bound to play a part in intellectual and moral life.[6]

Compared to Tocqueville's views on the process of democratization, his ideas on the social problem in Europe were relatively dependent, and relatively authority-bound. The extent to which this acceptance affected his general views of democratization and modernization has already been touched on and will again be considered in another context. At this point in the analysis it is enough to note that Tocqueville's reactions to poverty, as to European economic development in general, were more deeply embedded in the socio-intellectual ideas of his country and generation than his ideas on the political and social psychology of democratic man.[7] Perhaps this is only another way of saying that, in analyzing an individual's social thought, a sociology of knowledge will clarify it in inverse proportion to his areas of creativity and in direct proportion to his reliance on the "whole heap of facts and opinions which he has neither the leisure nor power to verify." The fact that Tocqueville was a liberal aristocratic landowner living in a postrevolutionary society with a relatively exclusive political and social structure may hopefully clarify the texture of his "dependent" thought, where it might water down an analysis of his genius.

6. *Democracy in America*, 398–399.
7. On the investigation of social assumptions, see C. B. MacPherson. *The Political Theory of Possessive Individualism* (Oxford, 1962), 4–8.

The French elite response to poverty was also clearly formulated, socially and ideologically, in the France of 1830. The movement to which Tocqueville and Beaumont had attached themselves by the end of the Bourbon regime was part of a social pattern that was historically well defined, international in scope, and highly restricted to the notable class in leadership and membership. The group of overlapping movements which in the nineteenth century were denoted by the name "humanitarianism" were direct descendants of similar movements that first clearly emerged in the second half of the previous century. The intellectual roots of humanitarianism were in the combination of religious and secular enthusiasms of the evangelical revival and the enlightenment. The humanitarian movement in France, led by highly educated aristocratic and bourgeois intellectuals, gradually formulated a broad program designed to systematize and secularize a national program of public welfare in matters of education, health, old age, criminality, and especially indigence and charity. The government of Louis XVI was by no means reluctant to proceed in limited experimentation in social reform. By the end of the old regime it had begun to implement some of the humanitarian projects and had accepted a good deal more in the way of its long-range goals.

Despite the formal denunciations by the National Assembly of the abuses of the old regime in the realm of public assistance, in practice the Revolution was more productive of a temporary acceleration of tendencies that were already prominent for a generation or more than of a sudden change in direction. For a brief moment at the beginning of the Revolution of 1789 it appeared likely that France would break free of its restraining structures and leap ahead of its neighbors in the eradication of the long-diagnosed social ills of the century. Members of the liberal nobility and upper bourgeoisie who had already made a reputation as welfare advocates and experts moved into guiding positions on parliamentary committees which were formed to draw up the legislative design for public welfare. The major committee on this legislation was significantly called the Committee on Mendicancy.[8] This reflected the large number of *cahiers de doléances* of 1789, which had singled out the growing problems of beggary and vagabondage as prime threats to social order, and demanded immediate action to reduce their numbers. Mendicancy was attacked in the name of the ideology of maximizing productivity, which was also directed against the regular clergy and their landed endowments. To the demands of the *cahiers* against beggars were added the combined pressures of the attack on the economic foundations of religious charities during one of the severest economic crises of the century.

The Committee on Mendicancy met three times a week for over a year and a half (February 1790–September 1791) and emerged with a plan for systematic public relief. The aim of charity was to encourage, not to direct, individual initiative and energy with the idea of making everyone a small proprietor. In accordance with the attack on idleness, most holidays were to be suppressed or incorporated with Sundays. The idea of savings banks was broached. Begging

8. See R. B. Du Boff, "Economic Thought in Revolutionary France, 1789–1792, the Question of Poverty and Unemployment," *French Historical Studies*, IV, no. 4 (Fall 1966).

was to be regarded as an antisocial crime and to be remedied by a penitentiary system encouraging the formation of work habits and skills. The penitentiary system was considered an intimate part of the continuum of poverty legislation. The committee's ideological thrust was far more significant than its operation. The entire scheme was buried amid the exigencies of war and inflation, which commanded far higher priority than public welfare. The Revolution left only a record of temporary expedients of charity workshops that provided models for dealing with the economic consequences of later revolutionary crises. After an initially enthusiastic acceleration of expenditures in the first flush of the Revolution, the workshops were closed by law on June 16, 1791.[9] The First Revolutionary government had the foresight to include in the decree of dissolution an appropriation of a million livres for specific public works. The limits of the right to relief and the obligations of the state were fixed. An attempt was made at categorization and preventive legislation. Public assistance and the right to subsistence through labor was recognized as the state's obligation to every citizen. An upper limit of relief, afterward known as the principle of less eligibility, was also introduced. Excessive public relief had to be avoided at all costs in order not to place a premium on "idleness, debauchery, and imprudence."[10] It was made a national and centrally regulated service since all hospitals, almshouses, corporations, and endowments were henceforth national property. A new tax system and administrative hierarchy

9. See Shelby T. McCloy, *Government Assistance in Eighteenth-Century France* (Durham, N.C., 1946), 289–291.

10. Ferdinand Dreyfus, *Un philanthrope d'autrefois: La Rochefoucauld-Liancourt, 1747–1827* (Paris, 1903), 174.

were envisioned for the care of orphans, the sick, the aged, and the infirm. For the able-bodied, temporary aid would be given only in exchange for productive labor, "less well paid than free labor; it must under no circumstance replace it."[11] The theory assumed on the one hand a socially disadvantaged portion of society with absolute claims to existence. On the other hand, it assumed the legal obligation of the state to distribute assistance uniformly as a right. Also, it assumed that the charity system was a net which caught only those on the edge of existence. To the helpless (orphan, aged, etc.) it provided relief to the extent of the disability; it kept the able-bodied and unemployed recipients at the lower limit of the "self-sustaining" realm. For anyone who chose to live by not working, e.g., a beggar, or a vagabond, it prescribed penal sanctions. It was a net, not an institution designed to foster an achievement ethic; it was a ladder of social mobility one rung high.

By 1794 the humanitarian program had either been radicalized far beyond the intentions of their originators, as with the abolition of slavery, or abandoned as a casualty of war and revolutionary priorities, as with the national welfare programs. Thermidor only brought a patchwork approach to social problems, and the Napoleonic regime, in its turn, concentrated on police repression in France and the restoration of slavery in the colonies as the quickest means of restoring discipline in the nether world. Its major innovation in public welfare was in the administration of the penal repression of beggary through the establishment of *dépôts de mendicité* throughout France. Public welfare projects lapsed, or reverted to the pre-Revolutionary pat-

11. *Ibid.*,180.

tern of private, church, and local initiative and responsibility. Institutionally and legally, large areas of French public welfare remained in this stage right through Tocqueville's and Beaumont's lifetimes. When Tocqueville died in 1859, Frenchmen still had no legal right to relief, and for three generations after the Revolution the original plans for relief still outdistanced the laws.

The entire project was tabled from one legislative assembly to another, despite some theoretical elaboration by the Convention, including the declaration of a right to work. Finally, the Directory simply returned or replaced the funds of the old charitable associations. At the end of the Revolutionary period nothing remained of national social duties and the legal right to assistance. The line of personal continuity was also broken. The Revolution dispersed the elite groups which had formulated the grand scheme of charity and welfare, and allowed the surviving charitable institutions to pick up the threads of relief piecemeal. In some areas public relief disappeared entirely and was only rebuilt bit by bit by municipal governments.

Socially, the framework of the humanitarian movement had also been shattered by 1792–1793. Its original leaders and carriers were either dead, exiled, involved in other political tasks, or scattered into the invisibility of private life. Slowly during the Napoleonic period and more rapidly during the Bourbon Restoration the humanitarian movement regrouped and co-opted membership among the new notables. It differed from the previous generation less in the social character of its personnel than in its attitude toward the methods of inducing social change. The fulfillment of the humanitarian program of the end of the old regime remained the goal of the movement, but the desire to control the pace and direction of reform had a new priority among the notables. In emphasizing the historical background of the humanitarian reform movement, it must be recalled that the continuity and divisions of opinions among the notability in early nineteenth-century France were related to its relative social and economic stability. The stable position of notable families as well as individuals contributed to the vitality of family political traditions. "In the majority of families, the opinion of the sons is determined by the political behavior of the fathers; in the provinces, even in the large cities, the sons of a great notable are quite often only the heirs of paternal influence."[12] Especially as regards their attitudes toward social evolution and class relationships, the breaks in post-Revolutionary patterns of geographical and familial influence and outlook is less apparent than the continuities.

The critical period of notable reconstruction therefore began in the authoritarian political environment of the Bonapartist and Bourbon regimes. In this environment, and after the enthusiastic omnibus projects of the Revolution, humanitarian organizations assiduously avoided massive social programs that might directly challenge political authority or require radical shifts in the disbursement of the very limited resources alloted to public welfare. It equally avoided open-ended and incalculable commitments such as national relief systems.

While remaining committed to the idea of progress, the movement identified itself as one that took great pains to proceed by empirical studies and carefully defined experiments free of explicit political identification. Its carriers

12. Tudesq, *Les Grands notables*, I, 107–109.

in their humanitarian capacity were nonpartisan. A clear distinction was drawn, both in and out of the parliamentary arena, between political questions and social questions. To call a question social was to assert that there was a common agreement by the entire political class that positions on the question would not follow, or be ascribed to, normal political divisions.[13]

The terms in which this type of social reform was conceived were, of course, always pacific. A premium was placed upon a total moral consensus on the end to be achieved, for example physical health or moral and technical improvement. This is illustrated by the Restoration emphasis on public health projects, the emphasis on technical education, and the frequent disclaimers against all socially disruptive ideas. Additional emphasis was placed on the need to achieve the voluntary acquiescence of all those in high social positions who could be adversely affected by any reform. By and large, persuasion and collaboration through long investigation in coordination with interested notables was preferred to instruments of mass appeal: the small society of interested notables was preferred to a mass movement; the scientific *Memoir* presented to the government or to an Academy was preferred to the popular meeting; the prize essay on a specific aspect of a question was preferred to the exposé article or romantic manifesto. In opting for forms of official action, the "inside" official investigating commission was preferred to the muckraking campaign, the parliamentary or royal commission to the mass petition.

In the notable approach to reform, a maximum of em-

13. See, for example, the debates on the child labor law in 1841, or on prison reform in 1844 in the Chamber of Deputies.

phasis was placed on scientific and pragmatic, as opposed to moralistic and messianic, approaches. In talking about race relations in the United States, Tocqueville might well talk in terms of total oppression and idealized dichotomies. But when one talked of institutions involving French notables, what were considered were statistics, institutional limitations, and a careful analysis of discreet interests. One has only to compare either *Marie* or *Democracy in America* on race relations to Tocqueville's later work on abolition in the French colonies to sense the narrowed emotional range and intellectual scope of social action in writings on an elite-controlled institution.[14] The humanitarian movement also dealt almost exclusively with problems in which there was a broad consensus on what constituted the problem. It might campaign to improve prison diets or hospital conditions, or attack the acknowledged inconsistency between legal commitments and enforcement, such as the toleration of the slave trade. The suggestions for innovation were usually as narrowly defined and as cautiously empirical as the definition of problems. Implementation and persuasion were based on the results of discrete projects, or more often on an evaluation of already functioning foreign experiments. Foreign experiments were described, recommended piecemeal, tested through pilot projects, and evaluated in terms of organizational simplicity, statistical effectiveness, and price. The Anglophile ideological orientation and the English personal contacts of a large number of French liberals in post-Napoleonic France insured a steady flow of reform data from across the Channel, and eventually from

14. See *Tocqueville and Beaumont on Social Reform*, ed. Drescher, Part III.

across the Atlantic. In the early decades of the nineteenth century the humanitarian movement in the Anglo-American world rapidly accumulated a body of legislative and institutional reforms while France's energies were focused on the exigencies of dynastic conflict, internal revolution, and war.

The personnel of humanitarianism in France were also selected to maximize elite control. For specific reforms, temporary educational or charitable associations drew on a pool of humanitarian notables and their wives. Broader and more permanent groups were constituted as educational, religious, and moral societies. They were restricted, elite associations. Formal and informal measures were adopted in order to avoid anything resembling mass movements or even the appearance of popularization. In this the notable moral societies were merely the counterparts of the narrowly restrictive political institutions of the French constitutional monarchy.

If there was one broad line of organizational conflict in the humanitarian movement it was as much historical and cultural as social and economic. The most prominent humanitarian organization in the post-Napoleonic period was the Society of Christian Morality, founded in 1821. Its president was La Rochefoucauld-Liancourt, who had also been the guiding spirit of the first Revolutionary assembly's Committee on Mendicancy. Its center of activity was Paris. Its membership was disproportionately Protestant. Although its members included Catholics, it was felt necessary to argue in favor of the right of Catholics to participate in the society. For its pronouncements against "fanaticism" it was continuously attacked as a coalition of Protestants and liberals *"nés catholiques* to decatholicize France . . . a society of skeptics, indifferents, of deistic hypocrites."[15] The society's most serious competitor of the Restoration period, the Congregation, engaged in similar humanitarian enterprises. Almost the entire future political personnel of the July Monarchy was linked with the Society of Christian Morality or published in its journal: the Duc d'Orléans, his son Rémusat, Delessert, Guizot, De Broglie, Benjamin Constant, Vivien, Dufaure, Lamartine, Thiers, and Mignet. Its Protestant and liberal membership had close personal links with the humanitarian movement in the English-speaking world.

The organization exerted influence primarily through its journal, but also through committees for political refugees, for placing orphans, etc. The topics treated by the journal show both the concerns of the society and the limits of the topics brought under discussion: the abolition of the slave trade, of gambling, of lottery, of the death penalty, and the reform of prisons, with the models in Geneva and America given special attention. Questions relating to slavery and to prison reform, with all their internationalist connotations, elicited the most attention from the society.

Certain social reforms were selected out of the political and cultural conflict between liberals and traditionalists as suitable fields of battle in the restricted atmosphere of the Restoration. However, one should not make the mistake of identifying the competitive moral societies of the Bourbon Restoration as two alien groups that led mutually exclusive social lives. The center of social and political life for both

15. Dreyfus, *Un philanthrope d'autrefois*, 177.

groups was Paris, and there was a good deal of informal interchange in the literary salons, which provided the circulatory system for contacts among the Paris notables. Members of the humanitarian affiliates of either society might end up in the other camp. During the Restoration Beaumont himself was a member of the *Société des bonnes oeuvres*, an action branch of the Catholic Congregation. Among the notables, plural social affiliation was quite high, and membership in a single group was not an accurate measure of one's position in the ideological or social spectrum.[16]

The conception of the problems of poverty began to change during the Restoration with the increased tempo of industrialization and mechanization. The conception of the able-bodied poor began to be discussed more in terms of pauperism than mendicancy, and of the urban worker rather than the rural vagabond.[17] At least in certain

16. Even Tocqueville's political break with his family has often been distorted, because of the emphasis placed on the legitimist outlook of his parents rather than the "liberal" outlook of his pre-Revolutionary progenitors. It must be recalled that Tocqueville's eighteenth-century reformist ancestor, Malesherbes, was also his chosen political model. As Tocqueville wrote in a note to himself: "I am the grand-child of M. de M. [Malesherbes]. No one is unaware that M. de M. after having defended the people before King Louis XVI, defended King Louis XVI before the people. It is a double example that I have never forgotten, and that I will never forget" (Ms from the Tocqueville archives, displayed by M. André Jardin in the Bibliothèque Nationale "Hommage à Alexis de Tocqueville [1805–1859]," Paris, 1959).

17. Tocqueville probably obtained his first information on the concept of "pauperism" from Say, who credited the English with inventing the term (J.-B. Say, *Cours complèt d'économie politique* [Paris, 1828], V, 352n.). For earlier anticipations of the "progress and poverty" conception of industrialization see Du Boff, "Economic Thought in Revolutionary France."

regions (Nord, Mulhouse, Rouen) there was increasing discussion of proletarianization after the economic depression of the post-Napoleonic period and the relative stagnation and decline of real wages in certain industries. On the part of legitimist and traditionalist agrarians there was an attempt to shift the cause of France's misery from the rural-mendicant-clerical nexus of the Revolutionary perspective to urban-prolitarian-industrialist variables. Certainly the prominence of Protestant and liberal elements in certain segments of the financial and industrial world, and their close commercial links to industrial England, which played an important role in the elite cultural conflict of the Restoration, was deepened by the July Revolution. Pauperization had already been accepted as a by-product of economic progress by J.-B. Say in his *Cours complét d'économie politique*, a work carefully studied by Tocqueville even before his journey to America. Opponents of English political economy went even further. The evil of pauperization was traced in seminal studies by the legitimist Villeneuve-Bargemont, and the agrarianists Bigot de Morogues and Charles de Coux,[18] to the foreign, Protestant, individualist, liberal, acquisitive philosophies of Adam Smith and his French counterpart, Jean-Baptiste Say. The social atomization of the French Revolution was merely the final stage in a centuries-long process of individuation.

Tocqueville accepted this acknowledged correlation of growing pauperism and industrialization as his point of departure. He also followed the main trend in French economic thought in at least one other important point: the

18. See Jean-Baptiste Duroselle, *Les Débuts du catholicisme social en France* (Paris, 1951), Chapter I.

idea that the industrial revolution and its concomitant pauperism were due primarily to a psychological over-stimulation of "artificial" needs. In the aftermath of the July Revolution a rapid rise in lower-class agitation and a combination of emergency relief and repression called forth renewed consideration of the possibilities of a legal systematization of a variety of relief and reform measures. There was little attempt to discriminate between categories of the poor. Global statistics, such as in Tocqueville's *Memoir on Pauperism*,[19] and broad geographical breakdowns were the common basis of analysis, whether intra- or international. One easily confused all the categories that applied to the lower classes. The result was an ambiguous continuum between "laboring" and "dangerous" (though not necessarily revolutionary) classes: the worker, the poor and the pauper, the indigent, the delinquent, the temporarily unemployed and the underemployed, psychological disturbance and moral depravity.[20] In such an ideological environment the upper-class humanitarian would slip quite easily from a conception of social to moral hierarchies. Especially in the early period, no distinctions were made within the main categories of rich and poor in order to take account of new occupational groups and classes.

As in England, most studies of public charity were a

19. See *Memoir on Pauperism* in *Tocqueville and Beaumont on Social Problems*, ed. Drescher.
20. See Tudesq, *Les Grands notables*, 568–569. French liberal humanitarians were not alone in being more concerned about the psychological effects of charity than physical suffering. Dependence was considered a moral disease elsewhere as well. See Jenifer Hart, "Nineteenth-Century Social Reform: A Tory Interpretation of History," *Past and Present*, July, 1965, 53.

function of the growing financial burden of relief on the taxpayer rather than an attempt systematically to isolate the variables in pauperization. Much was made of rising expectations among the poor. Misery in England, as Tocqueville noted, might be considered comfort in France and prosperity in Spain. In terms of basic human needs, physical suffering was carefully distinguished from "artificial" discontent. A good part of poverty, in this perspective, was due to the overgenerosity of the rich, who by misplaced benevolence had stirred the imaginations of the poor into a vicious cycle of escalating demands. The establishment of a legal right to public assistance was the ultimate outcome of such a trend.

Tocqueville's and Beaumont's own concerns with the problem of poverty arose from their French and European milieu rather than any American experience. They regarded their penitentiary mission in America as a part of the larger humanitarian movement.[21] But Tocqueville's first and only attempt to account systematically for the phenomenon of poverty and especially industrial poverty was in response to the request of a local scholarly society shortly after the appearance of *Democracy in America*. Tocqueville was asked to prepare a paper on pauperism by the Royal Academic Society of Cherbourg in La Manche. This department was statistically one of the more highly pauperized in the kingdom although its ratios ranked well below those of highly industrialized departments like the Nord. Indigence was by no means a novelty in nineteenth-century

21. Tocqueville was also the author of the short note on pauperism in America in the co-authored *Systemè pénitentiaire* (see Yale Tocqueville-Beaumont Mss B.I.f.3).

Normandy or France, although the extensive use of "pauperism" and some of its connotations was relatively novel.[22] In any event there was a growing apprehension in La Manche about the increasing tax burden resulting from relief and welfare demands. Concerted attacks in England on the old poor law had also just reached their climax. The debates in England, sharpened by a generation of discussion, loomed large in any treatment of the problem across the Channel. At the precise moment that Tocqueville was writing his *Memoir on Pauperism*, the English government had completed an enormous investigation of the administration of the poor law and had just passed into law what

22. In comparative percentage terms there was apparently something less than alarming about the indigency rate in Normandy at the beginning of the July Monarchy. Estimates of pauperism in Rouen at the end of the *ancien régime* (when there was a similar outcry against increasing pauperism) seem to point to the existence of a chronic or intermittent rather than an acute or novel indigency problem. See *Cahiers de doléances du tiers état du baillage de Rouen*, ed. M. Bouloiseau (Paris, 1957), I. The basis of assigning indigency might have been different in 1789, when beggary was still a profession officially sanctioned by religion, from what it was forty years later. Douai listed 26 per cent of its population as indigent but only 11 per cent were exempt from taxes. See Georges Lefebvre, *Paysans du nord* (Paris, 1924), 298, and Alfred Cobban, *The Social Interpretation of the French Revolution* (Cambridge, Eng., 1964), 134–135. But it would appear that the *cahiers* of 1789 and the Committee on Mendicancy concentrated on indigency as a rural problem. The studies of the late Restoration and the July Monarchy stressed the urban-industrial context of pauperism. While the *cahiers* of Cahors and Rouen wanted to close all caberets except in towns or within a quarter of a league of the main highway in 1789, alcoholism seemed to have migrated to the city and factory by 1830. Whatever the facts about the growth and distribution of pauperism and spirits between 1790 and 1840, the fears had certainly moved in the direction of a social redefinition.

promised to be drastic measures to drive the able-bodied worker, especially in rural areas, back into the free labor market, through a system of psychic punishment known as the workhouse test. Nassau Senior,[23] from whom Tocqueville requested information for his *Memoir*, was, along with Edwin Chadwick, the coauthor of both the investigation report and the new poor law amendments. Senior provided Tocqueville with both. It is against this background that the *Memoir*'s categorical pronouncement against any legal right to relief was written.

A number of points should be made about this essay. True to the pattern of Tocqueville's sporadic treatment of poverty, it remained incomplete. Precisely at the point where the essay was to deal with prevention and remedies, Tocqueville's publishing impulse died.[24] First an article on France before the Revolution, then the second part of the *Democracy* consumed his time. He never returned to the task at any point in his legislative career.

Even more important in terms of his own thought, Tocqueville's *Memoir* cast a stone at his own major historical premise. If "there were no longer classes of rich and poor," who were these unfortunates who risked misery of a new kind, who had received "from God the special and dangerous mission of providing for the material well-being of the rest of society"? This amplified Tocqueville's and Beaumont's earlier statement that the wages of advanced industrial societies, at least in Europe, naturally tended to hover around subsistence.[25] Permanent poverty and insecurity

23. On Senior's relation to Tocqueville, see Drescher, *Tocqueville and England*, 58–60, 76–77.
24. *Tocqueville and Beaumont on Social Reform*, ed. Drescher, 27.
25. *Penitentiary System*, 201–202.

were thus as providential and permanent for industrial workers as equalization was for the remainder of society.

In the *Memoir* the right to legal charity for the able-bodied was rejected on economic, administrative, and, above all, psychological grounds. It eventually destroyed productive capital and ultimately national wealth. The principle of less eligibility could never be enforced vigorously enough. The wealthy and their administrators would always prove to be victims of misplaced generosity. Finally, the assurance of charity inevitably depraved the poor and turned them into parasites and tax farmers of the rich. Legal charity, however administered, proved to be a system "by virtue of which all idlers become beggars and find in the imprudent providence of the law more material aid than they could hope to attain by their hardest work; they live upon alms, degrading themselves and ruining society."[26] Legal charity seemed to imply unearned comfort and security. And well it might, if one simultaneously accepted the iron law of subsistence wages for an entire productive class.

The implications of the *Memoir* epitomize Tocqueville's difficulty in approaching problems related to poverty. His general theory stated that the "dependent" so-

26. Beaumont, *Marie*, 43. See also *Du système pénitentiaire*, and its appendix on pauperism in America. Compare Tocqueville's formulation with the similar conclusion of J.-B. Say: "England is the country that has most havens available to the unfortunate, and it is perhaps the one where most unfortunate demand aid. Let public welfare or private associations open, a hundred, a thousand others—all—will be filled; and there will remain in society equally as many unfortunates who will request permission to enter or who will claim it as a right if one recognized it as such" (*Cours complèt d'économie politique*, V, 350).

ciety of the past was at an end. Economic self-sufficiency was the new norm. Only a new kind of nonmediated political dependency on the state was possible. Therefore, the chief danger to be avoided was an increase in the power of the state. Suddenly there appeared another economically and socially "dependent" class. It was not envisaged as a withering remnant or a mutant but the future of a large minority of the population. It was dependent for employment on a precarious and impersonal economic system, and on society for relief. Either direct or indirect state intervention was required for sheer survival. But for Tocqueville state intervention also threatened to create a false conception of the obligations of society among the idle. It produced a new kind of arrogant independence based on the very "rights" of dependency and put premiums on bastardy, shamelessness, and family disorganization. Even worse, it destroyed the psychological motivation of the free labor force for normal independence. Tocqueville posed a choice between security for the idle and the growth of bureaucracy on the one hand, increasing the opportunities for the new despotism, and limiting state action and keeping the sphere of independence as wide as possible on the other. Once the choice was thus stated, Tocqueville's option was clear. For the indigent, the despised state of personal inequality and even dependency was offered to him as a permanent condition. Patronage, banned from the larger world, could be maintained and strengthened in the underworld. Even ages of equality could still maintain the old moral tie between the rich and the very poor when such ties were rejected as degrading servility everywhere else in the society.

Finally, all state action on behalf of citizens who were not self-sufficient within the contemporary rules of the game was called charity. Free public education was charity. State underwriting of savings banks was charity.[27] With such a formulation of the use of state resources for the poor and only for the poor (subsidies and guarantees for railroads were never called charity, although Tocqueville disliked them, too), one can see how far Tocqueville was removed from the concept of universalized social rights as the basis for community in 1835.

From all their public statements, it seems clear that until the end of the July Monarchy, Tocqueville and Beaumont rejected a general right to relief as a means of alleviating poverty, of educating the poor in prudence, or of overcoming social alienation. Tocqueville put more faith in self-help institutions such as savings banks and mutual aid societies. He regarded the savings bank as an institution for all the poor rather than merely the most favored economic stratum among them. He even hoped that, in the absence of a poor law, the savings institutions would become more important in France than they were in England with its retrograde legal relief. (He ignored the fact that England with its poor law had a far higher total of deposits in savings institutions and a far higher rate of deposits per capita than France.) At one point he asked Beaumont to gather information for him on the operation of savings banks in England and Scotland.[28] Yet his main concern with regard to savings in the period following the *Memoir*

27. Letter of Tocqueville to Gobineau, Oct. 2, 1843, *Oeuvres* (M): *Correspondance Tocqueville-Gobineau*. See *Tocqueville and Beaumont on Social Reform*, ed. Drescher, 26n.
28. Tocqueville, *Journeys to England*, 77–78.

was not how it was affecting the question of poverty, but
how effectively it was increasing the power of the state. In
Democracy in America in 1840, as in the *Memoir on Pauperism*, his emphasis was identical. Savings banks were dangerous as well as beneficial, and their "gravest vice" was
that the deposits were "concentrated in the hands of the
Government."[29] The administrative implications of the
institution that reinforced the spirit of centralization captured his attention. The result of this approach, legislatively speaking, was that while Tocqueville quietly supported
a number of poverty measures he never developed *any* public statement on the means of encouraging preventives
against pauperism through even "indirect charity."[30]

29. *Democracy in America*, 656. See also *Annuaire des cinq de-
partements de la Normandie* (1842), VIII, 329.
30. There is an indication that by the mid-1840's Tocqueville saw
the problem of legal charity in a less rigid and legalistic perspective.
In a report to the *conseil-général* of *La Manche* on the problem of
public policy toward foundlings and abandoned children he wrote:
"We are still afraid of that terrible word, legal charity. What are our
hospitals, our asylums, our relief committees, our charity workshops,
our nurseries and so many other means by which society already
comes to the aid of its members, if not diverse applications of legal
charity?" (Edmonde L'Hommedé, *Un Département français sous
la monarchie de juillet* [Paris, 1933], 245–246). Tocqueville, like
Beaumont, had already been converted by 1844 to the need to systematize the existing system of relief, but not to guarantee a legal
right to relief as a long-range social tendency (see Tocqueville to
Richard Monckton Milnes [Lord Houghton], April 4, 1846 [Milnes
Mss, Trinity College Library, Cambridge]).
    In the discussion of public charity, the expansion of savings banks,
the expansion of education, the child labor laws, Tocqueville and
Beaumont were either negative in their judgment or lent only
passing support. For one reason or another, they did not choose to
devote a large portion of their time and energy to them. Foreign
policy and Algeria were much more absorbing. Fear of the leviathan

After the *Memoir on Pauperism,* Tocqueville and Beaumont, as potential legislators, began to narrow the focus on more specific causes and remedies for poverty than the industrial economy as a whole and the problems of a general system of relief. Especially after his trip to England in

---

state was an inhibiting factor. Another was the fear of violating an area of independence without any certainty that there were easily recognizable limits to the area thus infringed. Public relief threatened to corrode one area after another of the realm of individual initiative and wealth until it destroyed society. No discrimination could be made between the willing and educable and the unwilling or disabled poor. They totally rejected such an attempt. The child labor law obviously applied in one sense only to a dependent class of laborers. Yet even it was a step toward the regulation of labor, which needed liberty to live.

Stranger in the context of other liberal reformers' enthusiasms was Tocqueville's and Beaumont's limited participation in educational reform. Education was theoretically the most favored social right of early nineteenth-century France and was the model type of popular institutions. Equality, mobility, independence of character, integration in the social order—these were all attainable. If the state controlled the individual through it, it was only in his years of minority. Yet in early nineteenth-century France, education was the most politically loaded "social" question. As many nonpartisans discovered, to approach questions of education was to broach the problem of Church and State. (see Douglas Johnson, *Guizot: Aspects of French History, 1787–1874,* London, Toronto, 1963, Chapter 3). For Tocqueville, the best way to reduce the festering scars of the whole post-Revolutionary period was to let sleeping dogs lie, each in his own corner and as far away as institutionally possible. When he intervened in an educational question in parliament he was roundly berated by all sides for confusing and glossing over the real issues. He never tried his hand at educational policy again. Tocqueville and Beaumont rather threw their whole reforming energy into two consensus social problems that were limited in scope and almost precisely calculable in effect, and of minimum effect on the "free" or normal realm of French society. They turned their reforming energies to the prisoner and the slave.

1835, Tocqueville turned his attention toward the factory system and the manufacturing classes as the chief representatives of permanent poverty. Here again appeared to be a class of the poor stuck in the dependency stage of social evolution; its development was relatively retrograde with regard to the increase in wealth and mobility of the rest of the population. It was absolutely retrograde with regard to its general intelligence and self-sufficiency. It was even a deterioration from the old aristocratic framework, in that the relationship between the workers and the industrialists, who "use them and then abandon them to be supported by the charity of the public" was reduced to the cash nexus.

Since Tocqueville was set against having the public assume the burden of any comprehensive charity system, the position of the poor was at once precarious and a potential danger to the state: "For it is hard when the whole of society is on the move to keep one class stationary, and when the greater number of men are opening up new roads to fortune, to force some to bear in peace their needs and desires."[31] The status of the factory class, as viewed by Tocqueville and Beaumont, was a challenge to Tocqueville's general prognosis of social evolution and his talent and energy as a legislator. As he had warned Senior of the consolidation of land in England, there seemed to be two revolutions in process in Europe: "a political democratic movement and a social aristocratic one; that is to say, on the one side a general and equal redistribution of political rights amongst a continually increasing number of individuals and on the other a proportionately increasing concentration of wealth in the hands of the few. This anomaly cannot last

31. *Democracy in America,* 559.

long without grave danger to the State."[32] This danger to equality, to the security of the workers, and to the stability of society required the total concern of the legislator in Tocqueville's judgment. But he never published an essay or made a specific legislative speech on the matter. Once again the explanation seems to lie in the identification of centralization as the major threat to general independence and liberty. Manufacturing establishments required greater public surveillance but the state was already too powerful and too intrusive in the realm of social and economic legislation. Instead of bringing in the state to ameliorate immiseration, Tocqueville seemed to modify his conception of the total degradation of the worker.[33]

Beaumont's intervention in the debate over France's first factory legislation is virtually the only evidence we have of his and Tocqueville's public views on the social problems as they directly related to industrialization. It is also revealing of the social context in which the industrial revolution was met in France.

One of the few positive legislative accomplishments of the July Monarchy relating to the problems of industrialization was the child labor law for factories of March 22, 1841—the first modest step in a body of social legislation which was to follow it much later.[34] Despite its lack of effectiveness during the July Monarchy the law reveals the locus limits of reform as well as the ideology of the

32. Tocqueville, in conversation with Nassau Senior, May 24, 1835, quoted in A. J. White, *The Early Life and Letters of Cavour, 1810–1848* (London, 1925), 130.
33. See *Tocqueville and Beaumont on Social Reform*, ed. Drescher.
34. See Louis Guineau, "La Législation restrictive du travail des enfants," *Revue d'histoire économique et sociale*, XV (1927), 420–503.

articulate reformers and legislators in the period of Tocqueville's and Beaumont's participation in those two groups. It was of course an elite reform from beginning to end, with little manifestations of active approval or disapproval on the part of the workers and parents affected by the reform. The initiative, as with slavery and prisons, was disproportionately upper-class and Protestant. The principal initiative came from the Protestant industrialists of Alsace and especially the Industrial Society of Mulhouse. Guizot's law on primary education (1833) and similar legislation in England and the Germanies reinforced philanthropic and economic considerations arising out of the problems of adult unemployment and uncontrolled competition in the burgeoning factory system. Of the reforms on which Tocqueville and Beaumont spoke this seems to have aroused the least interest on their part as well as that of the public at large. Regions without mechanized or large-scale production (the law aimed only at those factories employing more than twenty workers) did not even stir. Indifference and a disposition to follow the law as formulated by the government and the most interested proponents seemed the most characteristic reactions of public and semi-official bodies, even when requested to respond by the government. Structural differences in industrial organization seem to account for the scattered and discordant regional opposition to legislation à l'Anglaise. Even in most cases where the reform was opposed, the principle of regulating working conditions in large-scale factories was not directly challenged, only the exaggeration of the relative evils of the condition of juvenile operatives or the economic effects of regulating the hours of labor. The normal political map of the Chambers bore little relation to positions for and against the projected law.[35] The essential dispute was more in the administration of the law than the law itself. Those areas which feared strict enforcement generally favored "decentralized administration," i.e., inspection by the local notables rather than agents of the central government. In this guise the principle of the freedom of industry against state control was invoked and debated. Usually even those who insisted on freedom for industry considered child labor an exception to the general rule. Eclecticism, and not principle, was preponderant in this consensus debate. In other words, the opponents of the reform wanted a statement of legal principles with as high a degree of voluntary "acquiescence" and as little administrative machinery as possible. Attempts to extend the law to adults were usually tactical maneuvers to defeat the proposal through radicalization.

The evidence points to the fact that the law of 1841 was a "manufacturers' bill" almost by default, even among the nonindustrial elite. A few attempts were made by legitimists and anti-industrialists such as Villeneuve-Bargement to convert the child labor debate into a general critique of industrialism, but the ideological critiques were limited to panoramic pictures of the whole spectrum of modern social evils. They contained no specific projects to extend the scope of the bill in question. The disaffected legitimist press made no attempt to treat the question as a *cause célèbre* in order to appeal to the masses over the heads of the *pays légal*. One should compare this generalized attack on industrialization in the Chamber of Deputies, "English"

35. Tudesq, *Les Grands notables*, 585–586.

political economy, competition, the acquisitive instinct, with Beaumont's warning against economic regulation.

For most of the speakers in the Chamber, it was the indirect rather than direct legislation that would be most effective in improving the condition of children in factories. The education of the child, tied to his leisure hours, was considered more essential to his social improvement than the reduction of working hours.[36] Thus the famous Article 5 of the law was inserted, making education compulsory for all factory workers under twelve. The suspicion of the state was equally translated into law by a notables inspection system, whose shortcomings became apparent almost immediately. The law was more a symbolic and humanitarian statement of intention than an act which regulated the day-to-day operations of even the large-scale factory owners and operatives. By 1847, amidst the ever-increasing pressure for a parliamentary study of poverty in France, the nonpartisan consensus had totally rejected the "benevolent" and local inspectorate and moved toward a professional salaried agency. When in 1847 Armand de Melun presented a petition to the Chambers requesting a revision of the law and a general study of social problems, he was warmly seconded by Beaumont of the Left opposition, by Benoist d'Azy on the Right, and by Salvandy, the Minister of the Interior himself.[37] Once again the legislative process spun smoothly in a vacuum until the handling process was interrupted by the February Revolution.

Although the institutionalization of poor relief was al-

36. See the *Moniteur,* Dec. 21, 1840, and *Tocqueville and Beaumont on Social reform,* ed. Drescher, 28–47.
37. *Moniteur,* May 28, 1840.

most totally restricted to private and quasi-private associations by a consensus among the elite before 1848, even private welfare could no more escape the process of centralization during a time of burgeoning growth than could the public sector of society under the same circumstances. Toward the end of the July Monarchy, a number of steps were taken to form a central clearing house for voluntary charitable institutions. The *Annales de la charité*, founded in 1845, with Tocqueville a charter member, was intended to coordinate and strengthen individual charity assistance programs, as well as to constitute a nucleus for the development of legislation for the poor, in much the same way as the abolitionist society founded in the previous decade. The *Annales* sought to consolidate programs through regularly scheduled meetings and publication of the proceedings, including plans for dealing with social problems. Its guiding spirit was the social Catholic Melun, but its initial membership was intentionally nonsectarian, including individuals not specifically affiliated with relogous organizations. Its net was extended to include non-Catholics.[38] Like the earlier abolition society it was limited to a handful of members and strictly avoided anything resembling even an elite membership drive, not to mention mass agitation. It was, in a word, the kind of self-enclosed reformist club in which Tocqueville felt most comfortable. He never gave the *Annales* anything more than his name and contributed nothing to its programs.

In 1847, as the discussion of social questions became more heated at all levels of society and was increasingly re-

38. Duroselle, *Débuts du catholicisme social*, 223; *Annales de la charité* (1845), 67.

ferred to as a single social question, two further steps were taken in the organization of the French charity movement. The *Société d'économie charitable*, growing out of the *Annales*, was a further attempt at coordination of the private poverty program at the national level. The French also participated in the founding of an international charity association at Brussels in the same year, at the very place that Marx and Engels were making their first attempt to found an international working-class association. Beaumont attended the first meeting of the Charity International as the French delegation's expert on prison reform. Both "internationals" were destined to be aborted within a few months by the Revolutions of 1848.

As usual in the July Monarchy, it was expected that the impetus for social legislation should come from a non- or extrapolitical association, which would establish a milieu for the production of an elite consensus. Programs were proposed and tested among prominent private figures, or at least public figures acting in private capacity, before being introduced into the formal political process. The government began its serious consideration of a systematic investigation of poverty as a whole only after it was challenged to do so by the elite charity movement in 1847. The government, as usual with such elite initiatives, adopted the principle of Melun's approach without debate. The Guizot government was in fact proceeding to introduce some minor bills into the Chambers when the Revolution intervened in 1848.

The French notables who recognized the necessity of state intervention in many areas of public assistance, if not a general public welfare system, therefore tended to formulate the role of the state as an extension of the obligation of the wealthy. It was to alleviate temporary and chronic sufferings in proportion to the resources allotted to it by the substantial taxpayers for that purpose. The allocation would increase in proportion to the resources of society as determined by the givers rather than the needs or the demands of the receivers. At the heart of the problem of the obligations of the state and the financial rights of individual taxpayers lay the problem of the social control of the state.

By the end of the July Monarchy the institutionalization of the charity movement in France had reached roughly the same level as the abolition and prison reform movements in the previous decade. The reason for the delay seems to have been twofold. First the question of poverty legislation was more highly charged (both financially and politically) than those affecting slaves and prisoners. The objects of reform were not isolated physically or geographically from the society at large. Socially, statistically, and juridically they were less sharply delineated from the society as a whole. They included temporary and permanent, violent and apathetic, organized and disorganized elements. Therefore the very problem of definition was a matter of dispute, both within and without the elite reform movement. Linked with this was a second consideration. The cost of constructing prisons or paying indemnities was significant but it could be predicted by the decision-makers, and they were relatively immune to further pressure from those affected by the change. Tocqueville and his parliamentary associates dealt with prison reform and abolition with at least as much attention to statistics of cost as to psychological models of changed behavior in their reform plans. While one could, and did, use methods of statistical analysis on problems of poverty during the July Monarchy, proposed reforms were couched in terms of moral and psychological effects without precise statements about the total economic costs to the society, or any systematic estimate of the proportion by each reform.

Over the whole discussion hung the vague but firm conception of the inability of French society and its taxpayers to pay the costs of extensive welfare programs, and the vague but equally firm belief that the poor were a vast horde of men with enormous "real" needs and limitless artificial ones which would be raised beyond the ability of the society to meet if the floodgates of welfare were opened. The possessors were haunted by the specter of expropriation. Social discontent might be described as the disease of envy or the ideal of communism, depending on the sympathies of the contemporary analyst. The notable conception of existing society's inadequacy to solve the social problem was reflected in a torrent of literature proposing radical transformations based on unlimited fulfillment, and another on a traditionalist current calling for a retreat from the acquisitive market society. Underlying most of these analyses was an additional conception of the masses as a great, hungry body with many mouths and one idea. The "masses" were an unrepresented majority, a poor majority, a potentially insatiable majority. To acknowledge the state's responsibility for raising the living standards of all its citizens was to voluntarily sign a commitment that was suicidal in terms of the society's potential. Both before and after 1848, it was thought preferable to couch the social problem in terms of the moral obligations of the rich rather than the social claims of the poor. The first gave the poor a part of the social surplus. The second gave them an equal or even preferential claim on the total social capital.

V

The War on Poverty: Prison Reform

OF all the problems discussed by elite humanitarianism in post-Revolutionary France, prison and penal reform seem to have stirred the most continuous dialogue during the period of the constitutional monarchy.[1] There were certainly other social causes that from time to time aroused more enthusiasm and antipathy in France, but this emotion usually reflected some mass interest in the outcome of the reform, in the extension of the franchise, the extension of public welfare, the abolition of military substitutions, the

1. For an extensive discussion on the background of prison reform in France see McCloy, *The Humanitarian Movement in Eighteenth-Century France*, as well as Moreau-Christophe's *Revue Pénitentiaire et des institutions préventives*, I (Paris, 1843–1844).

organization of labor, or even the abolition of slavery. Before 1848 popular pressure seemed to retard, rather than accelerate, the legislative process. On the other hand, compared with more trivial notable causes like the encouragement of increased investment in savings banks, the abolition of the lottery, and the reduction of the death penalty, prison reform most directly promised an automatic extension of governmental social control over one of the most disruptive elements among the lower classes.

From the government's point of view, prisons were already an institution with a highly developed administration that could respond without great difficulty to changes more radically affecting the inmate population than the supervisory personnel. No great break in continuity was necessary. Prison reform advocates also almost invariably held out the promise of both short- and long-range financial savings to governments and taxpayers from any prescribed innovation. It was increasingly apparent that the old forced labor institutions of the *bagnes* or galleys were not only totally obsolete militarily, but were grossly inefficient organizations of production. Moreover, the appeal based on the reduction of social costs to the nation as a whole was buffered by the promise of immediate savings to the taxpayers once initial construction costs were met. Almost all reformers at first hoped to make the prisons self-sustaining or even profit-making workhouses. It was the only part of the French Revolution's projected attack on poverty and indigence which had actually been expanded during the First Empire. Extension of the penal repression of beggary by the systematic establishment of *dépôts de mendicité* was Bonaparte's most important innovation in legislation concerning the poor. Furthermore the proportion of convicted criminals to the whole population rose almost every year of the early nineteenth century.[2] Every government was anxious to encourage studies directed toward a prison system that would either discourage crime or prevent recidivism. Not the least effective of the reformers' arguments to the taxpaying and legislative groups was that contemporary prisons resembled convalescent homes more than correctional institutions for the poor.

The prison reform movement had proceeded until 1815 by fits and starts, depending on the relative strength or favor of the liberals in government. In 1819 approval and patronage was obtained for a Royal Prison Society containing many prominent members of the Society of Christian Morality, but representing other shades of opinion as well: Rochefoucauld-Liancourt, Bellart, Bigot de Poreameneu, de Broglie, Chaptal, Chabrol, Daru, Benjamin Delessert, Guizot, de Laborde, Mollien, Pasquier, Seguier, Damas, Breze, Lafayette, Casimer-Perier, Barante, Royer-Collard, Feray, Hottinguer, Rothschild, Mallet, and Gerard. The Royal Society was much more closely tied to governmental initiative than the other reform groups. Its members themselves acted as inspectors of the Paris prisons. It was a government advisory board that permitted a good deal of peripheral participation by those who would otherwise have been deprived of social roles in their politically lean periods. Prison reform also appeared to be one of the best ways to begin the social reorganization of France, which, by the elite interpretation of the increase in crime, was one of the effects of the great social upheaval of the previous

2. See Henri Joly, *La France criminelle* (Paris, 1889), 8–9.

decades. It was the most direct means of reintroducing the broken authority relationships between the upper and lower classes, and of effecting the remoralization (i.e., socialization) of the lower classes in order to break the vicious cycle between the *classes laborieuses* and the *classes dangereuses*.[3]

The prison reform movement proceeded at a relatively uninterrupted and steady pace throughout the period of the constitutional monarchy in France (1815–1848). With the advent of Charles X, sympathetic to the Ultras and hostile to the whole socio-cultural identity of liberal humanitarian reform, the progress of the reform movement slowed, although it did not cease. It became more completely identified with the liberal opposition embodied in the Society for Christian Morality. Parliamentary initiative became more important than Royal Society initiatives. By 1830 immediate prison reform was bound up with the fate of the liberal movement as a whole, and it was one of the first social measures taken up by the July Monarchy on its accession to power in 1830. A regime of very insecure tenure, attempting simultaneously to halt lower-class agitation and to maintain its ideological thrust as a reform regime, hit upon the prison system as a subject of reform. To attack the problem of improving the prison system was to attack the problem of poverty, to do something concrete

3. See Louis Chevalier, *Classes laborieuses et classes dangereuses à Paris* (Paris, 1958); H. A. Frégier, *Des Classes dangereuses de la population dans les grands villes* (Paris, 1840), a copy of which is in Tocqueville's library at the Chateau de Tocqueville; the bibliographical references in Tocqueville and Beaumont's *Système pénitentiaire* and Beaumont's summary of penitentiary literature in France in the Chamber of Deputies, in *Moniteur*, April 24, 1844, 1069–1070.

for the poor. To start with the prison system was to start with that group of the poor institutionally most completely under the control of the government and the notables. To start with the prison system was to start with that group of the poor with the fewest possible claims on the sympathetic emotionalism that characterized reform movements in general. The July Monarchy thus encouraged the dialogue between reformers and the state that had gone on for over a decade before the July Revolution, and in which certain principles of desirable reforms in prison practice and administration had come to be widely accepted. It was also the area of the reform movement where the administration itself took the greatest initiatives.

The work of Tocqueville and Beaumont on prison reform thus developed within the main current of this respectable reformist and governmental tradition. It would seem that their interests in prisons predated the July Revolution, since their French investigations were already advanced even before the new regime was definitively established. Furthermore, following the revolution, Tocqueville and Beaumont, by virtue of their family backgrounds, found their loyalty under suspicion by the new government. They thus hit on their American penitentiary investigation as a means of enhancing their position within French political society while temporarily leaving its politics altogether, and of removing themselves from the uncomfortable political break with family and friends as well. It was also a means of establishing their political visibility without partisan labeling. This was precisely why Tocqueville was even more anxious to visit America than its prisons. A study of the United States might raise him above the crowd and fix public attention on him without the necessity of working his way up through the political jungle.[4]

The regime founded by Lafayette and Louis-Philippe was also more receptive than its predecessor to social experiments originating in the Anglo-American world. The early days of the July Monarchy probably marked the apogee of good feeling, official and otherwise, between France and America.[5] Thus when two young magistrates came forward with a proposal that they serve as official investigators of the American prison system, the government was interested. When the prospective investigators offered to pay their own way, the government was convinced. Thus Tocqueville and Beaumont, taking a new initiative in a well-developed reform movement, found themselves on a path that was to make them recognized experts and innovators in the prison legislation of the July Monarchy.

It was necessary, however, to prove not only that they were innovators but also conservatives. Although a study directed at the reduction of crime might be an attempt to reform one aspect of the social order, it was by no means being conducted by two young radicals turned loose in republican America. If modern society was stricken with economic insecurity and men driven to crime, a new country might offer striking examples of new cures for new social diseases. But even in the youthful flush of their departure

---

4. See the letter of Tocqueville to his friend Charles Stoffels, Nov. 4, 1830, quoted in Pierson, *Tocqueville and Beaumont in America*, 32.

5. Rémond, *Les Etats-Unis devant l'opinion française*, II, 655–659.

for America, Tocqueville and Beaumont assured society that they were out to prune, not to attack root and branch: "We no more harbor the childish plan of setting ourselves up as enemies of civilization, than we would want to deny the glory, the well-being, and the strength of modern nations."[6]

The nine-month journey of the two prison investigators in 1831 from one end of the United States to the other has been exhaustively treated.[7] Tocqueville's and Beaumont's inquiries ranged far beyond penitentiaries, yet they managed to fulfill their official obligations. They studied the system of New York, the famous prisons at Auburn and Sing Sing; Philadelphia's Walnut Street Prison and the new Eastern Penitentiary, later the basic model of the French system; the Connecticut state prison at Wethersfield; the prisons of Boston, Baltimore, and New Orleans. Tocqueville and Beaumont's subsequent study also contained lengthy interviews with prison inmates as well as administrators, a novel procedure in the period.

On their return to France, they completed the task of writing their penitentiary study, despite their departure from government service following Beaumont's refusal to participate in the prosecution of a political trial. Beaumont took up the task of writing the whole body of the text for

6. Beaumont and Tocqueville, *Note sur la système pénitentiaire, et sur la mission confiée par M. le Ministre de l'interieur à MM. Gustave de Beaumont et Alexis de Tocqueville* (Paris, 1831), 2. A draft of a letter by Beaumont (Yale Mss B.I.f.4) to the Minister of Public Works also condemned misguided "utopian" institutions of public welfare. It became the basis for the preface to the *Penitentiary System*.

7. Pierson, *Tocqueville and Beaumont in America, passim*.

the book published in 1833 over both their names: *Du Système pénitentiaire aux Etats-Unis et de son application en France [On the Penitentiary System in America and Its Application in France]*.[8] Tocqueville contributed a long note against penal colonies as an alternative to prisons, and some statistical notes and appendices. The work was quickly translated into English, German, and Portuguese. In France it was widely reviewed and went through three separate editions between 1833 and 1845, a remarkable accomplishment for an official report of its kind. In the course of the next decade it became one of the authoritative works in its field. During the debates on the French prison reform in 1844, it was a source of arguments for the adoption of alternate American systems.

The report, in accordance with the original spirit of its investigators and some good political advice from high places, was nonpartisan in its approach. It stated the need for reform and presented the two basic American alternatives, what came to be known as the Auburn and Pennsylvania systems. It contained carefully balanced statements on their respective advantages and disadvantages with regard to possible adoption by France. Like *Democracy in America*, two years later, it was noncommittal about the possibilities of adoption of individual reforms. It reiterated the generally acknowledged propositions that reform was urgently

8. The work, originally published by H. Fournier, *jeune*, was translated by Francis Lieber in America, and W. B. S. Taylor in England. It was also translated into German and Portuguese. It has recently been re-issued as the first volume of the Perspectives in Sociology series published by Southern Illinois University (1964), with an introduction by Thorsten Sellin and a foreword by Herman R. Lantz.

necessary, that America had worked out its reforms in the light of principles accepted throughout the Western World, had offered some good experimental examples, and could furnish important positive and negative data for any French reform. The report often emphasized the difficulties of introducing a penitentiary system. It was boldest in rejecting any system of transportation as an alternative to a prison system, although it favored experimentation in agricultural colonies for released convicts and "houses of refuge" for juvenile offenders. It departed most radically from French ideas in advocating a decentralized prison system.[9]

As regards the study's attitude toward the classes who were destined to inhabit the new prison system, the author's assumptions remained well within the common ground fixed by contemporary notable thought. A rising rate of crime, like a rising rate of pauperism, was an inevitable effect of civilization. Crimes against persons were decreasing while crimes against property were increasing, relative to population growth. Causal relations were drawn between urbanization, industrialization, pauperization, and criminality on the basis of positive statistical correlations in all four categories.[10] By the early years of the July Monarchy

9. Compare *Penitentiary System*, 125–129, with Tocqueville's report on the prison reform law for the Chamber of Deputies in Tocqueville, *Oeuvres (Beaumont* edition): *Etudes économiques*, 366–367.

10. In the second quarter of the nineteenth century most social analyses of crime utilizing statistics tended to measure one or two variables only. Many thereby arrived at very startling correlations. For example, Bigot de Morogues took total national figures on criminality and broke them down into northern and southern France. Since the more industrialized northern half had a higher rate of criminality than the more agricultural south, industrialization was the key

the concern with criminality had so shifted from a rural to an urban emphasis that contemporary studies might suggest segregation and differential treatment of prisoners according to their rural or urban origins and consider it a matter of course that the rural criminal should be exempt from isolation or silence, because having breathed the free air of the countryside he would suffer far more from the system of isolated confinement than his already more desensitized and confined urban counterpart.[11]

There was universal agreement, however, that a prison system was part of legislation for the poor, since poverty caused crime. An effective prison system was a better way to begin the attack on certain inevitable concomitants of poverty than poor relief laws. Crime, though arising from poverty, was a social disease that might be cured by an intensive system of desocialization for every convicted criminal.[12] The effect of unreformed prison systems was to

---

variable in the increase in criminality. Moreover, criminality was taken as the major index of public morality. Industralization was thus the key factor in the demoralization of France. Tocqueville followed Villeneuve-Bargemont in a similar correlation of pauperism and industrialization. On the other hand, when Tocqueville and Beaumont dealt with a specific problem like the effects of prisons in the deterrence of criminality, they were cautious to the point of total skepticism about the utility of international or even intranational statistical comparisons to prove the effectiveness of a given prison system. Impressionistically, one might assert that the tendency to leap to statistical conclusions varied directly with the novelty of the relationship being measured and with the attempt to make them serve as buttressing for philosophies of history.

11. Léon Faucher wanted to keep urban and rural offenders separated and to exempt the latter from isolated imprisonment.

12. *Penitentiary System*, Preface. Beaumont stated the issue as succinctly in 1843 as the *Penitentiary System* had done in 1833:

allow criminals to corrupt each other, to socialize antisocial behavior, to organize criminal activity. Criminals of different degrees of degradation were thrown indiscriminately together. The result was a high rate of recidivism and of more organized and serious crimes by recidivists. The objects of a system of prison discipline were, first, to prevent inmates from contaminating each other by forming associations for future activity, and, second, to form new habits of honesty and labor so as to enable them to lead an independent, noncriminal existence. Silence, separation, labor, and moral education were the means to achieve this end.[13] Secondly, for those who were poor but not yet criminals, the great problem was to devise a system of maximum deterrence. The leniency of the old "communal" prison and the temptations of a new life in a penal colony were rejected as nondeterrents. When French reformers envisioned the penal colony as an alternative to prisons in the early nineteenth century, they were thinking of something on the order of Australia, not Devil's Island. It was because Tocqueville considered the penal colony primarily as a permanent settlement and an extension of the mother country that he rejected it. Founded by criminal elements,

---

"Whatever universal equality may be in principle, we must surely recognize that it is the poor who furnish the annual criminal contingent" (see Beaumont, "Reform of the Prisons" in *Tocqueville and Beaumont on Social Reform*, ed. Drescher, 61). Crime was of the poor, prisons were for the poor, and hesitations concerning the proposed prison reform were indifference to the poor.

13. *Ibid.* The *positive* socializing content of Tocqueville's and Beaumont's early aims may be seen from a note for the *Système pénitentiaire* which listed the advantages of the Auburn system as "orderly habits, continuous labor, regulated life, daily obedience, silence (element of order and reform), reflection, introduction to a profession giving him the means of existence" (Yale Mss C. VIII).

a penal colony would be a source of weakness and rebellion, of enormous and ultimately wasted expense. In Tocqueville's conception, colonization should ideally be the prerogative of the independent middle classes. The best colony ever founded was religious, middle-class New England, the worst, Haiti—piratical, slave-ridden, and ultimately revolutionary. One kind of colony yielded wealth and prosperity, the other bloody servile wars.[14]

Since physical punishment and mutilation were also rejected as relics of medieval barbarism, only psychic punishment, applied with full rigor, could act as a deterrent. Nonassociation for the inmate, and deterrence for the potential inmate, were the referential basis for the disciplinary system for the criminal poor. Both objectives seemed superbly served by the methods of silence and noncommunication, which opponents called mental tombs and advocates called separation. For Tocqueville and Beaumont, as for the majority of reform experts, the choice was between the Pennsylvania system (separation day and night, with solitary labor) and the Auburn system (separation at night and silent, communal labor by day). It was around this point alone, whether noncommunication was possible in a cheaper communal work system, that the French debate over prison reform took place. On almost all other points there was nominal agreement.

The issue of Auburn versus Pennsylvania in France has subsequently been made to appear as a battle between two stable sets of committed antagonists.[15] The actual historic picture would seem to have been somewhat different. There

14. Appendix on penal colonies, reprinted in Beaumont's edition of Tocqueville's *Oeuvres*, IX,: *Etudes économiques*, 218–222.
15. See Rémond, *Les Etats-Unis*, II, 562–565, and Pierson, *Tocqueville and Beaumont in America*, 711–713.

was almost no opposition to the proposition that France required a fundamental change in her prison system, and no articulated third alternative to the American systems except transportation. By the early 1830's the inclination of French reformers, including Tocqueville, was generally in favor of the Auburn system because it seemed to accomplish the same basic goal of criminal de-socialization far more cheaply than that of Pennsylvania. By the end of the 1830's the overwhelming majority of articulate reformers shifted to the Pennsylvania system, although there was more latent emotional hostility to human isolation in the public at large than the reformers at first realized. The reason for the swing to Pennsylvania was apparently the result of further official inquiries during the 1830's and further data on the functioning of the two systems. The Demetz prison mission to America concluded that the "silence" of the Auburn system was constantly eluded, that discipline by the whip seemed the only way to ensure a modicum of silence, and that even silence could not prevent the formation of "visual" associations for post-prison contacts. It concluded that the Auburn system was not producing a sterile social environment, even using American methods of corporal punishment which were no longer conceivable in France. French investigators after Tocqueville and Beaumont discovered that in the Auburn prisons the goal of breaking through the system became the full-time occupation of convicts. And among veterans of the penitentiary system there evolved "a secret association of crime"—the original sin of the unreformed prison system. If de-socialization was the fundamental object of a prison system, Auburn yielded ambiguous, if not futile, results. Therefore by the late 1830's the most influential French experts with one notable exception, Charles Lucas, had declared in favor of Pennsylvania. In this instance Tocqueville and Beaumont were also converts rather than initiators. Convinced of Pennsylvania's superiority by 1837,[16] they were the leading authorities for it in the prison reform debates of 1844.[17]

Tocqueville and Beaumont were more convinced of the indisputable guarantee of nonsocialization through absolute separation than the possibility of moral reformation. The two Frenchmen were almost totally anti-utopian and skeptical about the possibility of institutionalizing the moral reform of criminals. It was fine for ministers and charitable visitors to believe in moral reformation, since it preserved high motivation among those in contact with the criminal. In fact, moral regeneration might be a possibility for individual criminals, even where it was statis-

16. See Beaumont's introduction to the second edition of *Du système pénitentiaire* (1836) and Tocqueville's letter to Beaumont, May 26, 1837 (Yale Mss C.I. a.2). The emphasis of their first work led later scholars, unaware of their subsequent legislative careers, to classify them as Auburnites. Charles Lucas was able to quote Tocqueville's *Système pénitentiaire* against his legislative option for the Philadelphia system (*Exposé de l'état de la question pénitentiaire en Europe et aux Etats-Unis . . . suivi d'observations de MM. de Tocqueville, etc.* [Paris, 1844], 10, 107).

17. Letter of Marie de Tocqueville to Francis Lieber, Paris, Dec. 2, 1844, Tocqueville and Beaumont letters, the Huntington Library. Since individual confinement was directed against the poor, both criminal and potentially criminal, it never achieved more transitory mass support. What opposition there was to the Pennsylvania system came from those who were most closely identified with the urban middle-class elements. Months after the prison reform bill had been passed by the deputies, Mme. de Tocqueville complained with exasperation of the opposition of M. Thiers and his corrupted party, who "are enemies to all measures that do not please the multitude."

tically a myth. But, "the moral reformation of an individual, which is an important affair for a religious man, means little to a politician. Or, to express it better, an institution is only political if it be founded on the interest of the mass; it loses its character if it only profits a small number."[18] For skeptics on moral reform, one supreme asset was contained exclusively in the Pennsylvania system. It was the principle of least corruptibility. The inmate who never saw or heard another prisoner in the entire course of his confinement could not possibly leave prison more educated in crime than when he went in. No other prison system could make a similar claim, and it formed the point of departure of Tocqueville and Beaumont's parliamentary argument. The only difficulty with the system was that, reduced to a less-corruptibility principle, the last therapeutic thread of the system was severed. One might add ministers, doctors, and teachers to the system, but only as supplements to the negative certainty of separation. What was being debated when the system came before parliament in 1844 was no longer a penitentiary system, but a system to prevent the socialization of criminality during the period of confinement, and to offer maximum deterrence to potential criminals.

To be that, a system had to be severely punitive in its sole repressive instrument—isolation. Tocqueville and

18. *Penitentiary System*, 89. Tocqueville was concerned that he and Beaumont should keep a careful distance between themselves and the "canaille pénitentiaire" (Tocqueville to Beaumont, Nov. [Yale Mss C.I.a.2]). Tocqueville later stated in the French Academy that the great question was not reform but that "the majority of criminals should not become worse in prison" (see Lucas, *Exposé de l'état de la question pénitentiaire*, 90).

Beaumont readily accepted its severity as the opposite side of the coin of a free society. When the citizen chose to break the law he lost his claims to general association with his fellow man. His right to be among men had to be limited to his teachers and administrators: "It must be acknowledged that the penitentiary system in America is severe. While society in the United States gives the example of the most extended liberty, the prisons of the same country offer the spectacle of the most complete despotism. The citizens subject to the law are protected by it; they only cease to be free when they become wicked."[19] The unreformed prison seemed, like the English poor law, to endow the offender with benefits not even available to the honest poor. "Something very strange is happening right now in our society," Beaumont told the Chamber of Deputies in 1844. "We have laws which prohibit associations between honest men, or which at least permit them to be established only with police authorization; and yet at the very moment these laws are being enforced, we have another law which institutes permanent associations between criminals who are obliged to live together, and who once having left prison, seek each other out."

With regard to its preventive social potential, Tocqueville and Beaumont felt it to be their duty to attack all false sentimentality and romantic utopianism in the reform movement. The physical pleasures of sexual contact and luxurious food were among the evils of the old system. No schemes and indulgences like Bentham's music for the prisoners' spirits or an advanced educational system for their minds would be permitted to destroy "the principles essen-

19. *Ibid.*, 79.

tial in criminal matters."[20] The poor might otherwise be tempted to get an educational diploma by overt crime, which they could not normally hope to obtain by any amount of honest labor. Mere confinement and loss of liberty was insufficient. "Less eligibility" haunted institutional reform as applied to the poor. It was as commonly accepted among this generation of humanitarian reformers as any in their common stock of assumptions. "If there is one point on which everyone seems just about agreed," wrote one legal and penal expert, "it is that the condition of the prisoner after his conviction must, as regards clothing, sleeping conditions, heat, food, etc., be slightly worse than that of the working class family in distress; excellent reasons are given for this position in principle."[21] French reformers were even familiar with Edwin Chadwick's interesting statistical finding that the less abundant the prisoners' diet was the more healthy they were, but they were somewhat skeptical about whether Chadwick wanted to carry his argument to its logical conclusion. That the principle of less eligibility was applied even to prisons shows how explicitly an institution for the poor they were conceived to be by nineteenth-century reformers. The same principle determined attitudes toward all institutional reforms linked to the prison system: houses of detention for juveniles and societies for released prisoners. Only political

20. The very desire to tighten the screws of Bentham's already ruthless Panopticon is symptomatic of a thrust for rigorous efficiency regarding prison reform. On Bentham's prison system see especially Gertrude Himmelfarb, "The Haunted House of Jeremy Bentham," in *Ideas in History: Essays in Honor of Louis Gottschalk* ed., Richard Herr and Harold Parker (Durham, N.C., 1965), 199–238.

21. Isidore Alauzet, *Essai sur les peines et le système pénitentiaire,* couronné par l'Institut (Paris, 1842), 272.

offenders, who more often came from higher and more educated social groups, were specifically exempted from the full rigors of the system.

Tocqueville and Beaumont's mission was only the first of a long and careful series of steps toward prison reform during the July Monarchy. A second official mission was dispatched to America in 1836 and another report appeared in 1837, supplemented by a steady stream of other international investigations.[22] The issues connected with prison reform were raised in the Chamber of Deputies and in the departmental councils with increasing frequency. The French Academy of Moral and Political Sciences offered prizes for essays on the "means of harmonizing our penal law system with a penitentiary system to be established with the aim of affording the most effective guarantees for the maintenance of public and private peace and security while procuring the moral improvement of the condemned." The French prison administration was continuously consulted, answered detailed questionnaires, and eventually played a significant role in the formulation of the reform legislation.[23] By 1840, when a French ministry finally felt ready to present a bill to the Chamber of Deputies, the documentation at its disposal was enormous. In the words of the Minister of the Interior, Rémusat, imprisonment had become "in a way, the unique moral sanction, the last guarantee of the social order." Mental punishment was conceived as the

22. F. Demtez et A. Blouet, *Rapports à M. le comte de Montalivet sur les pénitenciers des Etats-Unis* (Paris, 1837).

23. See *Analyse des réponses des directeurs des maisons centrales de force et de correction à une circulaire ministerielle du 10 mars 1834, sur les effets du régime de ces maisons* (Paris, 1836).

unique mode of enforcing the unique moral sanction. It became all important to assure that this last institutional barrier against criminal behavior was effective and "to give it a new force for the maintenance of public safety."[24] Only in this ideological framework can one appreciate why the issue of prison reform was one of the central issues before early nineteenth-century legislatures; why the legislators acquiesced with relatively few qualms to the prospect of sentences of eight or ten years of separate imprisonment as a unique brake to rising rates of crimes against property, those antisocial acts par excellence, in a society based on the proprietary Civil Code; why the certainty of deterrence took precedence over the possibility of moral reform; or why Tocqueville and Beaumont sought, as did the French government, the most certain deterrent to negative socialization.

As with most social legislation in the July Monarchy, the legislation approached fruition with agonizing slowness. A first bill was presented in 1840 and a parliamentary committee was chosen to examine the bill. Beaumont was a member and Tocqueville its reporter. After a careful examination of the relative merits of the Auburn and Pennsylvania systems, the committee, like the Minister of the Interior, opted for the latter, which more certainly guaranteed least corruptibility and greatest deterrence. Meanwhile the Guizot government withdrew the bill for revision. The presentation of Tocqueville's report to the Chambers was held up for the next two sessions. Finally in 1843 Duchâtel, the new Minister of the Interior, brought in a revised bill. Again the Pennsylvania system was chosen. It

24. *Moniteur*, May 10, 1840.

was to be applied to all age groups of criminals up to the limit of twelve years of confinement. A new parliamentary commission, again with Tocqueville as the reporter, approved the bill with some minor reservations.[25] It came up for general debate in 1844.

Once again the project proved to be politically nonpartisan, despite the relatively high degree of participation and sharp debate over the measure. Tocqueville and Beaumont found themselves in the doubly novel situation of being identified as the guiding spirits behind a piece of legislation, and as supporters of a government bill. But they were not unique in this situation. In a seventeen-day discussion in the Chamber of Deputies, the seventy members who participated in the debate again and again declared the nonpolitical nature of their ideas on a social question. The undercurrent of cultural conflict along Catholic and Protestant lines was muted when a number of the usually anticlerical dynastic opposition members added their reservations to those of the Catholic traditionalists. A few voices insisted that transportation had been neglected as an alternative, but the only substantial debate was over the relative merits of the Auburn and Philadelphia prisons. The goals of some forms of segregation and of deterrence by silence were virtually unchallenged in the French legislature.

When the Chamber passed the bill by a large majority at the close of the debate, Tocqueville and Beaumont seemed to have achieved their first reform of the July Monarchy. But further handling was in order before the legislature of the July Monarchy was willing to acquiesce in what would have been its biggest single social reform.

25. See note 9 above.

The Chamber of Peers and an extra-parliamentary committee spent four more years in an extended study of the bill. In February 1848 it appeared that the bill was about to clear its last hurdle when another revolution intervened. During the Second Republic, the Barrot Ministry, of which Tocqueville was a member, continued the construction of cellular prisons by executive order.[26] But Louis Napoleon Bonaparte's coup d'état of December 2, 1851, after giving Tocqueville and Beaumont a brief taste of collective imprisonment with their parliamentary peers, stopped all work on the cellular system and substituted penal colonies for the duration of the Empire. When the cellular system was reintroduced with the return of the notables to power after the fall of the Empire, Tocqueville and Beaumont were both dead.

In terms of their general social thought Tocqueville's and Beaumont's ideas on prison reform are interesting for a number of reasons. For a group that was antisocial by definition, the process of de-socialization was pushed to its limits. For the reservoir of criminality, which meant the poor in general, even punishment by compulsory confinement without normal human intercourse was considered insufficient as a deterrent. The fear of falling short of less eligibility was carried to extreme lengths in arguments about human contacts, education, and transportation as treatment for criminals. To establish totally effective de-socialization for the antisocial, the normal liberal image of human development was reversed. Free interaction among peers was abrogated. Association was reduced to rational contact with agents of moralization. Where any human in-

26. By order of Dufaure, Minister of the Interior, Aug. 20, 1849.

teraction took place it was in the context of a total authority-dependency relationship. The rules for the exercise of authority were fixed by a centralized agency. In opposition to the normal liberal world, centralization, and even despotism, were necessary to the breakdown of a perverted sense of self-sufficiency and independence vis-à-vis society. Limited to one clearly defined antisocial group, the new prison system seemed administratively desirable and politically self-enclosed. Despite the fact that Beaumont and Tocqueville had at first leaned heavily in favor of a decentralized system because of its general political and psychological effects on the "free" realm of society, they reversed themselves in the Chamber of Deputies.

It is significant that it was social reform in general and prison reform in particular which first brought Tocqueville and Beaumont to an awareness of the insidious nature of the modern tendency toward centralization. It is equally significant that they readily agreed to centralized administration in order to accomplish reforms in this area. The crucial problem of the tendency toward centralization as a natural response to the demands of democratic society did not first occur to Tocqueville and Beaumont in terms of the concentration of political power, which they observed varying in accordance with historical circumstances as disparate as those which created the American and European polities of the 1830's. Their perception of the centralization process came instead in their consideration of contemporary European responses to long-range social problems.

After returning from their prison mission to the United States, they had considered it logical and even probable that, as in the United States, European nations would seek to decentralize prison administration in order to ensure

responsiveness to local needs, and in order to maximize experimental competitive innovation along the lines of American prison development. Their first prison report looked
forward to the moment when political life "will enter
increasingly into the habits of the departments and administrative interests will increasingly tend to become localized."[27] The strength of administrative decentralization
seemed to be reinforced by the possibilities of social innovation. Decentralization itself seemed an ideal area for
democratic action.

Their observation of trends in English poor law and
prison administration in 1834–1835 altered their perspective. The thrust toward centralized administration was un-
deniable, and equally impressive was the passage of these
reforms on the heels of the reform bill of 1832. Tocqueville, recording a conversation with Henry Reeve on poor
law and prison administration, commented, "Centralization, a democratic instinct; instinct of a society which has
succeeded in escaping from the individualistic system of the
Middle Ages. Preparation for despotism. Why is centralization dear to the habits of democracy? . . . A fundamental
question."[28]

Their interests in social reform, in the process of democratization, and in the dangers of increasing centralization
had clashed. English reform experience had led to the conclusion that the primary cause of previously ineffective
initiatives came from lack of central coordination. The centralizing reflex of English democrats struck Tocqueville and
Beaumont as all the more dangerous in that it did not take

27. *Du système pénitentiaire* (1833 edition), 175–176.
28. Tocqueville, *Journeys to England and Ireland*, 77–78, May 11,
1835.

the form of overt demands for the concentration of political power. Innovations that directly tended to concentrate political power seemed to be effectively opposed by a large proportion of the notables who sat in European and American legislatures. In such cases the adverse effects of such concentrations to certain political interests were immediately perceived. The danger of the centralization of social welfare policies was more insidious because of the greater degree of unanimity within the political community that efficiency was the primary consideration in dealing with lower-class social problems. There was very little conflict along regular party lines on matters such as prison and poor law reforms.[29] When Beaumont had to compose a new preface to the second edition of the *Système pénitentiaire* in 1836, the whole nexus of democracy, centralization, and social reform was very much in his mind. In an unpublished draft he wrote under the heading "Centralization":[30]

29. For example, the debates over the 1834 poor law reform in England and the child labor and prison reform debates of 1841 and 1844 in France.

30. Yale Mss C. VIII: notes for *Du système pénitentiaire*; dossier entitled "2ᵉ edition. Système Pen *itre*. Intro *on*." Beaumont actually prepared more than one draft. Material from the supplementary draft appears in parentheses in this quotation. This passage was deleted, probably after the type was set, from the published edition; three dots in the published work indicate where it was to have appeared. Beaumont's second journey to England and Ireland in 1837 reinforced his initial impression. He noted after a conversation with Thomas M. Wyse: "The movement in England toward centralization is still more marked in Ireland.

    1.—Public Institutions
    2.—Public Works
    3.—The Poor"
(Yale Mss C.X.5: notes for L'Irlande: "Irlande-Centralisation-Grand Jury.")

This fact (of administrative centralization) has passed almost unnoticed (in England and France) because it is directed towards an object more social than political. However, it is bound up with the whole reform movement; democracy is centralizing by its nature. Since its principle is the equality of all, it tends in all things towards the uniformity introduced into Parliament with the aid of the ten-pound electorate.[31] This is what confers on the King's ministers the powers formerly belonging to cities, to corporations, to counties, not with the idea of increasing royal authority (Power) but in order to reduce (annul) powerful aristocratic local influences.[32]

In moving under the direction of a master, will they conserve the powerful and energetic allure of Liberty: Left to themselves they sometimes do well and sometimes badly. Managed by an expert—who I am ready to admit is more knowledgable—they will not commit mistakes so long as that superior intelligence takes the trouble to guide them. But what will happen if the guide happens to fail them? If that immense arm that stretches across the whole country and vitalizes it is pulled back, will death follow? That is the danger. Moreover, can't we see some good beneath the chaos presented in our dark portrait of the past? Is the variety of experiments that comes from a multitude of free and independent efforts, not significant in shedding light on the very question that concerns us? The government is certainly going to establish a better system than what exists in a large number of prisons. But can one be sure that no prison has a preferable system?

Centralization of prison reform would eliminate one more area of collective associational activity, and the state would take another long stride toward the reduction of the area available to associational activity between the individual and the state. In *Democracy in America*, in 1840,

31. Beaumont referred here to the rationalization of the franchise by English electoral reform of 1832.

32. See Yale Mss C.X.3: Beaumont's notes in England in 1835, "In what way the Whigs are democrats," and Yale Mss C.X.5: "Poor reform—aristocracy."

Tocqueville listed one area of social innovation after another as being removed from the associational realm and captured by the administrative apparatus.

Yet in Tocqueville and Beaumont's prison reports and articles of the 1840's, one finds no echo of the fear of centralization that haunted their theoretical musings, although the anxiety over centralization in general remained in full force. Nor did they feel required to show why in this instance they acquiesced in the centralizing concensus of their contemporaries. Perhaps it was because the arguments for efficiency and uniformity in matters concerning the punishment of criminals were overwhelming. Perhaps it seemed futile to question the historical association of prisons with central control when they themselves were uncertain as to how far they wished to push decentralization on any given social problem. But it seems more probable that they accepted the weight of arguments for central reform precisely because they wished to ensure speed of innovation and uniformity of application to control the *classes dangereuses* throughout France. Since prisons were an exclusive governmental concern there was no major extension of the area of central control at issue, even if there was no proposed erosion of centralization in the reform bills that they helped to write.

Ultimately, the prison was a uniquely nationwide institution operative on the nation's poor. The sedentary factory worker still occupied a relatively small niche in the social structure of the July Monarchy. The French workers were still conceived of primarily as a nomad class.[33] The alternative controls on his activity were checks on his geographi-

33. See L'Hommedé, *Un Département français sous la monarchie de juillet,* 105.

cal and economic movement in the form of the *livret*. For a rural proprietary society, these workers without land or homes were the reservoir of the criminal class. For a social group which moved from one end of France to the other, a national system of prisons seemed more logical than a decentralized departmental system on the model of the United States. The efficiency, the unity, and the ubiquity of centralized social power against the criminal was thus apparently more important than the indirect and ambiguous catalyst of local initiative in prison reform.[34]

34. The only concession to locality in the bill of 1844 was a provision for an inspection system that had to include elected notables from the department in which the prison was located.

VI

The Abolition of Slavery

AT the moment when the February Revolution interrupted
the political process in France, the prison reform law had
advanced almost to the point of complete acceptance and
seemed to have arrived at the last stage of the process, approval by the Chamber of Peers. Before the Revolution,
it was the nonpartisan reform most likely to have succeeded,
and Tocqueville was as close to being an effective innovator
as he ever came to be through any project of his disappoint-
ing legislative career. But the penitentiary movement in
France was only the most successful of the elite humanitarian movements. Not far behind it came the movement
for the abolition of slavery in the French colonies.

Their development was so strikingly parallel that they

might be regarded as parts of the same reform movement, in terms of their sources, the intellectual assumptions of their advocates, their political carriers, and the propaganda and handling processes during the constitutional monarchy. It is no coincidence that Tocqueville and Beaumont played a major role in both. Between them, they engrossed much of the national legislative reform energies of the July Monarchy.[1]

In its origins, abolitionism and prison reform sprang from the common sources of enlightenment and humanitarian ideas during the second half of the eighteenth century. Both moved along parallel lines of development from isolated, sporadic, and unsystematic criticism around 1750 through successive stages of articulation, organization, and radicalization on both the domestic and international levels. Both were at the level of isolated criticism roughly before 1770.[2] The next decade witnessed both general and detailed studies of the problems of the existing systems, not just sporadic discussion of the evil in the abstract. By the

1. See *Tocqueville and Beaumont on Social Reform*, ed. Drescher, Part III, as well as Beaumont, *Marie*, Appendix.

2. On the background of slavery and abolition in the French colonies see, among others, David B. Davis, *The Problem of Slavery in Western Culture* (Ithaca, N.Y., 1966); Edward D. Seeber, *Anti-Slavery Opinion in France during the Second Half of the Eighteenth Century* (Baltimore, 1937); McCloy, *The Humanitarian Movement in Eighteenth-Century France* (Frankfort, Ky., 1959); and his *The Negro in the French West Indies* (Frankfort, Ky., 1966); Augustin Cochin, *De l'Abolition de l'esclavage*, 2 vols. (Paris, 1861); Gabriel Debien, *Les Colons de Saint Domingue et la Révolution* (Paris, 1953), especially its bibliography; Lothrop T. Stoddard. *The French Revolution in San Domingo* (Boston and New York, 1914); Gaston Martin, *Histoire de l'esclavage dans les colonies françaises* (Paris, 1948), and *L'Abolition de l'esclavage* (Paris, 1948).

1780's the French government was itself considering systematic reform. In some cases experimentation was well underway by the time the Bourbon monarchy lost control of political initiative in 1787–1788. In 1789, as in 1848, the prison reform movement had made greater progress in governmental implementation and in public discussion than the colonial emancipation question. This seems to have been due to the large contribution of the colonial economy to French overseas trade,[3] and to the consequent identification of national interest with the well-being of the colonial planter class. Before 1789 the social policy of the mother country in the colonies was characterized by the acquiescence of the resident representatives of Church and State in the equation of order with racially defined social restrictions.[4] The combination of relative lack of governmental initiative, metropolitan apathy, and powerful social opposition may account for the fact that the French abolitionist movement was both more highly organized and more vigorously propagandistic than the prison reform movement at the outbreak of the Revolution. In this the French pattern appears parallel to the English.

In 1788 the *Société des Amis des Noirs* was organized after the example of the London abolitionist society formed the previous year.[5] The French *philosophes* proceeded through more literary channels than was the case in the

3. In 1789 Saint-Domingue was among the most prosperous and productive of the tropical colonies of Europe.

4. See Antoine Gisler, *L'Esclavage aux Antilles Françaises (XVIIe-XIXe siècle) contribution au problème de l'esclavage* (Fribourg, Switz, 1965), 17–127, 151–210.

5. See Léon Cahen, "La Société des amis des noirs et Condorcet," *La Révolution française*, L (1906), 481–511.

English reform, but with the jungle-growth of political and propaganda organization at the outbreak of the French Revolution, the abolitionists were able to appeal to a broad sector of at least the Parisian audience, and to attempt to integrate the questions of civil rights for free nonwhites, the slave trade, and slavery itself into the general attack on privilege.

The movement suffered a traumatic break in continuity and personnel during the Revolution, however. The early leaders, the *Amis des Noirs*, had represented the liberal aristocratic and moderate bourgeois sector of the Revolution. Most lost power with the Jacobin victory and many lost country or life as well. In terms of personnel, the *Amis des Noirs* were either silent or dead by the time Danton and Levasseur took the lead in bringing the question of complete emancipation before the Constituent Assembly on February 2, 1794. By then, the question of abolition had become merged with a complex revolution in Saint-Domingue (Haiti) and with a potential British invasion of the French possession. Perhaps equally important was the break with the previous assumption of emancipation as a controlled social experiment, protecting the economic interests of French trade and the planters, which had been central to earlier abolitionist thought. The *Amis des Noirs* had envisioned gradual and carefully controlled emancipation. In 1794 France's major West Indian possession was virtually out of the control of metropolitan France. The enthusiastic emancipation session of February 2, 1794, was as much a recognition of a *fait accompli* as August 4, 1789, was with regard to seigneurial rights. As significant for the nineteenth-century abolitionist movement in France were the events in the nominally French colony after emancipation. Of all the revolutions at the end of the eighteenth century, the Haitian revolution was easily the most bitter, violent, enduring, and thorough.[6] Social, economic, and racial conditions combined to produce a complex of class conflict and genocide between whites, mulattoes, and Negroes. While intensity and international significance are by no means identical, Haiti became a key symbol by which the edge of ideological arguments for emancipation in the West Indies was blunted. The issue of Haiti remained alive in France long after Napoleon lost the colony altogether in an attempt to restore slavery. Its restoration in France's remaining tropical possessions was promulgated in 1801, and these were also quickly lost to Great Britain. While the prison reform movement was reorganized with government sanction early in the Restoration, it was not until 1834 that an elite abolition society was reestablished in France,[7] and the petitions and demands for indemnity by ex-colonials through the whole period of con-

6. R. R. Palmer in *The Age of the Democratic Revolution* (Princeton, 1959), I, 188, attempts one measure of the relative intensity of the revolutions in America and France on the basis of the number of emigrés per thousand inhabitants in the two societies. If there were 5 emigrés per thousand from metropolitan France and 24 emigrés per thousand from the American colonies during their respective revolutions, the Haitian figure is at least 20 emigrés per thousand on the most conservative estimate. The proportion of violent deaths, however, was probably close to 200 per thousand, and the total population declined by at least 20 per cent between 1790 and 1805. Most significantly, the old white ruling class simply disappeared.

7. The *Société française pour l'abolition de l'esclavage*. There had been prior and more ephemeral groups devoted to the abolition of the slave trade.

stitutional monarchy tended to push the question of huge retroactive indemnities into the discussion of the abolition of slavery in the possessions restored to France in 1815. Colonists in the other islands used Haiti as a symbol of the opening afforded by emancipation to revolutionary violence, racial extermination, economic decay, chaos, and independence. It was not until the British government legislated for emancipation that the abolitionists could reverse the argument and insist on emancipation as the only means of preserving the French possessions against the potential threat of a British war of liberation.[8]

From the failure of Napoleon's venture in Haiti until the Restoration of the Bourbons, the question of slavery and abolition had no immediate relevance. Not only was the old leadership of the humanitarian movement disorganized, but France's overseas possessions had disappeared, with Haiti independent and the remaining colonies under British occupation. When the colonies were returned to France in 1815, slaves again came under her authority. Despite the diplomatic interest aroused by British initiatives to end the slave trade, and to some extent because of it, the abolition movement remained dormant in France. There was very little formal defense of slavery in principle, but also very little by way of attacks on it. It was less than a secret that the French government, while diplomatically pledged to end the slave trade, tolerated the fitting of ships for the slave trade in the Atlantic ports. The British consuls in French ports could accurately estimate the number of

8. See the first number of the periodical issued by the *Société française*.

slave ships that had left each year with perhaps more accuracy than for any other form of cargo.[9] Organizationally, the abolitionist movement—or perhaps more accurately, sentiment, for movement would be too strong a term—took refuge in fugitive articles and reviews in the Society for Christian Morality's journal. For the most part these articles stayed well within the most moderate limits. Attacks on the slave system were specifically directed against the slave trade, which the government itself had already officially condemned. Instead of systematic attacks on the whole institution, attack was concentrated on its most legally vulnerable appendage. Owners might still be respectable, powerful, and openly represented. Traders were not. Although in terms of organization and objective the movement had reverted to a lower stage of activity (learned article propaganda and administrative enforcement), it did not feel called upon to argue about the principle of the evil of slavery. Each side was content to deal with the problem on the level of organizational enforcement.

Most significantly, no serious attempt was made by the Bourbons either to integrate a justification of slavery into the defense of a hierarchical society or to list it among the glories of the old regime. At no point in the Restoration was there an ideological reversion to the pre-enlightenment era in terms of a sustained defense of permanent and complete civil inequality, nor any crusade to make the indefinite

9. A dispatch to French Foreign Minister Chateaubriand dated Jan. 5, 1824, declared that a minimum of thirty-six ships had recently sailed from Nantes rigged for slaving. Their names and tonnage were enclosed. Public Record Office F. O. (France) 146, Section "Slave Trade."

perpetuation of slavery a positive moral good.[10] For ardent legitimists as well as liberals the existence of slavery in the American republics was an absolute reproach to its pretensions to moral superiority as well as an index of its hypocrisy. When slavery again came under attack during the July Monarchy, the legitimists were too astute to defend it on the principle of the permanent inequality of human races, or to link their destinies with its survival. When such pro-slavery arguments were proposed by fringe intellectuals, as we shall see, they were rejected out of hand by liberals and not endorsed by the traditionalist groups. Institutionally, slavery had returned in 1815, but even those who gloried in the hierarchical past had no intellectual stake in the future of colonial slavery.

In a number of respects the genesis of the French nineteenth-century abolition movement differed from prison reform. The area of control was not the walls of a prison but the extent of an island. (One of the primary abolitionist arguments against the Haitian example was to emphasize the restricted uncultivated interior area available to runaways and revolutionaries in the remaining French colonies.) Secondly, the area of experimentation was not minutes or hours, but weeks, from the center of power. Thirdly, there remained a substantial, though much diminished, planter class which resisted changes in the status or organization of slaves and slave labor. Finally, while the prison reform movement was designed to give the upper classes increased control over every aspect of the life of

10. See for example *The Works of Joseph De Maistre*, ed. Jack Lively (New York, 1965), 143–146. Papal disapproval of slavery also became more emphatic in the period following the July Revolution.

the person within the reformed institution, the principal object of the emancipation was to release the slave from the total physical and moral control by the individual master. Much of the abolitionist concern in France was with finding a substitute social control that would ensure the general continuity of economic behavior and social structure in the colonies after the *Code Noir* had been abolished. In French abolitionism, labor control held pride of place.

When it finally reappeared, the notable abolitionist movement in France followed much the same lines as the prison reform movement. It presumed a consensus on the principle of abolition within the political class. It argued for a change in basic legal norms. It kept within the very narrow bounds of political agitation as prescribed by the regime of the July Monarchy.[11] It achieved throughout, the kind of sponsorship from the government of the July Monarchy that was reserved for very few social questions. A steady stream of ministerial inquiries and reports, Royal Commissions, and administrative initiatives was made to prove that the regime was interested in a solution to the question and in resolving it in favor of abolition at some undetermined point in the future. No minister of the Crown ever spoke publicly against the idea of abolition during the July Monarchy.

The movement also repeated some of the organizational patterns of the prison reform movement. The penitentiary movement and the anti-slave trade movements were both represented in the Society of Christian Morality during the

11. The French abolitionist society formed at the very moment when the government had just initiated new legislation to minimize political associations.

Restoration. The English orientation of the movement and the disproportionately large Protestant, liberal, and free-masonic elements in the early movement kept the legitimist and Catholic participation low until the late 1840's.[12] Even more than in prison reform, the opposition to immediate or rapid emancipation identified its antagonists as Anglo-philes. While prison reform had been identified as unpatriotic by virtue of its Anglo-Protestant origin and tendencies, abolitionists were identified as conscious agents of an English conspiracy against French colonial ambitions. And when, as in the right of search controversy, French policy seemed to be too subordinate to the English, many abolitionists, including Tocqueville, voted vigorously in favor of French national prestige even at the temporary expense of abolition.[13]

If there was a consensus in principle, the abolition issue was tactically more divisive than that of prison reform. It directly affected important notable economic interests. And it was obviously a more radical measure in the eyes of the proprietary classes, because it called for a drastic and even revolutionary interference in private property as enshrined

12. For the Anglophile connections of the movement in the Restoration, see Reboul, *Le Mythe anglais dans la littérature française sous la Restauration*, 19. This Restoration linkage was part of the process of picking up the threads of the humanitarian affiliations of the pre-Revolutionary period. On Catholic suspicions of the Protestant and anti-clerical activists in abolitionism, see Tudesq, *Les Grands notables*, II, 834.

13. See Mary Lawlor, *Alexis de Tocqueville in the Chamber of Deputies: His Views on Foreign and Colonial Policy* (Washington, D.C., 1959), and Tocqueville's clash with Lord Brougham reproduced in Brougham's *Discours sur le droit de visite*, transl. A. Claudet (Paris 1843). For the general background of the right of search affair, see Paul Thureau-Dangin, *Histoire de la monarchie de juillet*, 7 vols. (Paris, 1904), V, Chapters III and IV.

in the Civil Code. It was with the symbols of property, economic stability, and social order that the opposition made its most cogent appeals to the metropolitan governing class.[14] Among the most conservative ministries, like that of Count Louis Mathieu Molé, this kind of argument found its greatest receptivity. The sharp edge of economic interests also cut across the "natural" lines of the humanitarian alliance as well. Social Catholic opinion, vigorously exercised about the condition of the poor in France, was generally little concerned with emancipation until very late in the day. The Chambers of Commerce of Bordeaux and other ports were far from enthusiastic about further disruptions in the already enfeebled colonial trade.

The moderate liberal tradition, represented by Victor de

14. The *Revue coloniale,* which spoke in behalf of the colonial interest in Paris, based its defense against abolitionism primarily on the proprietary principle and explicitly denied themselves any defense of white domination on racial grounds. The *Revue* insisted that the colonists applauded the abolition of the legal color bar, or at least accepted it without bitterness and sabotage. See *Revue coloniale* (T.I. vol. 1 "Prospectus," 6). The *Revue abolitioniste* (T.I. vol. 1, "Declaration") was equally circumspect. It did not ask its supporters for the fervor of early Christians but for a plan to render abolition as palatable as possible for the proprietor and as "rapid, complete, moral, and religious" as possible for the slave. An entrepreneurial joint stock company in Paris offered to emancipate the slaves, indemnify the owners, and exploit the colonies on the model of French railroad companies, with state-guaranteed interest on capital investment for a fixed period. See A. Cachut, "De la Société coloniale. Abolition de l'esclavage," *Revue des deux mondes,* T. III (13e année) (1843), 207. Some colonial councils had no objection to emancipation on condition that the state bought out the colonists entirely, slaves, land, machinery, and capital—in other words paid the cash value of the colony. This was probably no more than a ploy to make emancipation financially unfeasible, since property was so encumbered and credit so tight as to render unaided private liquidation a rather pleasant fantasy.

Broglie, Charles de Remusat, Tocqueville, Odilon Barrot, Beaumont, and Passy, formed the core of the elite abolitionist movement with the concurring but immobile Guizot on its conservative wing, and the ardent abolitionist Victor Schoelcher on the more polemical and strident radical side.[15] While there had been a good deal of agitation for the enforcement of the prohibition of the slave trade by the Society for Christian Morality in the 1820's and governmental steps toward more effective enforcement after 1830, the abolitionist movement at the time of the July Revolution was organizationally where it had been in the 1780's. As before the Revolution, it was an elite concern, carried out by the descendants and heirs of the liberal enlightenment.

The precipitating event that crystallized a formal organization was one that occurred in England, as it had forty years before. In 1833 Parliament decreed the abolition of slavery in her colonies following a period of apprenticeship. For French liberals and for many administrators this was the handwriting on the wall for French slavery. If abolition were not achieved with all deliberate speed the colonies might be lost as well. The Society for the Abolition of Slavery was founded in 1834. Tocqueville and Beaumont entered in the first co-option of 1835. The Society was, of course, immune from laws against subversive associations

15. The measure of this Right-Left scale would be based on two elements: (1) the extent to which the rights of property were considered equal to the rights of the slaves (the compensation corollary); (2) the extent to which immediate and total emancipation was supported against partial and gradual proposals. In France the elite abolitionist group was also paralleled by a distinct mulatto group as well as by the radical middle-class branch as represented by Schoelcher and Arago.

passed in 1834. Its president, the Duc de Broglie, was president of the Council of Ministers at the time of its formation. One of its vice-presidents was Odilon Barrot, leader of the dynastic opposition. The organization did not conceive of itself as a mass movement or mass propaganda group, and it succeeded quite well in maintaining its elite restrictiveness. Its rules for admission resembled those of its ancestor, the *Amis des Noirs,* and were more than enough to ensure a highly restricted and moderate society. To enter the French abolitionist society one had to be introduced by two other members, as well as nominated by the central committee, which consisted of *all* the charter members, and one had then to make a minimum voluntary contribution of 25 francs. According to contemporary statistical estimates, this sum was the equivalent of between thirteen and seventeen days' wages for the average adult worker in 1840.[16] But the social barrier was far more restrictive than the financial one. When an English abolitionist asked Beaumont why Bissette, a prominent and wealthy West Indian mulatto resident in Paris, was not a member of the society, he unhesitatingly responded, "Why! He is a colored man!"[17] Bearing in mind the fact that Beaumont had written the most vehement book of his generation against the psychological effects of racial prejudice, the low "Negrophile" content of the movement becomes clear, colonial and administrative accusations notwithstanding.

16. Based on the estimates of Edouard Dolléans and Gérard Dehove, *Histoire du travail en France,* 2 vols. (Paris, 1953), I, 168–169.
17. See Edward S. Abdy to Maria (Weston) Chapman, May 24, 1844, Weston Papers, Boston Public Library; also cited in Leon F. Litwack, *North of Slavery: The Negro in the Free States* (Chicago, 1961), 219 and note.

When parliamentary and Royal Commissions were selected to hear testimony on the question of emancipation, Negroes, whether slave or free, were not asked to appear.[18] At its inception the abolition movement was a dialogue within and between the interested parties of the *pays légal*. The Society for the Abolition of Slavery could more accurately have been called the abolitionist section of the Chamber of Deputies and the French Academy.[19]

This self-limitation of means and methods and the very clear determination to move totally within the confines of legality, reflected the *pays légal*'s commitment to abolition in principle. The semiofficial *Journal des débats*, which represented the general principle of social conservatism even more than it represented the Orleanist regime, reaffirmed the value of emancipation at every debate in parliament. If it always added, "with just indemnity," so did the abolitionist society. The Chamber of Deputies was always far more impatient with the handful of representatives of the planter interest who frankly defended the institution of slavery than with the abolitionist speakers.

The continuation of slavery was not even allowed to be an "academic" question. On one occasion in 1839 Tocque-

18. See Archives Nationales, C795 (1839), *Commission chargée d'examiner la proposition de M. de Tracy relative à l'abolition de l'esclavage.*

19. The Academy of Moral and Political Sciences, of which Tocqueville and Beaumont were members, refused to award the *Prix Grégoire* in 1839 to a memoir on the causes of prejudice because it was "not free of that virulence which is reproachfully attributed to their European adversaries; we must henceforth eschew polemic where reason needs only its own weapons to emerge victorious" (*Société française pour l'abolition de l'esclavage*, XIII [July 1839], 8).

ville himself intervened to prevent Charles Dunoyer from suggesting the relative utility of slavery as an institution as a topic for discussion in the French Academy. Dunoyer raised the question whether "at the moment" forced labor was not preferable to liberty for the Negroes of the French colonies. Tocqueville, who had not attended the preparatory conference in which Dunoyer had first formulated the question, protested against allowing such a proposition to be entered on the Academy's program. Dunoyer's project was promptly tabled. No historical or economic rationale was to be suggested that would diminish the fundamental moral clarity of the question of slavery either for the nineteenth or the seventeenth century: "The illustrious author of *Democracy in America* rejected the idea that slavery might have been necessary at its origin [or] useful and necessary to insure labor, since it merely degrades it."[20] It was not the first time that Dunoyer had been ruled out of order by French liberalism.

The entire debate took place in an atmosphere of relative apathy. Thomas Jollivet, one of the principal representatives of the colonial interest, used the absence of a mass movement in French abolitionism as an argument against government action. Where, he asked, were the French equivalents of the English electoral mandates, of her mass meetings, of endless clamor in the press, of the innumerable petitions, with eighty thousand signatures, of the associations of clerical wives and devout women, of

20. Cited from the account of the newspaper *Le Siècle*, published in *Société française pour l'abolition de l'esclavage*, XIII (July 1839), 32–33.

the religious fanaticism, of the long lists of localities demanding abolition?[21] Few areas of France were as economically interested in the question as the merchants of Bordeaux or the sugar beet producers, and their concern was marginal. The yearly departmental resolutions on public questions may be taken as an index of this apathy. Only about a dozen departmental councils (*conseils-généraux*) even bothered to pass a resolution on the question of abolition during the whole July Monarchy, and only three did so with any regularity.[22] Neither Tocqueville nor Beaumont ever got their respective departments to pass resolutions on the question. More accurately, they probably never attempted to have their *conseils* formulate such a resolution.

Aside from the maintenance of orderly transition, the problem within the *pays légal* seemed to boil down to a careful, documentary discussion about two questions: (1) what should be the timing of emancipation, and (2) what would be a fair slaveowners' indemnity, funded at the lowest possible cost to the taxpayers? The government was also reluctant to push through a radical change in the status of the slaves without at least the reluctant acquiescence of the slaveowners. The slaveowners and their sympathizers within the colonial administration and the French overseas trade seemed satisfied if only they could keep a definitive mechanism for emancipation from being agreed on by the Chambers and approved by the government. For

21. Thomas Jollivet, *Observations sur le rapport de M. de Tocqueville relatif à l'abolition de l'esclavage dans les colonies et quelques mots sur la loi des sucres* (Paris, 1840), 10.

22. Archives Nationales, Section Colonies, Généralités 156 (1301): "Voeux des Conseils-généraux pour l'abolition de l'esclavage."

more than a decade, interpellation followed interpellation, report followed report, petition followed petition, discussion followed discussion, improvement followed improvement in the legal situation of slaves, but no definitive date or plan for emancipation was in sight when the February Revolution shattered the political framework. During the July Monarchy only a small group of radicals, led by Victor Schoelcher and another group of mulatto expatriates in Paris, with an occasional working-class petition, gave any hint that the question was of any interest to a larger audience.[23] Popular petitions were confined to two large cities, Paris and Lyon, and scattered rural areas. The maritime towns, with their large notable element hostile to immediate emancipation, seem to have been either unsolicited or unresponsive. Whatever degree of anti-Negro feeling there was among the French lower classes was also localized in the Atlantic ports.[24]

The techniques of the "opposition" to abolition, or at least to any practical steps toward implementation, reveal the nature of the movement more clearly than the arguments of the abolitionists. Perhaps the most telling evidence of consensus on the principle of abolition even by those most opposed to it in France was the advice the newspaper *La Guienne* gave to its readers. Located in Bordeaux, the most "pro-colonial" city in France, the paper was in addition vigorously anti-liberal, anti-Protestant, anti-abolitionist, and anti-Orleanist: "The colonists," it warned in 1844, "commit a great mistake when they ac-

23. See Raphaël Tardon, *Le Combat de Schoelcher* (Paris, 1948); Léonard Sainville, *Victor Schoelcher* (Paris, 1950), and selected works of Schoelcher in *Esclavage et colonisation* (Paris, 1948).

24. See McCloy, *The Negro in France*, 115–116, 127–128.

cept debate on the grounds of abstractions and syllogisms. . . . Their evident interest is discussion on exclusively economic grounds." On the level of values, *La Guienne* obviously felt uncomfortable before the symbols of "Christianity," "Humanity," "Liberty," and "Equality" combined in all abolitionist arguments. Neither they nor the creoles were prepared to reject the Christian doctrine of the unity of the species, nor to embrace a thoroughly antiegalitarian or racist metaphysic. They preferred to speak the common language of their class and of their metropolitan contemporaries, which was also the language of capitalism and property and of liberalism and Christianity.[25]

While the leaders of the anti-slavery movement represented no direct economic interests, the anti-abolitionist leaders were more closely aligned to specific economic sectors. Their appeal was to these sectors and to a far larger group of those who feared anything that might resemble social revolution, to all the groups who supported a policy of low taxes, or who wished to progress as slowly as was politically possible. In a situation where they were fighting a moral consensus, only a portion of the creole element itself opposed emancipation in principle. The mainland representatives of the slaveowners never seriously raised any questions of racial inferiority in the Chamber of Deputies, or at the hearings of parliamentary commissions, where they had ample opportunity to speak without contradiction from nonwhites. The creoles might take the position that the Negro population was not yet fully civilized or socialized; they might say that the Negroes would always be in a

25. Cited in Tudesq, *Les Grands notables*, II, 843.

state of relative social inferiority to the whites. But the most ardent abolitionists for their part did not intend to reverse that situation except in the very long run by individual social mobility.[26]

Through their representatives, notably Jollivet and Dupin, the creoles argued on the basis of the economic and political dangers that would arise out of abolition, not on the merits of the slave system itself. Loss of the colonies, potential revolution, a breakdown of the colonial trade, these were counters which they manipulated with dexterity. They attacked the abolitionist movement as an English pawn, or attempted to show that the entire question really served the domestic sugar beet interests in attacking colonial sugar cane interests. The most telling argument against abolition, however, was the procedural and financial argument against precipitate action. This was the argument that most appealed to those who were neither economically interested in the question nor swayed by the abolitionists' appeals to controlled revolution in the name of Christianity, liberty, or equality. Here the fears of colonial and domestic economic confiscation and dislocation played an important veto role. But apparently even more decisive was the argument that the enormous cost of the required indemnity to the French taxpayer was reason enough to postpone action. This combination of social and fiscal conservatism was probably best represented by the Parisian press through the pens of Granier de Cassagnac

26. See the report of the [*Royal*] *Commission du 26 mai 1840 pour l'examen des questions relatives à l'esclavage et à la constitution politique des colonies.*

and Emile de Girardin and by the Molé[27] faction in the Chamber of Deputies.

The July Monarchy presented a pattern of continuously reiterated consensus on the necessity of abolition and an equally continuous evasion of implementation. The colonists used every technique to make the machinery of government spin in a void. They challenged the constitutional power of the Chambers to alter property relations. They refused to recognize the competence of a Royal Commission. They demanded their own collaboration in all projects. They succeeded in winning the support of the ministry for indefinite postponements. If they failed to veto minor legislation,[28] they postponed its promulgation or its enforcement. Reckoning on the principle of no aboli-

27. When the first (Guizot-Rémusat) report on emancipation was being brought before the Chamber of Deputies, Molé wrote to the French ambassador in Washington expressing satisfaction with a victory of Calhoun against the abolitionist movement: "The Senate . . . has again justified its reputation for wisdom and lofty rationality. A lively and healthy awareness of the rights and interests whose inviolability is the chief guarantee of the maintenance of the American federation . . . condemns the passionate attempts of abolitionism." Then followed a passage which was penned out: "This method of handling a matter in itself so delicate and irritating could serve as a lesson for the men in Europe who, with more zeal than prudence, raise the question of the [aboli] suppression of slavery in the colonies, which is tied to so many other interests of the highest political and moral order" (Archives des Affaires Etrangères. Correspondance politique. Etats-Unis, 93 (1838) P. 164). Prudence was also to be the characteristic of the Guizot ministries throughout the 1840's. It reflected the view of the king as well. In its reluctance toward any move involving costly indemnities, the apathetic "center" of the pays légal did not represent merely its own sentiments.

28. The laws of July 18 and 19, 1845, concerning the control and redemption of slaves.

tion without the consent of the slaveholders and a huge indemnity, they postponed a decision for the life of the July Monarchy.

On the ideological level, then, Tocqueville and Beaumont wrote in a friendly atmosphere of consensus. Within the vocal political classes of continental France during the July Monarchy there was well-nigh universal agreement that slavery was morally evil and, at least in the long run, historically doomed. The principle of abolition in France aroused much less general interest or polemical debate over the question of human inequality than in the Anglo-American world because that issue was regarded as settled in the civil realm by almost the entire elite in France. The literature that proposed to scientifically question the abolitionist premise of fundamental racial equality received a reception in France which was cool to the point of indifference.[29] The shrug with which Arthur de Gobineau's

29. Before and after the Revolution, a number of writers and historians flirted with the idea of racial diversity as an explanation of French history (Aristocratic Franks versus bourgeois Gallo-Romans), but no thinker attempted to use race as a key to human action in anything like a rigorous causal analysis. Race, in French writing of the early nineteenth century, was apparently used more as a term of social than of biological differentiation. It was frequently used interchangeably with the term "class," even with reference to the social structure of the French colonies, by the most anti-abolitionist newspapers. The Christian doctrine of the unity of the human race was so strong that even Gobineau, as a Catholic, felt himself impelled to state that the unity of, or diversity of, the species was not a settled question. Only those who had broken more radically with the contemporary religious framework could take so radical a stand. Attempts to classify the human species in terms of racial characteristics should not be confused with doctrines which used race as a determinant of individual or social behavior. The history of the idea of race in France has been treated in Theophile Simard's,

Essay on the Inequality of Human Races was greeted within the French intellectual establishment when it appeared in 1853 is well known. Even when Tocqueville tried to assuage the bitter disappointment of his friend and protégé, he stretched the historical truth. The unwillingness of his fellow countrymen to become excited about the hypotheses of human inequality was characterized as part of the general lassitude of French political thought following the crises of 1848 and 1851. Twenty years before, wrote Tocqueville soothingly, the work would have received the serious attention it deserved.[30] Yet slightly less than twenty years before, Gobineau's key to human history had in fact been presented to France by Victor Courtet de L'Isle. It was received with deep silence.[31] At the outset of his own work

---

*Etude critique sur la formation de la doctrine des races au xviii*e *siècle et son expansion au xix*e *siècle,* Memoires de l'Académie royale de Belgique, 2e série TXVI (Bruxelles, 1922).

30. Letter of Tocqueville to Arthur de Gobineau, July 30, 1856 (*Oeuvres* (M): *Correspondance Tocqueville-Gobineau*). This correspondence is translated in *"The European Revolution" and Correspondence with Gobineau,* ed. and trans. John Lukacs (Garden City, N. Y., 1959), 292–294.

31. Victor Courtet de L'Isle, *La Science politique fondée sur la science de l'homme, ou étude des race humaines sous le rapport philosophique, historique et social* (Paris, 1838), 110–113. Alphonse Ride, who also launched a frontal attack on the principle of human equality, declared that the weight of opinion was all on the side of the *philosophes,* with their "immense mass of partisans and innumerable readers . . . indeed I am obliged to confess that almost all these men, endowed with more or less superior intelligence, are completely misled in this matter." He bitterly complained about his inability to even get his works published in a land dominated by the tyranny of the egalitarian majority. See Ride, *Esclavage et liberté. Existence de l'homme et des sociétés en harmonie avec les lois universelles* (Paris, 1843), 57–58.

Courtet traced the unhappy fate of the doctrine of a natural racial hierarchy in France. He stormed against the refusal of certain authors to frankly confront the evidence of contemporary socio-racial relationships and the implications of physical anthropology. Twenty years before his own works were snubbed, claimed Courtet, Charles Dunoyer had raised the hypothesis of racial inferiority as a possible explanation of social hierarchies throughout the world. And what had been the response? The doyens of liberalism, Charles Comte and Benjamin Constant, had both rejected the suggestions not as untrue, but as politically dangerous and therefore undiscussable. "This system," Constant wrote of Dunoyer, "has its portion of truth; it is interesting to examine it, and science might be enriched by it, but we think that it must be carefully set apart from politics."[32] What, after all, concluded Constant, was the greatest and really undisputed achievement of the French Revolution, if not in having established the principle of civil equality beyond question? To throw the one basic accomplishment of the Revolution back into the cauldron of political debate would have been too much for this weary liberal at the beginning of the Bourbon Restoration. Nor did the traditionalist or legitimist writers bring this scientific hypothesis into the political area. Their perspective was tied too closely to the Christian tradition to radically question the unity of the human species.[33] Thus Tocqueville only echoed generations of French liberalism when he wrote of Gobineau's ideas: "I believe that they are

32. *Ibid.*, 113.
33. Charles Comte observed that race prejudice along color lines was not a characteristic of contemporary European aristocrats (see his *Traité de legislation*, 4 vols., 2d ed. [Paris, 1835], IV, 312).

probably quite false; I know that they are certainly very pernicious."[34]

One must not confuse these tangential defenses of Constant and Tocqueville and the reticence of Remusat and Renan with an attempt at a scientific refutation of racial inequality or as an absolute denial of the possibility of racially determined differences in group characteristics. Both positions were based essentially on the perceived political potentials of racist arguments. Constant opposed it at the beginning of the nineteenth century because it would reopen one of the positively settled questions of the Revolution. Tocqueville fought it as part of his general attack on deterministic fatalism within the French elite. Gobineau biologically closed political and human freedom to certain

34. Tocqueville to Gobineau, Nov. 17, 1853 (*Oeuvres* (M): *Correspondance Tocqueville-Gobineau*; Lukacs, *The European Revolution*, 227. Even Gobineau's sponsor in the French Academy, Charles de Remusat, held back from speaking out on the book. As he told Gobineau, "If what you say is true, I prefer that someone else should affirm it" (Gobineau to Tocqueville, Teheran, May 1, 1856 [*Oeuvres* (M): *Correspondance*], and Lukacs, 289–290). Ernest Renan, willing to agree to certain points in Gobineau's argument, was also eager to avoid being identified as the man who publicized it. See Michael D. Biddiss, "Gobineau and the Origins of European Racism," *Race*, VIII (Jan. 1966), 255–270, 268. Renan's response shows that more was involved in the reluctance to be linked with popularizing Gobineau's work than the religious conformity of the early Second Empire as suggested by Tocqueville. Had Gobineau been less well connected with the eminences of the French Academy, the reception would have been, as with his predecessors, virtual silence. One need only see Tocqueville torturing himself to find compliments and excuses to soothe Gobineau's distress at the general indifference to his work in France. In the light of the sources cited in Gobineau's work, the overwhelming dependence on German rather than French scholarship is clear, although eminent French scientists such as Cuvier had hypothesized the diversity of human species.

human groups, including the French nation. In the same letter in which he emphasized the anti-libertarian political dynamite in Gobineau's ideas, Tocqueville, trying to be accommodating, also wrote: "If your doctrine were to relate merely to the *externally* recognizable differences of human families, and through these enduring characteristics assign them to differences in creation, it would be less fantastic and easier to understand. But when one applies it within one of these great families, for example, within the white race, then the thread of reasoning becomes entangled and loses itself."[35]

Tocqueville universalized the pernicious aspects of racism: "What purpose does it serve to persuade lesser peoples, living in abject conditions of barbarism or slavery, that, such being their racial nature, they can do nothing to better themselves, to change their habits or to ameliorate their status? Don't you see how in your doctrine are inherent all the evils produced by permanent inequality: pride, violence, the scorn of one's fellow man, tyranny, and abjection in every one of their forms?" But he most feared its reception in France: "Those who approve your fundamental thesis or those who wish it to be true (and, in our days, after the wear and tear of sixty years of revolution, there are many in France who may want to believe something similar) must read it with great enthusiasm, since your book is well constructed, it proceeds straight to its conclusion, and it is argued most intelligently."[36] Irrespective of the merits of Gobineau's arguments, the book en-

35. Tocqueville to Gobineau, Nov. 17, 1853 (*Oeuvres* (M): *Correspondance Tocqueville-Gobineau*; Lukacs, "The European Revolution," 227).
36. *Ibid.*

couraged the spiritual lassitude of his already weakening contemporaries.

For both political and intellectual reasons, Tocqueville and Beaumont were in agreement with their contemporaries in opposing any justification of permanent domination through arguments based on inherent racial inferiority. Like Constant they were willing to treat the question of racial intellectual differentiation and inferiority as an open academic question, but their own personal experience in America had evoked in them a far more determined response than mere agreement with the mass of their liberal contemporaries. Beaumont launched his literary and political career by an exposé of the evils of Negro slavery and the extension of racial hatred in free as well as slave America. His novel *Marie* was an illustration of the racial tragedies created by the hatreds, the guilt, and the violence which the institution of Negro slavery had caused to be built into American democracy.[37] Both *Marie* and Tocqueville's *Democracy* contained lengthy arguments on the extent to which the institution of slavery brutalized one segment of those connected with it, demoralized the other segment, and distorted the economic and social progress of the entire society in which it was embedded. *Marie*, in fact, was one of the most effective and widely read works on the subject in France.[38]

37. Beaumont also attacked English racism directed against the Irish.

38. See Rémond, *Les Etats-Unis devant l'opinion française*, I, 379, 380, 387–389; II, 736–737. The heroine of *Marie* was not a Negro but a Caucasian with some Negro ancestry, and the major episode of racial hatred took place in New York, closely following an actual race riot in New York in 1834, occasioned by an interracial marriage (see *Marie*, Chapter 13, Appendix L).

There are two important features to be noted about Beaumont's attack on American Negro slavery as a background for Tocqueville's work on emancipation in the French West Indies. Slavery was not simply a moral evil that had to be wiped out immediately, or at all costs. It was an institution. The economic interests, psychological attitudes, and political structure of the United States made it impossible for one to predict or to recommend a probable mode of abolition. Beaumont and Tocqueville instead emphasized the difficulties of the proposed solutions in America to such an extent as to discourage any hopes for controlled abolition with the peaceful acquiescence of both races. It is no wonder that, despite their condemnation of the principles and practices of slavery on moral and economic grounds, their works on America furnished ample material for the spokesmen of the anti-abolitionists in France. Secondly, emancipation did not imply for Tocqueville and Beaumont a stage in the process toward an integrated society. "If I absolutely had to make some guess about the future," wrote Tocqueville from his experience in the North," I should say that in the probable course of things the abolition of slavery in the South will increase the repugnance felt by the white population for the blacks."[39] This idea of permanent segregation was reflected in Tocqueville's relegation of the race question to the parts of *Democracy in America* which were "American" rather than democratic. He likewise excluded statistics on Negroes in his comparisons of American and French prison systems.[40]

39. *Oeuvres* (M): *De la démocratie en Amérique*, I, 373; *Democracy in America*, 328.

40. See *Penitentiary System*, 93–99, and note 18 of Chapter 3; and Tocqueville's speech to the Chamber of Deputies in *Tocqueville*

Tocqueville and Beaumont apparently did not compose their studies on American slavery with the problem of abolition in the French West Indies in mind. Although the two men became members of the French abolition society almost at the very moment when their books on America appeared, one of their conclusions on the implications of abolition was to be hurled against them again and again in parliament and the press. This was that, given the context of past racial oppression, abolition could not ward off a struggle between the two races in the South. Even more emphatically, Tocqueville affirmed as a general principle his disbelief "that the white and black races will ever come to live anywhere on an equal footing." If the whites of North America remained united it would be difficult for the Negroes to avoid being destroyed or, at the least, being isolated along the Gulf Coast littoral. The fate of the whites on the Caribbean Islands seemed equally clear: "In the Antilles the white race seems destined to succumb; on the Continent, the black."[41] If in the West Indies emancipation was a step toward black supremacy, it is no wonder that spokesmen for the French slaveholders accused Tocqueville of attempting to have the French government

---

and Beaumont on Social Reform, ed. Drescher, Part II. Negroes were clearly distinguished from the native white population because the emancipated Negroes, according to American statistics, produced convicted criminals out of all proportion to their numbers; "In fact," wrote Beaumont, "to separate the Negroes from the whole population of the United States, would be equal to deducting the poorer classes of the community with us. That is to say, those who commit the crimes" (see *Penitentiary System,* 99).

41. *De la démocratie,* I, 372, 373; *Democracy in America,* 327, 328.

act as the executioner of its own colonials.[42] Nor is it surprising that Tocqueville shifted the emphasis of his argument away from America in connection with French abolition. He realized that since the West Indian slave system was no longer based on rapidly expanding production and markets, the French abolitionists had a far better argument from obsolescence than their American counterparts.[43] From a European abolitionist's viewpoint the less said about the American example the better. After 1835 Tocqueville's attitude toward slavery was molded less from his American experience and more from the contingencies of the French situation.

In one respect the later outline of the future of the Indies was the reverse of Tocqueville's prognosis in the *Democracy*. There, projecting from his idea of the rise of the masses and the omnipotence of the majority, he had predicted the triumph of the black race and the disappearance of the white in the Antilles. To Tocqueville and Beaumont, French emancipation implied the end of the total ownership by individuals of the lives and labor of other individ-

42. See Archives Nationales, section Colonies. Generalités (1375), dossier 10, *Memoire* of M. Ronmy, chef de battaillon; and Le Pelletier du Clary, *Rapport . . . chargée de repondre à celui de M. de Tocqueville au Conseil colonial de la Martinique . . . session de 1839, passim* (1839), 1, 2, 6, 10, 15, 25.

43. See the letter of Tocqueville to Jared Sparks, Oct. 19, 1840 (Houghton Library, Harvard University, b Ms Sparks, 153). When the American Civil War broke out its abolitionists were also anxious to know whether Tocqueville had ever changed his mind about the possibility of black and white living together peaceably. See the letter of John Murray Forbes to Marie de Tocqueville, June 14, 1861 *(Letters of John Murray Forbes*, ed. Sarah F. Hughes, 3 vols. [Boston, 1905], I, 275).

uals, that is, the end of an aristocratic relationship in its purest form. It never meant the necessary extinction of relationships of domination and subordination between racial groups taken as a whole, and certainly not the destruction of economic power and social superiority of white Europeans by European governments. Whites and blacks could nowhere exist without either subordination or racial conflict. Only an outside, centralized, power could avoid civil war after abolition, and only for as long as it remained unresponsive to local power conflicts. In his report in 1839 to the Chamber of Deputies he noted, apparently without caveat or temporal qualification, "If it be thought necessary to the cultivation of colonial produce, and to the continuation of the white race in the Antilles, that the services of the enfranchised Negro may be permanently hired by the great proprietors of the soil, it is evident that we should not create for him a domain, where he can easily live by laboring for himself alone."[44]

Before the Chamber of Deputies a vision of general European expansion and dominance took the place of the egalitarian upsurge. Moreover, at the very moment when Tocqueville looked to white European governments to be the principal agents of the abolition of legal individual slaveholding, he expected an ever more extended domination of non-European peoples by Europeans throughout the world. Ironically, one of his most important arguments against Gobineau's theory of the decline of the Western races was the providential fact that "the few million men, who, a few centuries ago, lived nearly shelterless in the for-

44. *Tocqueville and Beaumont on Social Reform*, ed. Drescher, 129.

ests and in the marshes of Europe, will within a hundred years have transformed the globe and dominated the other races. Nothing is more clearly prescribed beforehand by Providence."[45] For once Tocqueville's prophetic timing was a little off, for within that century the European races had already transformed the globe and begun a headlong retreat from political domination as a final consequence of the transformation. The significant point here is that extended public domination was perfectly compatible with the abolition of private slaveholding and the indefinite extension of legal equality. Tocqueville's deep commitment to both the abolition of slavery and the extended conquest of Algeria, for example, was predicated on this distinction, as it was for most liberal expansionists in France.[46]

In the political arena Tocqueville was among the most radical of the abolitionist notables. He was not a full-time abolitionist crusader like Victor Schoelcher, but it was not in the nature of any of the notables to be totally absorbed in any reform movement. Tocqueville was, however, as closely identified with the cause of abolition as any prominent political figure of his day. On January 1, 1838, all

45. Tocqueville to Gobineau, Nov. 13, 1855 (*Oeuvres* (M): *Correspondance Tocqueville-Gobineau*), Lukacs, *The European Revolution*, 268; see also Tocqueville's letter to Gobineau of Nov. 17, 1853.

46. The connection between abolitionist and expansionist ideas was by no means confined to Tocqueville or to the French elite. It had an even broader base in England than in France. But Tocqueville's expansionism was more closely tied to the salvation of French patriotism than to the humanitarian ideology of ameliorating the social condition of non-European peoples. With Tocqueville the Machiavellian symbols of power and vitality were invoked more frequently than those of improvement.

slaves in the British colonies were completely emancipated, two years ahead of the schedule contemplated in the original abolition bill of 1833. The following month Hyppolite Passy, a deputy and vice-president of the French Abolitionist Society, presented to the Chamber a bill calling for the gradual abolition of slavery in the French colonies. The parliamentary commission that studied the Passy proposal with Guizot as its presiding officer and Rémusat its reporter asked the government in June 1838 to begin a serious study of emancipation. But the Molé ministry pigeon-holed the commission's resolution. Molé's fall in February 1839 was the signal for new elections, and Tocqueville won his seat in the Chamber of Deputies. The new Soult ministry, in which two avowed abolitionists (Tracy and Passy) held ministerial posts, took up the suggestion of the Rémusat-Guizot commission and in June 1839 a new commission (de Sade presiding) was formed. Tocqueville was elected its reporter. His report was presented less than two months later on July 23, 1839.[47] It drew upon the materials gathered by the previous commission as well as its own hearings.

The novelty of Tocqueville's report was the commission's decision in favor of immediate and simultaneous abolition. This report also languished. With the advent of another ministry (Thiers-Rémusat) in May of 1840, also containing an abolitionist, a Royal Commission was formed, consisting of peers, deputies, and high functionaries. Tocqueville was also nominated to this commission, presided over by the Duc de Broglie, president of the

47. See *Tocqueville and Beaumont on Social Reform*, ed. Drescher, Part III.

French abolition society. The members of this commission, by their participation, all formally accepted the principle of abolition. But the parliamentary representatives of the commercial ports and the administrative personnel were "moderates." They refused to go as far in their recommendations as the previous Sade-Tocqueville commission. The result was a division in the final report, the majority (including Tocqueville) favoring a plan calling for universal and simultaneous emancipation on January 1, 1853, and the minority declaring in favor of partial and progressive emancipation for everyone born after 1838, with total emancipation twenty years after the law took effect. The Guizot-Soult ministry (constituted in October 1840) made a decision to wait for the slaveowners to choose between the two suggested plans and the colonists simply refrained from any choice.

The first of Tocqueville's writings on French abolition, the parliamentary report, was undoubtedly his most famous reform essay. Published while he was completing the final draft of the second part of *Democracy in America*, it was intended, as were all of his major political reports, to be written within the consensus of the political class. Following the well-tested and eminently successful approach of the *Penitentiary System* and the *Democracy*, Tocqueville intended his report to be lofty in tone and nonpolemical in its style. He wanted to treat slavery as an institutional reality as well as a moral problem, to recognize the legitimacy of the anxieties of the slaveowners as well as the goals of the abolitionists. There were to be no purple passages about the oppressed and exploited in his work. When he sent a copy to his English friend and translator, Henry Reeve, he commented: "I think you will not find, along with a great taste for liberty, any of those revolutionary passions which sometimes trouble my abolitionist brothers."[48] Tocqueville was anxious that his support of reform causes like abolition and pentitentiary reform not be identified with the "mummeries of the philanthropists which succeed in making noble passions almost ridiculous."[49] The report was designed in the style befitting its conception, to appeal as much to the self-interest of the slaveowners and the colonies as to the demands of humanitarian France. Tocqueville was in fact complimented by an adversary of abolition for having treated slavery as a complex institutional fact rather than as a simple moral imperative. Even some of the official colonial defenses of the status quo used his report to bolster their case.[50]

48. Letter of Tocqueville to Henry Reeve, Nov. 15, 1839 (*Oeuvres* (M): *Correspondance anglaise*). See also his letter on the same subject to John Stuart Mill, Nov. 14, 1839, in the same volume of correspondence.

49. Letter of Tocqueville to Beaumont, Oct. 9, 1843 (*Oeuvres* (M): *Correspondance Tocqueville-Beaumont*, II).

50. Archives Nationales, section Colonies Generalites (1379), *Conseil colonial de Guadeloupe, rapport*, 75. The earlier views of Tocqueville's *Democracy* and Beaumont's *Marie* on abolition were in fact so evenly balanced between general moral principles and the enormous practical difficulties of implementation that they appear to have excited no hostility toward *Democracy in America* in the South. They caused no indignation among slaveholders. Tocqueville's report on slavery in 1839 probably caused more violent response than any of his other writings. A number of polemic replies were written by the representatives of creole interests. The report made a transatlantic ripple as well. (It certainly occasioned more reaction in America in 1840 than the second part of the *Democracy*.) An abolitionist friend of Tocqueville's, Mary Sparks, translated the report and had it published. The French consul in New Orleans

The report established a frame of reference which is as revealing of its author's view of his audience as his conclusions.[51] No arguments were marshaled against the system of slavery, or in support of its inevitable and proximate demise. It assumed that his audience would neither defend its existence morally, nor maintain that it could exist for too much longer. The questions were not if and why, but simply how, and how soon. Secondly, any program of emancipation had to minimize economic costs to the planter and maximize social controls over labor. Ensured economic prosperity was the most effective lubricant not of a social revolution but of a controlled legal transformation. The maintenance of nonviolent social processes was assumed to be tactically simple because of the smallness of the islands, thus brushing aside the nightmare of another Haiti. The real danger was economic chaos rather than race war. France, at least indirectly, had to assume the obligation of providing the colonies with a cheap labor supply. The government had to provide three types of incentives, indemnity for the planter, discipline for the freedman, and low costs to the metropolitan taxpayer.

Once again, two separate worlds demanded two different relationships to the state. In the exceptional, transitional realm of labor in the islands, the state was to have its com-

---

entered a special dispatch in his political correspondence on Southern reaction to it (see *Tocqueville and Beaumont on Social Reform*, ed. Drescher, 98–99n).

51. *Tocqueville and Beaumont on Social Reform*, ed. Drescher, 98–100. For Tocqueville's assumption of a consensus in favor of emancipation and its inevitability, see his parliamentary report in the same book. On its validity and limits, see Tudesq, *Les Grandes notables*, II, 838–840.

petence and its power increased to the full extent necessary to accomplish and maintain the social transformation.[52] The relationship between the state, the slaveholding aristocracy, and the masses was to be deliberately and consciously a reenactment of the democratic revolution in Europe. The centralized state was to be the legitimate and the only conceivable agency of transformation. The real difference between the islands and the European model was that the agency was to be external to the society, responsible for but undetermined by either major social group within the affected society. External despotism was the surest guarantee against internal tyranny, and above all against the incalculable risks of violence.

Tocqueville's second essay on the abolition of slavery was written in the fall of 1843 for the opposition newspaper *Siècle* and dovetailed with Beaumont's articles on prison reform in the same paper. It was occasioned by the publication of the Broglie commission's report on methods of abolition. Although Tocqueville's ideas on state-controlled immediate emancipation had not been accepted, he had been with the commission majority in advocating simultaneous emancipation in ten years. He regarded the report itself as a masterpiece and accepted the offer of Chambolle, the *Siècle*'s editor, to publish his own background observations on the subject.

It is a commentary on Tocqueville's relatively advanced position on the slavery question that, contrary to his usual practice, he consented to publish his ideas in a newspaper. Moreover, the newspaper was an organ of the dynastic Left, which expressed views, especially on the Catholic Church, that Tocqueville openly repudiated. In the case of aboli-

52. *Tocqueville and Beaumont on Social Reform*, ed. Drescher, 133–134.

tionism there seems to have been a real coincidence of aims with the left and a mutual desire to goad the Guizot government into legislative action. The essay appeared in six installments between October and December of 1843. Tocqueville's anonymous articles were produced with as much care and polish as work appearing over his own name. Finding himself without the qualities or experience of a journalist he wrote what were, in his own words, more like chapters of a book than free-flowing articles, with his usual condensation of ideas.[53] The reader was only told that they were produced by "a man who owes his untainted renown and high position in politics and letters to conscientious works."

The sequence of topics is a measure of the priorities with which Tocqueville presented the subject to his audience. He first emphasized the logical continuity of abolition with the democratic revolution in France and the English emancipation in the West Indies. He next attempted to arouse highly apathetic readers to think of the broader commercial and imperial importance of the colonies. This was obviously aimed at convincing a taxpayers' audience that the benefits of emancipation, indemnification, and colonial possessions in the West Indies were worth the time, money, and risks projected by the Broglie report. The essay was climaxed not by a sermon on liberty and equality but by a long discussion of indemnity-funding procedures. Implicitly, for a middle-class Parisian audience, cost accounting was more crucial than democratic vistas.

Moreover, the question of moralization was now presented far more as a question of controlling labor costs and labor than as a more broadly conceived crusade for restruc-

53. Tocqueville to Beaumont, Oct. 9, 1843 (*Oeuvres* (M): *Correspondance Tocqueville-Beaumont,* II).

turing family and religious relationships. The mechanism of change was conceived primarily in terms of maintenance of economically competitive labor costs in the sugar refineries. The central thesis, derived from the English experience, was that French emancipation legislation had to include a total prohibition of the purchase of land by the freedman for a certain period of time. The idea was to produce legislatively a landless proletariat from the slave population. Here the conception of the free Negro's future converged with Tocqueville's conception of the role of the metropolitan proletariat. In Europe it was economically "almost impossible for a worker to become a landed proprietor." By legally preventing Negroes from owning land, one only artificially proletarianized and Europeanized them. This, of course, also reflected Tocqueville's conception of the relatively high position of the nineteenth-century worker vis-à-vis the colonial slave, despite the contrary claims of colonial apologetics.

In this sense the essay of 1843 represented a radical simplification of the problem of social control as conceived in 1840. A restrictive land law was to act as the great agency of social and economic stability, while the legal position of the slaves was revolutionized. The role of the state was correspondingly no longer conceived of in terms of a multifunctional enlightened despotism.[54] Education and regu-

54. Tocqueville's plan in the report of 1839 was enthusiastically received but was later attacked as requiring far more administrative expansion than implied by the report. It was also ironically attacked because of its "statist" implications by the liberal economist Rossi on the Broglie commission. The Broglie commission did not adopt Tocqueville's plan and he seems to have acquiesced completely by the time he wrote the newspaper articles.

larized family life were described as flowing *naturally* and automatically from the very permissiveness of emancipation. Since the sole immediate problem of English colonial emancipation came in the area of labor costs, the state's role, aside from negative police action, was narrowed to enforcing two important restrictions on the free market economy—the mobility and price of Negro labor.[55] This was the principal obligation of the state after the moment of emancipation. And this restriction, being also temporary, easily conveyed the idea of a gradual progression in the colonies to the liberal state and society.

Tocqueville's slavery articles strike one as the most assured of his reformist work. They approach closest to his great diagnostic classics, the *Democracy* and the *Ancien Régime*. They were less indecisive than his works on poverty and less defensive than those on prison reform. Despite his suspension of habitual positions on decentralization and administratively controlled social evolution, he wrote with a clear sense of the role and the limitations of contemporary public power in effecting social change.

Tocqueville's work on abolition was obviously inspired by a sense of moral and historical certainty. Tocqueville devoted so much time to the financing of emancipation because the problem seemed, in the final analysis, both relatively remote and relatively exorbitant to the French electorate. But the abolitionists were obviously inspired by more cosmopolitan and internationally oriented values. The question of liberty versus servitude was nowhere so clearly posed or so easily answered. If, as Constant had

---

55. *Tocqueville and Beaumont on Social Reform*, ed. Drescher, 163–164.

said, civil equality was the first and surest victory of the French Revolution, slavery was the most blatant anomaly in a polity founded on that Revolution. Rarely did liberty, equality, and religion so clearly converge in Tocqueville's perception, and where they converged he moved with seven league boots. If liberty, equality, and Christianity harmonized so well on the moral plane, emancipation also united the themes which were to Tocqueville of greatest historical significance. The history of the modern world was the development of equality of conditions. It was the great providential fact. In the introduction to *Democracy in America*, Tocqueville had written to his fellow Frenchmen: "Is it wise to suppose that a movement of such duration can be suspended by the efforts of one generation? Does anyone suppose that democracy, which has destroyed feudalism and conquered kings, will bend before the *bourgeois* and the wealthy?" He could easily have added, "Will it yield to a remote and insignificant colonial aristocracy, after having destroyed the greater aristocracy of the mother country?" And what history prophesied, strategy specified. If Europe's principal democracy hesitated to declare the death of slavery, her strongest aristocracy already had. England's emancipation had fixed the extreme time limit of French slavery: the first outbreak of Anglo-French hostilities. And in 1840 this was more than a remote contingency.

Not only did international conflicts demand the emancipation of France's 250,000 enslaved beings; so did France's ambition to participate in Europe's ever-expanding economic and military ascendency over the rest of the world. The West Indies represented a strategic emporium for France's New World trade and a token of her bid for a share of world domination. The expansionist and egalitarian revolutions seemed intimately linked to the question of rapid emancipation. When completing *Democracy in America,* Tocqueville had decided to turn his talents only to something as significant and as appealing to the historic imagination as the advent of democracy.[56] Emancipation was the subject that, after democracy, first challenged his political imagination. Tocqueville had also written that one was aroused only by what partially coincided with a great familiar problem, and had something novel to offer as well. The abolition of slavery in the French colonies, uniting the themes of liberty, equality, Christianity, and national greatness, seemed sufficiently significant to evoke the commitment of his talents.

In an important sense, Tocqueville's writings on slavery in the West Indies are far more closely related to his total perception of the domestic scene than his other colonial studies. In the West Indies his primary problem was to raise the legal status of the lowest class in the colony in order to make it indistinguishable from the European proletariat. In his other colonial interest, Algeria, his concern was with the exportation and duplication of French middle-class society. The fate of the subordinate indigenous population was peripheral to this primary aim.[57] He condemned the Europeans of the sixteenth century for having reintro-

56. Tocqueville to Royer-Collard, Nov. 20, 1838, Bibliothèque de l'Institut, Ms 3992.

57. Tocqueville wrote to Beaumont on Oct. 28, "It is evident that however important the question of the Arabs and the war is to the government, I can consider it only as accessory to my concern. For me, above all, with no desire to leave the region of Algiers, the highest priority is the administration and establishment of the European society" (*Oeuvres* (M): *Correspondance Tocqueville-Beaumont,* I, 592).

duced slavery into the world as one might condemn original sin. But with all his own consciousness of the inevitable triumph of democracy, he did not express a twinge of uneasiness at the creation of new dependent peoples by European colonization in the nineteenth century or how it might affect democracy. This is only to say that the religiously inspired doctrine of the unity of the human race far from precluded the acceptance of providential domination by one society or culture over another. The providential ordinance of equality pertained to an individual's personal control of other individuals. For most Europeans, including Tocqueville and Beaumont, international domination was an equally providential ordinance of unknown historical duration.

Those who elaborated democratic visions of human relations did not shudder at the perils to equality afforded by the economic, technological, and military opportunities for European penetration and domination. It is significant that, faced with a choice of subject to which to devote himself in the decade after he completed his *Democracy*, Tocqueville devoted most of his time to studying Algeria rather than the Antilles, turning toward colonization rather than emancipation. Psychologically, the dynamism of African expansion appealed more to his imagination than the fate of a few stagnant settlements in the Caribbean and the Indian Ocean.[58] Algeria was "not a colony like the Antilles and Bourbon, where it is a question of enabling

58. Although Tocqueville spoke on abolition again in the Chambers and presented a small petition on behalf of some Parisian signatories, the movement of the notables lost momentum after the Broglie report. While petitions slowly accrued and more popular and radical elements increased their polemical output, the political elite seemed to reach a stalemate. Ideologically slavery was almost

a hundred thousand Europeans to exist with privileges, with slaves, with mulattoes, all hemmed in by the sea. We don't want to organize knights of Rhodes or Templars on a grander scale [in Africa]. Alongside the Arab society which did not know how to hold on to its inheritance, we want to establish our own society such as it is and must be, . . . a European Christian people numbering in the

---

without a public defender by 1848. Administratively it was virtually untouched after fifteen years of agitation. The February Revolution of 1848 suddenly reversed the situation. The notables, including Tocqueville and Beaumont, were thrust from their positions of prominence. Among the few immediately obvious results of the revolution was the death knell of slavery. The immediate and universal abolition of slavery was declared in all French possessions on April 27, 1848. After the installation of the new Constituent Assembly and the June uprising of 1848, one after another of the reforms of 1848 was rescinded or denatured. Of all the major legislative innovations of the revolutionary period, only the abolition of slavery survived the tide of reaction. Nothing could better indicate the degree to which the traumatized notables, returning to power, had already accepted the inevitability of emancipation.

Tocqueville was again briefly involved in the abolition movement. He was chosen to the advisory commission on indemnification of the ex-slaveholders. Tocqueville played a fairly neutral role here. His major contribution to this committee was in maintaining, along with the more radical members, that the indemnity was compensation for lost labor power, not property loss. Once the indemnity had been voted in 1849, further interest in the colonies declined precipitously among the former abolitionist notables. It does not appear that Tocqueville ever again gave thought to the French island possessions after abolition.

Tocqueville's and Beaumont's interest in abolition did not totally expire with their participation in the French anti-slavery movement, however. As the United States moved toward disintegration Tocqueville's and Beaumont's interest moved back to its point of origin as an adjunct of their concern with the survival of the first democratic nation. When the Civil War broke out Tocqueville was already dead but the Union became a joint cause of Tocqueville's

millions."[59] Rejecting the principle of totally dependent individuals, Tocqueville and Beaumont embraced the principle of dependent peoples. Colonization required explicit domination backed by force "for a century, if not forever."[60]

---

widow and the Beaumont family. Beaumont participated in the French liberal campaign to make slavery the central issue of the American Civil War, a campaign which was as much an attack on the foreign policy of the emperor as on slavery. He was an active member of the revived anti-slavery society and was recognized as one of the first determined Continental antagonists of slavery in America. At the war's end Beaumont wished that he were young enough to write the history of reconstruction as a sequel to his first work on American racial oppression. Yet the basic emphasis in Tocqueville's and Beaumont's ideas on the process of emancipation remained fixed. Beaumont especially feared the advent of an uncontrolled social revolution in the South. His primary concern for the South, at the end of the Civil War, was for the social security of the embattled ex-slaveholders.

59. Beaumont, "Note sur l'organisation de l'Algérie," Mss 42 AP 123, Beaumont Papers, Archives Privées, Archives Nationales. It was written ca. 1844–1845.

60. *Ibid.*; see also *Oeuvres* (M): *Ecrits et discours politiques*, 289. Tocqueville emphasized the point in his report to the Chamber of Deputies concerning special funds for Algeria (1847): "It is neither necessary nor useful to give our Moslem subjects exaggerated ideas of their own importance, nor to persuade them that we are obligated to always treat them precisely as if they were fellow citizens and equals." The subjects were aware of who ruled and expected to see the rulers maintain that rule (*ibid.*, 324). Tocqueville and Beaumont seemed to view the future of the Arabs as analogous to that of the free Negroes in the United States (separation from, and domination by, the European society), after some rejected analogies to the fate of the American Indians (see *ibid.*, 275, and Beaumont, Commission de colonisation de l'Algérie, *Rapport fait au nom de la seconde sous-commission . . . le 20 juin 1842. Organisation civile, administrative, municipale, et judiciaire* [Paris, 1843], 5). Tocqueville's report on Algeria also suggested the abolition of Negro slavery in the Moslem community.

Ironically, France's real agony over emancipation would come where she had undertaken to found a replica of herself in Africa uninfected by the institution of chattel slavery. And when the tide of colonization had ebbed once more, she would be left with almost nothing but her old slave colonies. But at her nineteenth-century colonial point of departure, France's acknowledged prophet of democracy was in the vanguard of a new aristocratization of the world.

VII

Social Revolution and Class Conflict

BETWEEN them, penitentiary reform and the abolition of slavery virtually exhausted the positive social legislative efforts of Tocqueville and Beaumont during the July Monarchy. They also nearly exhausted the social reforms seriously considered by that regime. Legislative action was meager and sporadic.[1] It was not until the rising tide of lower-class agitation and economic depression in 1846 and 1847 that the government and the Chambers bestirred themselves to launch a systematic inquiry into working-class conditions as a whole. If one compares the French and

1. See Ferdinand-Dreyfus, *L'Assistance sous la Seconde République (1848–1851)* (Paris, 1907), and Tudesq, *Les Grands notables*, II, 566–595.

English records on social legislation in the broadest sense during the period 1830–1848—and many opposition members, including Beaumont, did just this—one sees why a member of the Chamber in 1848 protested that the government did "nothing, nothing, nothing!" This is not to suggest that social problems were low-priority items in public discussion. Few periods have been so rich in projects for vast and fundamental changes at every level of the national community, and in discussions of the values and the social structure in which it expected its citizens to exist and fulfill their lives. Two generations after the outbreak of the French Revolution the legitimacy of the existing political and social order was still challenged at every turn, and by a whole range of possible techniques, from prophetic visions to armed uprisings.

While Tocqueville and Beaumont were at the forefront of humanitarian reform during the July Monarchy, they paid scant attention to writers and systems who proposed more fundamental change. Not that they were ignorant of the utopian outpourings of their age. They could hardly help being familiar with the most flamboyant, well-publicized, and well born of the new socialist sects of Paris, the Saint-Simonians.[2] Tocqueville's personal concern with "socialism" in the 1830's and 1840's seems to have been limited to keeping Michel Chevalier from obtaining a

2. In the period before 1840, Tocqueville's notes for Part II of *Democracy in America* contain references to the Saint-Simonians, and Beaumont's notes for *L'Irlande* show that he took notes on the writings of William Godwin. See Yale Tocqueville-Beaumont Mss C.V.g, paq. 9, cahier 1, p. 183; and C.X.3 (2). Tocqueville's reference to the sect "celebrated for its talents and its extravagance" in *Democracy in America* (423) also undoubtedly referred to the Saint-Simonians. It is the only concrete reference to socialism in that study.

place in the Academy of Moral and Political Sciences in 1838. When Chevalier, "all *pimpant,* all elegance from head to toe," complained to Beaumont that Tocqueville had attempted a character assassination by calling him an ex-convict for having been sentenced to prison along with "Père" Enfantin for his early participation in the Saint-Simonian sect, Beaumont replied, inasmuch as he was well informed about the incident, that Tocqueville "had indeed raised an [objection] against him, but less [because] of him than because of public opinion, which had severely judged the doctrine which claimed him as one of its most distinguished apostles; and that it seemed . . . that the distinction given to the man could be considered a sanctioning of the doctrine."[3] Significantly, in terms of Tocqueville's options, Chevalier's successful competitor for the vacancy was Blanqui, the ultra-liberal economist. Perhaps more significant for posterity, Tocqueville had to defend the academic holy of holies against a man "enchanted" with administrative centralization at the very moment that he was preparing the final chapters of *Democracy in America.*

Tocqueville and Beaumont were more impressed by the extravagance than by the talent of the Saint-Simonians and kindred movements before 1848. As political sociologists, they noted the handful of followers that constituted the upper limits of socialist recruitment in the first decade of the July Monarchy. It seems safe to say that by 1840

3. Beaumont to Tocqueville, June 10, 1838 (*Oeuvres* (M): *Correspondance Tocqueville-Beaumont,* I, 301–302 and note). Four years later, again commenting on Chevalier's candidacy as a possible alternative to Duchâtel, a member of the Guizot government, Beaumont declared that he would "rather vote for the minister than for the Saint-Simonian" (letter to Tocqueville, Nov. 16, 1842, *ibid.,* 482).

Tocqueville was less concerned with socialist theories than were a large number of notables who were less wedded to the liberal value of the independent and autonomous man. Many of Tocqueville's contemporaries, including some of the most traditionalist, treated their theories as the point of departure for their own critiques of modern society.[4] There again seems to be a rough cultural division between the concerns of elite liberal humanitarianism and those of the Catholic-social reform groups.

It is significant, however, that the single important tendency that Tocqueville perceived in socialists' theories, even while he still considered them to be minor contenders in the modern democratic world, was the centralist element to be found in their writings, especially in those of the Saint-Simonians. Thus, in the *Democracy* of 1840 he wrote that "the unity, ubiquity, and omnipotence of the social power and the uniformity of its rules constitute the most striking feature of all political systems invented in our day. They recur in the most fantastic utopias. The human mind still pursues them in its dreams." In the early 1840's Tocqueville tended to view social revolutionary ideas more as the nightmares which follow a great revolutionary trauma than the formative ideas of a new, or continuing, revolution. He drew an analogy between the "extraordinary, anarchic and tyrannical" doctrines of contemporary revo-

---

4. A number of Catholic and legitimist intellectuals located the main social problems in industrialization as early as the beginning of the July Monarchy. Tocqueville was a borderline case here as in other contemporary French elite dualisms. His humanitarian options were definitely "Anglo-liberal," while his immediate family was Catholic-legitimist. But he was a leader of the "Anglo-liberal" movements, and only a peripheral member of the "Catholic" ones.

lutionaries and the extremists of the revolutions of previous centuries. The conclusion, of course, was that there would be an analogous outcome:

> When an entire nation undergoes a great political movement, it is impossible to hope that all its citizens will halt together or even at the same moment. The reasonable taste for necessary or useful innovations always becomes transformed by a few into a disordered taste for novelty. After having accomplished the practicable, there is always a residue disposed to attempt the impossible. The sight of extraordinary events stirs up curiosities and monstrosities. . . .
>
> Moreover, history has shown us that these extraordinary doctrines and eccentric parties who want in every way to push to extremes the principles of the revolution that spawned them, have ordinarily appeared only at the very time when the great revolutionary movement began to subside, and when the new society was in the process of consolidation. To see and hear [these revolutionaries], one would have thought that the nation was about to embark on a new and more violent voyage just as it was moving into port.[5]

The socialist systems were considered to be only pathological manifestations of a general social evolution.

It is clear that by the time their political philosophy had reached maturity and they entered active political life at the end of the 1830's, Tocqueville and Beaumont considered major social or intellectual revolutions in France as less likely than at any time in generations. The chapter of the *Democracy* of 1840 which Tocqueville selected to appear as a separate article was his analysis of why great revolutions would become more infrequent. If anything, the possibilities of a political coup, remote as they were, were

5. Tocqueville, unsigned letter to *Le Siècle*, January 5, 1843. See also *Democracy in America*, 645–646.

considered more likely than any rapid change in the contemporary social or economic order. Given the high degree of centralization in the "democratic" and apathetic France of 1840, it was still conceivable that a small group of revolutionaries, whom Tocqueville fashionably referred to as barbarians and condottieri, might conspire to seize control of the machinery of the state by an uprising in the capital.[6] But any more widespread social or economic trans-

6. This possibility, which appeared in the last published note in *Democracy in America*, was probably an afterthought produced by the brief return to political instability in 1839, the most prominent of which was Louis Auguste Blanqui's abortive "conspiracy of the seasons." But this type of conspiracy was considered ephemeral. Both Beaumont and Tocqueville considered the July Revolution to be a triumph of the middle class with the aid of the popular movement. As Tocqueville wrote soon after that event, "The middle classes made the Revolution. God grant that they may not soon repent of it. Already the lower classes treat them as a new aristocracy. The newspapers fan the fire; the people have become a power and seek to have their flatterers. Will the middle classes be able to organize to resist the movement which is pushing them on? Are thy acute enough to realize the present dangers in their position and to unite to remedy it? I hope so but I do not dare to count too much upon it. In any case, upon the solution of that problem depends our future" (Tocqueville to Charles Stoffels, Aug. 26, 1830 [Yale Mss A.VI], cited in Gargan, *Alexis de Tocqueville*, 11). On the elite perception of the July Revolution, see David H. Pinkney, "The Myth of the French Revolution of 1830" in *A Festschrift for Frederick B. Artz*, ed. David H. Pinkney and Theodore Ropp (Durham, N.C., 1964), 52–71; Alfred Cobban, "The 'Middle Class' in France, 1815–1848," *French Historical Studies*, V (Spring 1967), 41–52; and Vincent Starzinger, *Middlingness* (Charlottesville, Va., 1965) 85–94. Tocqueville's and Beaumont's fears of another popular uprising fluctuated in proportion to the incidence of violence. For the most part, until 1847, they considered a lower-class revolution to be impossible without middle-class leadership: "While it is true that if it is the people who *carry out* revolutions, it is the middle class which *make them*" (Yale Mss A.V.b [Beaumont's notes] Dec. 21, 22, 1830. See also Beaumont's

formation was highly improbable for the foreseeable future given the presumed property-owning and conservative outlook of the bulk of the nation's citizenry. Those who predicated reconstruction of society on the basis of instability of the economic structure or its inevitable collapse seemed as harmless as the social base to which the appealed was a helpless and disorganized minority. The appropriate stance for a concerned member of the advantaged class was thus neither statically repressive nor desperately reformist, but a humanitarianism more cautious than urgent.

Intellectual, like institutional, novelties were interesting only if they were "founded on the interests of the mass."[7] This point is illustrated by Tocqueville's approach to a study on tendencies of modern moral doctrines, which he

---

analysis of the July Revolution in A.V.c). Two years later, Beaumont wrote, "Civil war in Paris for the first time since the Revolution of 1830. Grave fact . . . the symptoms are almost the same as those of July 27, the day after the ordinances of Charles X. However I don't think that the consequences will be the same for the present government. Today the movement seems to be the work of the lowest class of the people set in motion by the republicans. . . . It will have against it the greater part of the national guard—organ of the middle class" (A.V.b, June 5, 1832). By 1833 Tocqueville was certain that in general lower classes were incapable of a lasting revolution (*Journeys to England and Ireland*, 45, London, Aug. 15, 1833). In terms of its power to change the social system, the lower classes were steadily discounted as a factor by Tocqueville and Beaumont from 1830 to the mid-1840's. Their emphasis on *classes* in the analysis of French society can therefore be correlated almost exactly with outbreaks of class hostility in France. A decade after his conviction about the power of the lower classes had been severely shaken by the Revolution of 1848, Tocqueville moved back toward the idea that the "people" alone could make no revolution. See letter to Beaumont, Feb. 27, 1858 (Yale Mss D.I.c; *Oeuvres* (M): *Correspondance Tocqueville-Beaumont*, III, 544).

7. Beaumont and Tocqueville, *Penitentiary System*, 89.

agreed to undertake for the Academy of Political and Moral Sciences in 1843. His correspondence with his protégé and assistant, Arthur de Gobineau, clearly reveals his judgment concerning the relative significance of contemporary French socialist literature on the subject. He expressed familiarity with Saint-Simonian thought from the angle of its indulgence of "material pleasures" and the "rehabilitation of the flesh." The main tendencies of modern moral systems seemed to him to be found rather in the individualist doctrines of self-interest as expressed by the English utilitarians. He was also cognizant of conceptions of the state's obligations toward the poor, but when Gobineau pointed to novel ideas about the rights of the worker and of the criminal as extensions of moral ideas beyond eighteenth-century utilitarianism, Tocqueville insisted that they were rather extensions of Christian charity than new ethical points of departure. In Tocqueville's sense even mass education was a variety of state charity. Characteristically their correspondence drifted quickly from a discussion of state welfare into an argument over the historical role of Christian morality in the modern world.[8]

Despite the fact that Tocqueville expressed a passing interest when Gobineau mentioned the "right to work," neither of the correspondents seemed to feel any necessity to venture further into the "too special" and "too adventurous" works of the Fourierists and other socialist sects. Gobineau placed them *hors de discussion,* and Tocqueville

8. Tocqueville to Gobineau, Oct. 2, 1843; Oct. 22, 1843; Gobineau to Tocqueville, Sept. 8, 1843; Oct. 16, 1843 *(Oeuvres* (M): *Correspondance Tocqueville-Gobineau).* Characteristically, the discussion of "Public Instruction in the United States" was located in the *Système pénitentiaire,* not in *Democracy in America.*

raised no objection. The thinkers to whom Gobineau turned Tocqueville's attention were Kant, Fichte, Schelling, and Hegel, who were summarized in one essay, and Bentham, Priestly, and Godwin, who were each accorded separate essays. Hume and Pestalozzi also received some attention. There is no evidence, however, that Gobineau followed up Tocqueville's request for more information on the right to work, or that Tocqueville ever repeated his request.

Somewhere between the Academic project of 1843 and Tocqueville's alarmed manifesto of 1847 "on the Middle Classes and the People,"[9] Tocqueville's and Beaumont's interest in socialism apparently rose quite sharply. Beaumont's reform articles on the parliamentary session of 1844–1845 are evidence of this.[10] Tocqueville was initially surprised by the sudden spurt of interest taken by his political colleagues, but he too began to consider the right to work

9. See *Tocqueville and Beaumont on Social Reform*, ed. Drescher, Chapter IX. Tocqueville was so far from believing in the probability of a social revolution in the early 1840's that he accused the Guizot ministry of attempting to capitalize on the fear of revolution in France to whittle away French liberties. He regarded the fear of revolution as a political device. "Fear is a feeling that must first be shown by all who want some favor. Trembling has become the prior condition to making one's way in the world. . . . I believe . . . that no greater service can be rendered to the liberal cause than to show how ill-founded are these fears of social upheaval and political revolution" (unsigned letters in *Le Siècle*, January 1 and 3, 1843). Revolution was, on the contrary, the *least* likely possibility envisioned by Tocqueville for the immediate future.

10. *Ibid.*, Chapter III. On a sheet dated 1844 Tocqueville noted: "The imagination of my colleagues is quite tormented by what is happening in the working class, by what it does and thinks" (quoted by R. P. Marcel, *Essai politique sur Alexis de Tocqueville* [Paris, 1910], 254).

as a discussable issue. Beaumont still considered them as "vague and mad" in 1845, as Tocqueville had considered them five years before. The real problem was that the laboring classes were taking them seriously because the government was refusing to enact any legislation whatsoever in behalf of the poor. Using the example of legislation already adopted elsewhere, especially in England, Tocqueville and Beaumont began to advocate the lowering of grain tariffs, the abolition of marriage taxes for the indigent, and a reassessment of taxes in favor of the poor. Beaumont became a leader of the banquet campaign of 1847. At the first great banquet in Paris, it was he who injected the social problem into the reform program.

Tocqueville refused to join the campaign both for personal reasons and because of the revolutionary potential which he perceived in the mass appeal that it involved. In his own characteristic way, however, he too increased his personal participation in social action. He was a charter member of the *Annales de la Charité*, founded in 1845, and of the *Société d'Economie Charitable*, organized in 1847. These were organizational ventures of the conservative branch of the social Catholic movement in France.[11] Its guiding spirit was Armand de Melun, a disciple of Villeneuve-Bargemont. Although Tocqueville's participation in these movements was nominal, his adherence testifies to the importance he attached to the handling of the social problem by the notables after 1845.

There is no doubt that by 1847 Tocqueville and Beaumont were convinced that France was approaching a revo-

11. See Duroselle, *Les Débuts de catholicisme sociale (1822–1870)*, 217–227.

206 DILEMMAS OF DEMOCRACY

lutionary crisis, if not a revolution, and that its activists
were now imbued with "social" rather than just "political"
passions. The convergence of the revolutionary coteries
with working-class discontent and an economic crisis called
forth Tocqueville's famous prophetic warning to the Chamber of Deputies on January 27, 1848. It was the first as well
as the last time that he raised the social question before
that half-skeptical, half-fearful audience. If he had dismissed
socialism much more lightly than a good number of his
fellow notables before 1845, by 1847 he perceived the political seriousness of the crisis far more acutely than most.
However, he still believed that a revolution could be
avoided by the mildest of reforms, or even by simply a
change in the psychological attitude of the government toward the country in the framework of existing institutions.[12]
Why were his suggested measures so mild in relation to the
gravity of the crisis? The answer seems to be that Tocqueville still dealt with the socialist ideas as socio-psychological
phenomena. He spoke more of the socialist "passions" than
of socialist ideas or programs. He believed that working-
class discontent was not founded on economic misery. The
workers, despite the recent depression, were economically
far better off than they had been a generation before, and
their situation had steadily improved over the long run. In
fact labor's proportionate share of wealth had virtually
reached the "upper limit" possible in mature societies.[13]

12. This speech is included in the Mayer and Lerner edition of
Democracy in America, Appendix III; see especially 730.
13. See Tocqueville to Nassau Senior, April 10, 1848, *Oeuvres*
(Beaumont edition): *Correspondance d'Alexis de Tocqueville;
Tocqueville and Beaumont on Social Reform*, ed. Drescher, 96, 165;
and the *Recollections of Alexis de Tocqueville*, 79.

For Tocqueville, then, the increasing misery theory of the working class was belied by observable facts. The theory that revolutions occur at the end of a growth cycle was to be one of the more interesting hypotheses about the causes of revolution in Tocqueville's *Ancien Régime*. Secondly, and more significantly, Tocqueville believed that there was no realistic or viable alternative to the economic system founded on the competitive free market and individual proprietary ownership. The French economic system, he assured Nassau Senior in the summer of 1847, would "continue to rest on its present foundation because even if some wanted to place society on another one, they would not know how to go about it."[14] One could simply not arrive at an economic system that dispensed with individual property, as distributed by the impersonal market "and the inequality of conditions which flows from it." "Socialist" ideas could act only as catalysts of millenarian hysteria, not as models of social reconstruction. It was more important that they be channeled or handled as indices of pathological resentment, than as rational legislative demands. As early as the *Democracy* Tocqueville surmised that the way in which the rich treated the poor was more important than any substantive issue. Thus Tocqueville, in January 1848, was essentially recommending a gesture which would temper the pressure of hostility and the expectations that had accumulated among the "people." And it was for this reason that he was able to demonstrate real sympathy for certain socialists on the very eve of the Revolution, precisely because they were not preaching revolution or class conflict.

14. Letter of Aug. 25, 1847, *Oeuvres* (Beaumont edition): *Nouvelle correspondance*.

They were hopefully doing what he himself was attempting in the legislature, to channel the crisis. For the moment at least the pacific socialists seemed preferable to the activists.[15]

The French Revolution of 1848 at once broadened and narrowed the discussion of the social question. Issues passed from the self-controlled "legal country" into the realm of universal suffrage and uncensored discussion. Before 1848 the notables had constituted the principal participants in legally recognized associations, the principal writers and readers of newspapers. With the disappearance of cautionary bonds and the press laws of the July Monarchy, democratic and socialist presses mushroomed. The audience of political discussion suddenly shifted from chambers of notables to popular political clubs. The dialogue, or at least the chorus, was national, and the options of the peasantry of the provinces became as important as the more concentrated groups of the capital.

The change in the effective interlocutors also involved a change in the attitudes toward the questions at stake. The carriers and potential carriers of formerly utopian doctrines were now competitors for public representation. The objects of debate shifted quickly and the social stakes involved in their outcome were high. Arguments tended to be produced in the form of slogans, manifestos, and demonstrations, rather than in discreet sequences of problem raising, information gathering, discussion, and decision. Tocque-

15. See the letter of Tocqueville to the Saint-Simonian, Enfantin, Nov. 2, 1847, cited in Marcel, *Essai politique*, 259n. After the Revolution of 1848 the Academic candidacy of Michel Chevalier came to seem respectable enough to warrant the support of Beaumont and Tocqueville, who had also in the meantime developed family connections with the former Saint-Simonian.

ville and Beaumont probably expressed only a typical sense of disorientation when they compared French society to a ship suddenly thrust onto a boundless sea without knowledge of its position, course, or destination. Old political leaders, noted Tocqueville, "who had almost all been trained to public business amid the regulated, restrained movement of constitutional liberty, and upon whom a great revolution had unexpectedly come, were like river oarsmen who should suddenly find themselves called upon to navigate their boat in mid-ocean. The knowledge they had acquired in their freshwater trips would be of more trouble than assistance to them in this greater adventure, and they would often display more confusion than the passengers themselves."[16] All that needs to be added to this picture is that it applied equally to Tocqueville's own position in the new ship of state. His initial reaction was as disoriented and pessimistic as those of the colleagues whom he describes with a tinge of contempt in his *Recollections*. But as the old political class reorganized and, to a limited extent, regained some power of direction in society, exhilaration over the prospect of a victorious conflict overtook fear of that conflict. And it was precisely on the question of social revolution that the notability moved back into positions of leadership.

Until February 1848 Tocqueville had worried about the fact that social passions were becoming revolutionary passions. Afterwards his chief concern was preventing the variety of revolutionary passions from becoming socialist. Before the Revolution, socialism was less dangerous than revolution because it was, in his vision, further removed

16. Tocqueville, *Recollections*, 85.

from reality. Now it was more dangerous than the Revolution itself because it might give the ritualized Revolution of February a new content. Socialism, in short, was suddenly "the essential characteristic and the most redoubtable remembrance of the Revolution of February."[17]

In another sense, the Revolution of 1848 progressively narrowed the social question. As the divergence of aims between the bourgeois and social democratic elements became more clearly defined, the choice was narrowed to one between order and a social revolution of unknown dimensions. The social world divided itself into two hostile segments. Tocqueville identified totally with the "party of order" and welcomed the battle when victory seemed assured. His pattern of reaction followed that of the bulk of the old elite class. He despised Lamartine, the most prominent member of the provisional government, for his theatrical role in overthrowing the monarchy. He supported him in the aftermath of February as the "last bulwark of order,"[18] while the notables were in a state of disarray and disorganization. He discarded Lamartine as soon as the party of order had won a clearcut victory.

Tocqueville was elected in April 1848 to the new Constituent Assembly almost at the top of the list in his department on a platform in defense of the rights of property. He was probably more committed to the new Republic than were most of the former parliamentarians who campaigned in the first French election by universal manhood suffrage.

17. *Ibid.*, 79.
18. Letters of Tocqueville to Paul Clamorgan, Feb. 25, 27, 1848, cited in Pouthas, "A. de Tocqueville, Representant de la Manche (1837–1851)," in *Alexis de Tocqueville: Livre du centenaire, 1859–1959*, 27.

The June Days found him at the barricades, in the capacity of a special liaison of the National Assembly to the army regulars and national guardsmen fighting the insurgents. Psychologically, Tocqueville welcomed the crude options and heroic situations offered by the division of France into two hostile camps. The relatively ingrown political arena of the July Monarchy had been profoundly dissatisfying for him. He was a respected member of the legislature but definitely not one of its leaders. The greatest parliamentary debates had been struggles of nuances within an almost total social consensus. Tocqueville could never convince himself that honor, utility, truth, and virtue were located on one side of the Chamber or with one of its leaders. The distribution of alignments seemed too transient to warrant the self-deceptions of party devotion, although on almost all "partisan" issues, Church questions excepted, he voted with the opposition to Guizot. Tocqueville had opted for the role of the independent statesman in parliament, devoting himself wholeheartedly to the issues on which the partisan lines were least clear: colonization, prison reform, and abolition, questions where one could support legislation without a specific political commitment.

The situation suddenly changed in 1848. Tocqueville became first a partisan, and then a party man. He was no longer a free-floater but a potential minister, voting with the right, and with the majority, on every issue. He became the leader of a parliamentary faction within the assembly, then Foreign Minister (1849), and remained *ministeriable* until the end of the Second Republic. The choices were narrower, sharper, and more palatable. Before 1848 he had been unable to convince himself that his "own advantage was one and the same with the general good." Now he was able to do precisely that. Honor, utility, and truth, if not intelligence, were now to be found on one side of the Assembly. "We were to walk in broad daylight, supported and encouraged by the crowd," wrote Tocqueville, in retrospect, although both facts were only clear after the general elections. But psychologically the most important change in Tocqueville's perception was that there was "no field left for uncertainty of mind."[19] On one side lay order, liberty, and national salvation; on the other the vague and mad theories of total equality, the destruction of property, and a new form of servitude.

Tocqueville's *Democracy* had located class society in the past, in the old regime. There might be rich and poor but there were no longer races of poor or wealthy. In 1848 two worlds again seemed violently opposed to each other. The sense of rigid class lines predominates in the *Recollections*. It was the central sociological fact of his description of the Revolution. Hostility and social violence were no passing phenomena. On the contrary, Tocqueville tied the Revolution to permanent and stable variables in modern development: the increasing centralization of power in Paris, the growth of an industrial population, materialism, periodic unemployment, the natural limits on labor's share of wealth, the vision of a more perfect equality, and above all the elite's failure to impose a sense of stability on a society racked by continuous changes of regime since the Great Revolution.

Tocqueville's metaphors and descriptions reveal his psychological perception of a "race of the poor" as well as any extended analysis on the permanence of class resentment.

19. Tocqueville, *Recollections*, 86–92.

Without any sense of altering his own earlier vision, in the *Recollections* he refers to "the two parts of which the social body of France is mainly composed"—the upper classes and the mass of the people—"that is to say the classes who work with their hands."[20] In the June Days large numbers of the lower classes either remained apathetic or were recruited to fight the uprising, yet in the eyes of Tocqueville it was a struggle between one whole section of the population and another, a slave war. Even more vivid are Tocqueville's character sketches of his opponents in the *Recollections*. His descriptions of popular leaders invariably connote clinical pathology or moral depravity. They are either madmen or demagogues who could appeal more easily to the passions of the people. In her own *Memoirs*, George Sand remarked that in the public mind a republican socialist was an infanticide, a wife beater, a drunkard, and a thief. Tocqueville characterized a hostile porter in his house as a mentally disturbed cafe-crawler and wife beater, "in short, a Socialist by birth, or rather by temperament."[21] Tocqueville's account of the invasion of the National Assembly by a mob on May 15, 1848, emphasizes the sound of coarse and vulgar voices, the smell of sweat and wine, the sight of men without shirts. He was struck by one leader's old clothes, his lack of underwear, his sickly repulsive expression, dirty pallor, and corpse-like appearance. He was told it was Blanqui, and his memory recorded horror and disgust: "He seemed to have passed his life in a sewer and to have just left it."[22] The remark was as much a commentary on French prisons as on its sewers.

20. *Ibid.*, 74.
21. *Ibid.*, 172.
22. *Ibid.*, 130.

Tocqueville by no means lost his sharp sense of detachment and clarity even in the climactic situation of 1848. His portraits of colleagues and friends on his own side of the barricades are often as acid as anything he had to say about the enemy. Even the accounts of his own motives and reactions reveal that his sharp analytic sense did not disappear when it became self-scrutiny. His portraits of Blanqui and Barbès showed less nuance only because they were personally remote as well as physically distasteful.

The important point is that Tocqueville clearly saw the growing alienation of the two classes of society and the approach of a solution through violence on a scale undreamed of in his previous experience. Unlike intellectuals such as Lamennais or George Sand, who had strong commitments to rectifying social injustices, or Lamartine, who had a political stake in the nonpolarization of the revolution, Tocqueville welcomed a resolution of the conflict once the relative weakness of the hostile element in the lower classes became clear. That Tocqueville underestimated the power of the Parisian proletariat only serves to emphasize this. In the Assembly, Tocqueville and Beaumont, like most of the old parliamentary notables, hung back from precipitating the civil war written on its walls. But reluctance to start a conflict was subordinated to the determination to revoke the social innovations of February, including the feeble beginning of the organization of labor.

The "right to work" and the "organization of labor" were the first and most explicit demands presented by the Parisian working-class crowds to the Provisional Government in 1848.[23] The right to work as it had developed in

23. The "organization of labor" had no legal or institutional

the forties was an attempt to extend the claims on society of workers as producers.[24] It varied from a call for the right of individuals to the full value of their labor (the abolition of "surplus value") and the abolition of a wage system, to more modest demands for more adequate wages and guaranteed minimums of social welfare. It was at bottom an attempt to legitimize the claims of producers on society to certain material and moral conditions. But it emphasized these not as claims of a dependent sector of society, but as a fulfillment of implicit contractual and reciprocal obligations. For those who formulated social claims in terms of a right to work, every man was equally entitled and obliged to work for society and society obliged to satisfy certain specified social needs. The literature on the right was so infused by the dependency issue that the state was viewed more as an economic and organizational catalyst than as a permanent source of social welfare. Cooperative and "associational" socialism rather than state-regulated industries

status before the February Revolution, although there were of course institutional precedents for state-supported workshops in time of revolutionary crisis. The Revolutions of 1789 and 1830 had produced attempts at special public relief works and workshops. This was also the intention of the majority in the provisional government in 1848. They were in fact little more than the old "charity" workshops, except in name. The real difference in this case was that the workers, at least, apparently considered the national workshops as only the beginning of a permanent innovation. On the background to the national workshops see Donald C. McKay, *The National Workshops: A Study in the French Revolution of 1848* (Cambridge, Mass., 1933).

24. See Anton Menger, *The Right to the Whole Produce of Labour*, trans. M. E. Tanner (New York, 1962); E. Labrousse, *Le Mouvement ouvrier et les idées sociales en France de 1815 à la fin du XIXe siècle* (Paris, 1948); and Jacques Benet, *Le Capitalisme libéral et le droit au travail* (Paris, 1947).

were seen as the ideal means of extending social independence to the working class. Without some form of "industrial association," it was claimed, the most extensive political and civil rights would be meaningless, or at least deceptive to the economically insecure segments of the population.

In 1848 Louis Blanc was forced upon the Provisional Government by the crowd at the Hotel de Ville precisely because he had already formulated a plan for overcoming the competitive, alienating, economic system through the *Organization of Labor*.[25] Labor was to be organized in state-initiated "social workshops" through state loans, leading ultimately to a noncompetitive society. The government's acceptance of the right to work and the creation of national workshops were the immediate result of workers' demands on the eve of the February Revolution. Blanc was thrust upon the Provisional Government, but the workshops themselves were placed under the effective control of a man who was not committed to their permanence. Since socialist ideas about property were never incorporated into the policies of the Provisional Government, the right to work became the central focus of debate over the nature and direction of the February Revolution. It was the first slogan against which the old notables rallied and the issue on which they were certain of having greatest mass support. Although the national workshops were largely a stopgap unemployment and pacification measure, their dissolution in June, 1848 seemed not only a matter of sound financial policy, but a means of destroying the

25. The title of Louis Blanc's most famous work, first published in 1840.

Provisional Government's concession to dangerous theories about the rights of labor.

Tocqueville's intervention in the issue of the right to work in the National Assembly was on the occasion of the debates on the constitution for the Second Republic in September 1848.[26] The affirmation of the right to work in its preamble was the final legacy of the Provisional Government's social innovation. It was Tocqueville's first public commentary before a national audience on the meaning of the Revolution of 1848. But it was not his first encounter with the issue. Along with Beaumont and a number of the old dynastic opposition he had been previously elected by the National Assembly to its constitutional drafting committee. The old dynastic group constituted the committee's right wing, the legitimists having been excluded altogether. When the issue of rights in the preamble was raised, it was Beaumont who initiated the argument against the inclusion of a right to work clause, for which he wanted to substitute only a right to subsistance.[27] Because of the republican majority on the committee, but even more because of the

26. On the debates see P. de la Gorce, *Histoire de la Seconde République française*, 2 vols. (Paris, 1909). The "old republicans" were more strongly represented by Armand Marrast, Martin de Strasbourg, Coquerel, Thouret, Dornés, Vaulabelle, Pagès de l' Ariege, and Woirhaye. Victor Considérant constituted the committee's theoretical socialist, and Corbon its worker. Lamennais, an unclassifiable radical, and Cormenin, who came prepared with an entire outline of a constitution, completed the list.

27. The committee debates are in Archives Nationales, C918, "Procès-verbaux du Comité de Constitution de 1848." The deliberations on the right to work clause can also be found with other interesting materials in Yale Mss D.IV.b: Beaumont's notes on the "Comité de Constitution," paq. "Droit au travail," and are quoted at length in Dreyfus, *L'Assistance sous la Seconde République*, 50–72.

threat of class war, Beaumont's proposal was voted down. By July, when the draft constitution was discussed in the *bureaux* of the assembly, the atmosphere had changed. The constitutional committee's right "to live by working" was replaced by a right "to assistance."

The September debates in the Assembly therefore represented the final efforts of the social democrats to retain at least one value commitment of the February Revolution to the working class, the one which had clearly been accepted in principle by both the Provisional Government and the constitutional committee.[28]

When Tocqueville spoke, the personnel, the institutions, and the provisional norms that symbolized the recognition of workers' claims on the state as members of a peculiar class had already been successively abolished. What remained at stake in September 1848 was no more than a recognition of their claims on the most abstract value level. The right to work clause was to be inserted in the preamble to the constitution. If passed it would have had no legally binding status. Since the outcome of the vote was certain, Tocqueville's decision to speak was an opportunity to debate the long-range effect of a fundamental declaration of value on the social psychology of a society.[29] Purely technical arguments were of course also possible. Thiers presented the main argument of the Party of Order in terms

28. Ledru-Rollin, Crémieux, Lamartine, Arnaud (de l'Ariège), Billault, and Mathieu (de la Drôme) successively appealed to the Assembly to recognize the right to work as a means of dissolving the bitter legacy of the June Days.

29. It is conceivable that Beaumont, having originally entered the lists against the clause, would also have taken the issue to the Assembly. But in the interim he had been appointed special plenipotentiary to England by the Cavaignac government.

of the disastrous economic consequences to the workers that would proceed from any implementation of a right to work. But Tocqueville avoided this strategy. In the style of his writings on slavery or democracy, he was attempting to define a fundamental choice of society. In his eyes the issue was one of conflicting values and not one of timing or instrumentalities. If other opponents of the right to work spoke in terms of the economic or technical impossibilities, the author of *Democracy in America* stuck to the sociopsychological implications expressed in the right to work principle as it affected his fundamental value, liberty.

Tocqueville no longer spoke on a consensus issue within the legislative body, but he certainly spoke "in broad daylight, supported and encouraged by the mass." His avowed purpose was to sharpen the resolve of the majority against any innovations in social values.[30] If he did not at all wish to liquidate the democratic political results of the February Revolution, he clearly wished to strengthen the trend against further social experimentation and to establish as wide an ideological gulf as possible between political and social democracy. It will be necessary to return to this point later.

Tocqueville's method in this speech follows the pattern of his tried and tested stylistic strengths. He reduced the argument for the right to work to a monolithic tendency of social organization and carried its logical implications "to the verge of the false and impracticable." As Tocqueville said of other institutions, they were by nature so imperfect that to destroy them "it almost always suffices to

30. *Tocqueville and Beaumont on Social Reform*, ed. Drescher, 181. For another analysis of Tocqueville's speech, see Gargan, *Alexis de Tocqueville*, 115–121.

draw from their principles all the consequences."[31] The more iron-clad one could make the inevitable steps from point of departure to ultimate social model, the more rigorously inhuman the principle appeared. This tactic was applied to the right to work in 1848 as rigorously as it had been to the right to relief in 1835.

A right to work statement in the preamble would lead to a total transformation in the nature of the relationships between the state, the individual, and the economy. The obvious intent of this argument was to narrow the range of historical alternatives. The right to work necessarily implied either socialism or communism. These in turn were associated with the violence of the June Days and the confiscatory rhetoric of ancestral revolutionaries like Babeuf and Buonarotti. Socialism was characterized as an appeal to materialism, not philosophical materialism, but material gratification and physical passions. Its second characteristic was an attack on individual property, civilization's oldest achievement and the source of man's independence within society. Its third and fundamental characteristic was contempt for the individual "taken by himself" as the basis for dealing with the human condition, and the consequent substitution of the bureaucratic state for the self-governing community of free individuals. Socialism, in short, represented the return of all individuals to a condition of social dependency, more totalitarian than the despotisms of the old regime.

Despite the formidable appearance of this three-pronged assault, only socialism's attack on property went beyond Tocqueville's projection of the normal democratic pattern

31. *Oeuvres* (M): *Ancien Régime*, II, 347.

outlined in his *Democracy in America*. John Plamenatz has noted of Tocqueville's accusation of materialism that this could have been applied equally well to the Encyclopedists in France and the utilitarians in England.[32] But one can go further. The appeal to the expansion of state responsibility was strikingly similar to that outlined in *Democracy in America*. Although the point was naturally not emphasized to the National Assembly, the process of centralization perceptibly flourished in states ruled by princes and parliaments, as well as in the imaginations of populist revolutionaries. In 1840 Tocqueville treated the process of centralization at least as much as a co-variant of an egalitarian social condition as of socialist theories arising within that condition. When he had begun to write the concluding part of *Democracy in America* (on the influence of democratic ideas and feelings on government and politics) exactly a decade before, Tocqueville had used almost the identical words in describing the relationship of democracy and the state as he applied to socialism and the state in the right to work speech. "You see," he had declared to Beaumont, "that I have moved far beyond the perspective of administrative centralization which primarily consists of replacing

32. Tocqueville to Beaumont, July 8, 1833 (Yale Mss C.I.a.2; *Oeuvres* (M): *Correspondance Tocqueville-Beaumont*, I, 311 [Tocqueville's emphasis]). See also John Plamenatz, *Man and Society. Political Social Theory: Bentham Through Marx*, 2 vols. (New York, 1963), II, 59. Tocqueville drew a direct line from the physiocrats to nineteenth-century socialism in his *Ancien Régime*, Part III, Chapter 3. In 1843 Tocqueville had written of revolutionaries in France, "Among them as among their [status quo] adversaries, the love of well-being is the mother-passion . . . the only difference comes from the fact that to satisfy some, this passion needs stability, while for others it inspires revolutions" (unsigned letter published in *Le Siècle*, January 5, 1843).

secondary powers by the central power. I want to show not only this, but also the state successively seizing everything, interposing itself from every direction in place of the *individual* or putting the individual under tutelage, governing, regulating, *standardizing* all things and all persons." Tocqueville also added that this was the state's pattern, whoever represented it—people or king. If one substituted "proletarians or proprietors" for the previous alternative the argument could have been repeated by an advocate of the right to work without further alteration. It was in fact a line of reasoning taken up in Tocqueville's *Ancien Régime* after the dust of the Revolution of 1848 had settled. Materialist and centralist tendencies were not just intellectual monsters of the nightmare world of socialism, but the most permanent, fundamental, natural tendencies of the middle-class world of 1840.

In casting socialism out of the democratic fold, Tocqueville implicitly acknowledged its paternity while denying its legitimacy. His *Recollections* were more explicit. There his characterization of the ruling class of the July Monarchy was as materialistic as democracy in 1840, or socialism in 1848. Even the attack on property was recognized as a natural offspring of revolutionary democratic psychology. "Property, which is, as it were, the foundation of our social order—all the privileges which covered it and which, so to speak, concealed the privilege of property having been destroyed, and the latter remaining the principal obstacle to equality among men, and appearing to be the only sign of inequality—was it not necessary, I will not say that it should be abolished in its turn, but at least that the thought of abolishing it should occur to the minds of those who did not enjoy it?"[33] Tocqueville did not bury socialism in his historical imagination as easily as he buried the right to work in the National Constituent Assembly. Tocqueville's separation of socialism and democracy, attacking the June insurgents' slogan, "Long live the democratic and social republic," was underscored in the speech by an even more startling divorce between democracy and equality. Previously, "democracy" had been used to define a general equality of conditions compatible with a number of political regimes whether libertarian or despotic. The year 1848 marks the beginning of a narrowing of the conception of democracy which was to linger on in the *Ancien Régime*. A clear distinction was now drawn between individualistic, proprietary democracy and centralist, confiscatory socialism. They were made possible only by a sociological sleight of hand, but one at which Tocqueville was already the supreme though not entirely conscious master. It involved shifting models of society. In 1835 he had published a work using America as his major source for his investigation of democracy. In 1840 under the same title, and without being entirely clear or conscious about it, he increasingly relied on France as his basic democratic example. In 1848 he switched back to America, the liberal and stable egalitarian society against which the unstable one

33. *Recollections*, 80. Tocqueville in Jan. 1853 carefully filed a remark of his close political colleague, Victor Lanjuinais, among the notes for his history of the French Revolution: "Socialism is our natural disease; it comes naturally from our laws, our ideas on government from the political structure and administrative structure of our society. It is to centralization what the wild fruit is to the cultivated variety." It became Tocqueville's principal conclusion about socialism in the *Ancien Régime* (see II, 332, and I, 214).

could be compared. Her individualistic, liberal, proprietary, decentralist society was the most effective argument
that could be used against the legitimation of the socialist
argument for a pure democratic pedigree.

One significant difference between Tocqueville's descriptions of democracy in 1840 and 1848 is that the first was the
basis for a careful sociological projection of modern society
and the second was the basis for a legislative project. The
first was concerned with what was probable in the future,
given certain stable elements in the present. The second
was concerned with what was best in the present, given
certain bitterly contested choices about the future. By
branding the claims of one class as statist and centralizing,
Tocqueville was not changing his hostility toward centralization, but was obscuring one of his fundamental sociological conclusions—that most members of society in democracies, including himself, continuously appealed to and
benefited from state intervention in social organization.
An increase of state power and responsibility was to be
averted in one particular instance, but the calculated gain
to the whole society in less bureaucracy and greater autonomy was to be borne by that class which had already
benefited least from the already elaborate machinery of
state and society.

The relationship between democracy, socialism, and centralization was presented from the vantage point of one
social class even though it now claimed to represent the
view of the majority of the adult male population. The
speech was exclusively addressed to, and concerned with
independency, rather than poverty and misery. Two thirds
of this one major speech on the social problem was an attack
on the right to work clause, one third was an attack on the

"social," as opposed to political aims of the French Revolution, and two closing sentences were allotted to the role that the state should in fact play in solving the social problem under discussion. Here again ideology was substituted for sociology. Although the division of France into proprietors and proletarians was perhaps never so sharp as in 1848, although class relationships were in later reflective moments the significant units of social analysis for Tocqueville ("I speak only of classes; they alone concern the historian"[34]), the assembly was asked not to recognize the existence of privilege in post-Revolutionary France: "The French Revolution willed that there be no classes. We must will what our fathers wanted." Even Beaumont's concession, in committee, of the right to existence as a substitute for the right to work was not clearly implied in Tocqueville's treatment of the relationship of the state to the poor. The state had an obligation to the poor, but the poor were not thereby granted a legal right to relief. Nothing, Tocqueville bluntly declared, gives laborers a right vis-à-vis the state.[35] All citizens, whatever their degree of affluence or poverty, were equal. The state was obligated to help its citizens only in total destitution or emergencies commonly known as acts of God. Welfare was only an extension of Christian almsgiving, discontinuous, temporary, and forthcoming only after all other resources had been exhausted.

Every part of Tocqueville's speech points to a continuity of perception of the relation of the working class to society across the trauma of 1848. The central social problem was the problem of liberty. Liberty was defined in the context of psychologically and economically independent man. It

34. *Oeuvres* (M): *Ancien Régime*, I, 179.
35. *Tocqueville and Beaumont on Social Reform*, ed. Drescher, 192.

was his social base which was threatened. The minimized role of the state, the maximized role of individual choice, and voluntary association were the areas at risk, requiring hard choices and fixed resolve. The problems of poverty and deprivation were as much a coda to the speech as they were to Tocqueville's thought. The question of poverty had to be tacked on to the question of liberty, not vice versa. The first French Revolution had secured equality before the law. The Revolution of 1848 had introduced effective universal suffrage. Legal rights and political rights had been universalized. They were congruent with extensions of liberty. But extensions of the sphere of rights in the economic sphere could only *contract* the sphere of liberty. They would sooner or later return all of society to a dependence on the state so complete as to negate liberty. In his evocation of the possibility, Tocqueville already writhed in darkness and suffocation.

It might be observed that the speech did no more than reveal the political sociologist, like any man in an emergency, responding (and less hysterically than most) to the hatreds and fears of the moment. Tocqueville's ingrained habits prevented him from making overtly personal attacks. Only Babeuf, dead fifty years, came close to being the socialist scapegoat, and as a member of the Left aptly shouted in rubuttal to Tocqueville's allusion, there were no Babouvists in the Assembly. Tocqueville sublimated his emotions into socio-ideology rather than venting them in personal polemics, expressing emotional intensity in higher degrees of generalization. But Tocqueville's speech was not exactly rendered *in extremis*. The battle over the workshops had already been decided. Tocqueville was already anticipating an overreaction. The reflex of the old social mediators was to conciliate, and although the role of radical reformer was alien to Tocqueville, that of intellectual mediator was not. He signed up for a speech against the last symbol of working-class integration in a republic faced by a social reaction that threatened to engulf liberalism as well. The threat was perceptible, if not critical, in September 1848, but Tocqueville's priority of evils had not altered even three years later on the eve of Louis Napoleon's coup d'état.[36] A good part of his life had been spent probing the range of democratic societies. Yet his approach to "socialism" was to narrow rather than to widen the focus of social possibilities, even where he privately recognized them. He was not stimulated to explore the Parisian working class as he had once explored the bustling democracy of America. To this challenge the response was fear and withdrawal.

36. Tocqueville, *Recollections*, 184–185. Tocqueville still conjured up the threat of the torrent of socialism before the *conseilgénéral* of La Manche during its debate over the revision of the constitution of 1848 on Aug. 28, 1851. See *Annuaire de la Manche* (1852), 215–217. The speech was also circulated as a separate publication (Bib. Nat. #Lk[16], 177).

On July 27, 1851, he wrote to Nassau Senior: "I believe that the bonapartist current, if it is deflected, can only be so by a revolutionary current that would be even more dangerous. . . . Having little faith in the possibility of maintaining the Republic, which had it been possible would have been the government of my choice, I would find no difficulty in seeing Louis Napoleon become our permanent ruler, if I thought it possible that, on the one hand, he could rally the elite of society around him, and, on the other hand, that he were able and willing to be a constitutional prince. . . . Thus his reelection, especially if unconstitutional, could have the most unfortunate consequences, and yet it is almost inevitable unless one turns to revolutionary passions that I don't want to see reawakened in the nation" (*Oeuvres* (Beaumont edition): *Nouvelle correspondance*). Tocqueville's dilemma and paralysis before the coup is deftly treated by Gargan, *Alexis de Tocqueville*, Chapter VII.

Despite the fact that in terms of invective Tocqueville's speech was mild, it was a model of high analytical rigidity. He stuck close to his talent for analyzing the psychological and political implications of the organization of labor judged against the preservation of liberty as it was commonly perceived. The right to work, however, was not an attempt to strike at the values of property, at the separation of state and society, or at a pluralist social structure populated by autonomous, independent individuals. It was an attempt on the part of a vocal portion of the urban working community to remove themselves from the general category of indigence, to be accorded recognition as a new social category of intermittently threatened independent workers, and to be distinguished from unemployables, vagabonds, and beggars. The psychological implication of a demand for a right to work implied that as creators of value, or as at least members of the productive segment of society, workers deserved a socially guaranteed right to security of employment as no more than an exchange for past and future production, and a more rational use of potential productivity.

The right to work was, in fact, inextricably embedded in a mutually shared value system of property and autonomy. It seemed crucial to those who argued for a right to work, as distinguished from relief or assistance, that it was similar to a right to any other property, as much a part of claims on specific national wealth as a government bond.[37]

37. This contractual conception of social justice was later incorporated in the ideology of the Radical Party in France at the end of the nineteenth century, precisely because it permitted an extension of the realm of independency. In a society prescribing independence as a prerequisite to dignity, what was "most terrible in poverty is the fact that there are human beings who, in their social position, are nothing but poor" (Georg Simmel, "The Poor," *Social Problems*, XIII [Fall 1965], 140).

The constitutional question was fundamentally socio-psychological for both sides. The right to work was a claim to special status on the part of the able-bodied worker at the expense of the disabled poor as well as the securely rich. It was a demand that the workers be permitted to rise out of the ranks of the dole receivers as a class through recognition of their most valuable personal property—productive power. Their difference from the rest of the proprietary class lay in their need to have the state guarantee the exchangability, if not necessarily the full value, of this property. The state or some form of public institutional mechanism thus had to underwrite their independent status. The right to work was therefore thoroughly inegalitarian with regard to the poor in general. Although Tocqueville interpreted the right to work as the decisive step toward socialism, it presupposed a claim to a wage, not "the whole product of labor." It therefore also presupposed the maintenance of private ownership of land and capital. It was a class-specific claim which did not imply the negation of the right to relief, or the right to property, also guaranteed in the constitution.[38]

In the most fundamental sense the working class was asking for a status between proprietary independence and indigent dependence. The state was to be the institutional guarantor of that status. Tocqueville and the majority in the assembly refused to recognize any intermediate status between dependency and independence that enhanced,

38. On the general adaption of the egalitarian and individualistic frame of reference to the "equality" concept of social rights, see T. H. Marshall, *Class, Citizenship and Social Development* (Garden City, N. Y., 1964), and Bendix, *Nation Building and Citizenship*, 77–104.

without visible limit, the power and obligations of the state. They suggested that no alternate means of creating this quasi-independence was conceivable. Thus the working class remained identified with indigence and dependency. Yet the workers were not dependent and suppliant in the middle of the nineteenth century. They were conscious of common interest, of their potential power, and of the incongruity between their legal independence, their social permanence, and their periodic economic dependence. Tocqueville himself thought them to be the "real political class" of his final years, the group who were most liable to radical innovation in politics. The relation between their real and nominal social position in society was, as Tocqueville could have noted, the very condition that had permitted the destruction of the old social order at the outbreak of the first French Revolution.

Tocqueville's role as pallbearer of the right to work in the constitution of the Second French Republic was almost his last public action on the working-class and social revolution in France. His *Recollections* of the February Revolution, begun in 1850, recognized that the issues raised by 1848 remained open even after the June uprising and the final vote on the constitution. Yet he fell silent. His position as Foreign Minister in 1849, his long illness in 1850, his involvement with the constitutional crisis and the impending coup d'état of 1851 sufficed to distract him from the memories of the June barricades. Socialism continued of course to be the synonym for anarchy and revolution for the party of order. Beaumont countered Victor Hugo's plea for more poverty legislation in 1849 by reminding the legislative assembly how false sentimentality and social romanticism had fostered extravagant visions of the power of society to affect the problem of economic misery. Tocqueville's concern with working-class hostility had risen in direct proportion to his perception of its imminent danger. It declined for the same reason after 1848.

The political fact which most clearly affected Tocqueville's and Beaumont's own lives was the Bonapartist triumph, which cut short their careers. Even when Tocqueville found himself among the politically unemployed after December 2, 1851, his attention did not turn toward France's social legacy of 1848, but toward her socio-political problem as rephrased by the anti-parliamentary coup of 1851. The continuities of administrative centralization, and the alterations of revolution and plebiscitary despotism in French history were the focus of Tocqueville's final years, not the novel economic and social strains produced during the nineteenth century. The *Ancien Régime*, insofar as it was a study of class relationships, centered on the breakdown of communications and sentiments among the elite groups in society: the nobility, the clergy, the bourgeoisie, the administrators, the intellectuals. When it did turn to the rise of a working-class population in the capital as an important factor in the Revolution, it was within the framework of administrative centralization. Tocqueville was preoccupied with Paris as a dominant factor in French national history rather than with urban or industrial development. The notes to his unfinished sequel to the *Ancien Régime* indicate very little work on the Parisian crowds. Of course Tocqueville died in the midst of this study, but the fact remains that it was an object of analysis that came later rather than sooner in research priority. Yet his emphasis on the continuity of the nineteenth-century Parisian working class with that of the eighteenth century has also been increasingly acknowledged by recent historiography.[39] Pre-Revolutionary continuities rather than post-Revolutionary innovations were evident in every passing remark in the *Ancien Régime* about the working classes. The crucial period for the development of the working class was traced well back into the eighteenth century and even to the reign of Louis XIV. As he read the history of the old regime more closely, the sharp edge of contemporary novelty disappeared. Nineteenth-century socialist ideas were treated as mere replicas of the eighteenth-century economists' notions. Since the advocacy of the social concentration of power was regarded as the *sine qua non* of all doctrines tending to community control of property, socialism was embedded, and virtually embodied in the despotic physiocracy of the old regime. Socialism was only a less domesticated fruit. Revolutionary liberalism, not socialism or Bonapartist centralism, provided the real but shallow-rooted novelty of the French Revolution.

The degree to which Tocqueville linked socialism to the despotism of the old regime through the thread of centralization was based on his perception of the Second Empire as the latest link in France's historical development. Louis Napoleon's confiscation of the Orleanist estates, combined

39. R. Gossez, "Diversité des antagonismes sociaux vers le milieu du XIXᵉ siècle" *Revue économique*, I (1956), 439–458; David H. Pinkney, "The Crowd in the French Revolution of 1830," *American Historical Review*, LXX (Oct. 1964), 1–17; Charles Tilly, "Reflections on the Revolutions of Paris," *Social Problems*, XII (Summer 1964), 99–121. George Rudé, *The Crowd in History, A Study of Popular Disturbances in France and England 1730–1848* (New York, 1964), 175–177; M. Girard, *Etude comparée des mouvements revolutionnaires en France en 1830, 1848 et 1870–71*, 3 vols., Cours de Sorbonne (Paris, s. d.).

with his authoritarian regime and rationalization of economic investment, struck him as the fulfillment of demagogic despotism.

Yet the most terrifying long-range social fact of Louis Napoleon's political economy for Tocqueville was the rebuilding of Paris, which was depositing an ever-increasing residue of workers around the city. The urban workers, however much at the periphery of Tocqueville's and Beaumont's analytical concerns, were considered to be hopelessly imbued with socialism. Concentration of a working-class population was regarded as an unmitigated danger to the social order. As with Bonapartist politics, he believed concentration was the essential fact of the reconstruction of Paris during the 1850's. How important Tocqueville considered the fact may be judged from an incident during his final and triumphal visit to England in 1857. In the course of an interview with Lord Clarendon, the Prime Minister, the visitor was asked to sum up his impressions of the conditions of his nation. Tocqueville's reply was "that the working classes in Paris were by no means well affectioned to the Emperor and that the vast numbers of workmen who have been attracted to Paris and who cannot be expelled from it, do what the authorities will, must some day, he does not pretend to say when, be the cause of an enormous catastrophe."[40] Tocqueville could look forward propheti-

40. Clarendon to Cowley, June 24, 1857 (Public Record Office F. O. [519] 177). On Tocqueville's fear of a revolution of unemployed workers in Paris see also *Correspondence and Conversations of Alexis de Tocqueville with Nassau William Senior*, ed. M. C. M. Simpson, 2 vols. (London, 1872), II, 37 (conversation in Paris, May 17, 1853); and *Oeuvres* (M): *Correspondance Tocqueville-Beaumont*, III, 102. In the *Ancien Régime* the royal authorities were retroactive-

cally to the Paris Commune of 1871. But he could not see what the Saint-Simonians and Louis Napoleon perceived, that in the long run some of the acute problems of industrialization and urbanization might be alleviated by both more rapid and more controlled industrialization.

There was little evolution in Tocqueville's and Beaumont's thought on the lower classes after 1848. The enormous personal upheaval consequent to the overthrow of the parliamentary regime only served to remove them even further from the problems of poverty, latent alienation and violence, and collectivist ideas of any variety. They both grudgingly conceded the necessity if not the desirability of some kind of poor law in France, presumably based on the English model.[41] This would have resolved none of the

---

ly reproached for having so foolishly allowed a hostile army to accumulate in the capital which could control the city in time of revolution.

41. "Less elegibility" was of course the assumed basis for any such law. "If we give this right, we must, of course, make this relief disagreeable; we must separate families, make the workhouse a prison, and our charity repulsive" (Tocqueville in conversation with Nassau Senior [1851], *Correspondence and Conversations of Alexis de Tocqueville with Nassau William Senior from 1834 to 1859*, ed. Simpson, I, 204). See also Senior's *Journals Kept in France and in Italy from 1848 to 1852*, ed Simpson, 2 vols. (London, 1871), I, 276–277. As foreign minister in 1849, Tocqueville was converted to, or acquiesced in, the idea of deportation as a temporary solution to European social problems. He spent much of his brief tenure (June–Oct. 1849) in searching for permission from the British to deport French political prisoners to South America or the Pacific, in forcing the Swiss government to disgorge their political refugees from the center of Europe, and in persuading the Austrian and Russian governments to permit the revolutionary leaders of Hungary and Poland to go into exile outside Europe. Furthermore, despite Tocqueville's earlier warnings against allowing "bad seeds" into a

ambiguities of the confusion of relief and punishment so closely linked to the ideology of independence. The relatively novel precipitation of an articulate working-class consciousness required an explanation in terms of its origins and possible futures amidst the futures of other classes, but in the eyes of Tocqueville and Beaumont it was frozen into hostile quiescence. It had a degree of common traditions and feelings. It knew how to will and how to act. That it would remain in a state of latent violence was assumed. Another unyielding fact was simply registered in the providential equation.

In one essential way, however, Tocqueville's prognosis was dramatically altered by the Revolution of 1848. It had less to do with any change in perspective toward the industrial classes than toward France as a whole. Tocqueville had always viewed a part of the lower class as hopelessly alienated. He was primarily surprised in 1848 by its organi-

---

European colony, Beaumont in his capacity as French ambassador to the Austrian empire in 1849 suggested to Schwartzenberg, the Austrian foreign minister, that the Polish and Hungarian revolutionaries who had sought political asylum in the Ottoman empire be allowed to proceed to Algeria. Beaumont was now convinced that exile to North Africa could convert dangerous Europeans into good proprietary colonials. See Archives des Affaires Etrangeres: Correspondance politique, *Autriche* (440), Beaumont to Tocqueville, Oct. 22, 1849. In the wake of 1848 Tocqueville and Beaumont both completely scrapped their general arguments against deportation as a solution to "anti-social" behavior. See also Tocqueville's *Recollections*, concluding chapter, as well as Lord Normanby, English ambassador to Palmerston, Paris, July 3, 1849: "Conversation [with Tocqueville] on political emigration to Monte-Video" (first proposed by Beaumont, as ambassador to London, in 1848), P.R.O. F.O. 27/846, No. 357; also No. 369, July 9, 1849; 370, July 9, 1849; 417, Aug. 5, 1849.

zation and collective hostility. The real change in his thinking was an only half-recognized decision that class analysis
was more appropriate to an understanding of contemporary France than the mass society framework. The upheav-
als of 1848–1851 had been repetitive as well as traumatic.
The novelties of the nineteenth century seemed like mere
improvisations in the reenactments of history. The "special
spirit" of the Revolution of 1848 emerged only momentarily between the ritual-ridden act of February 24, 1848 ("bad
tragedy performed by provincial actors"),[42] and that of
December 2, 1851. Another contemporary, Karl Marx, commenting on the same drama, had observed that history re-
peats itself, the first time as tragedy, the second time as
farce. For Tocqueville the significant fact was the bank-
ruptcy of social change revealed by the second performance.
The real historical tragedy was in the repetition.[43]

42. Tocqueville, *Recollections,* 54–55. See Marx's similar theme
in the *Eighteenth Brumaire of Louis Bonaparte* (New York, 1963).
For two good studies of their parallel treatments of the 1848 period,
see Gargan, *Alexis de Tocqueville,* Chapter XI, and Aron, *Main Currents in Sociological Thought,* 233–260.

43. On the role of repetition in the choice of Tocqueville's subject of study, see his letter to Louis de Kergorlay, *Oeuvres* (Beaumont edition): *Correspondance et oeuvres posthumes,* 383–385. In
the midst of his research for the *Ancien Régime* he felt that the
world no longer seemed launched on a new era. He complained
that "fatigue and discouragement sometimes take hold of me. Not
only discouragement with myself, but with men as they daily reveal
themselves with greater clarity, with how few things we know, with
even their uncertainty, with their incessant repetition in novel
terms for three thousand years; lastly, with the insignificance of our
species, with our world, with our destiny, with what we call our
great revolutions and our *great* concerns" (letter to Beaumont,
March 23, 1853 [Yale Mss D.I.c.; *Oeuvres* (M): *Correspondance
Tocqueville-Beaumont,* III, 95–96]).

The class struggles of 1848–1851 left a durable mark in Tocqueville's work. If the urban working classes had roused his bitter enmity by their threat to the social order at the birth of the Second Republic, every other class in France had earned his disgust by its indifference to constitutional liberty at the end of the Republic. Those who had interred the "democratic and social republic" in the June Days also sanctified Louis Napoleon's burial of the liberal republic, while parliamentarians including Tocqueville and Beaumont were relieved of their offices and carted off to prison for a token incarceration in response to their symbolic resistance.[44] For Tocqueville, the new government was distastefully "founding itself on peasants and soldiers, the most brutal elements of democracy."[45] But the betrayal of the elites left him far more bitter than did that of the masses. In an intimate letter he made the relative distribution of his political indictment unmistakable:

In the quote you send me, he has said something quite true that I myself have long been thinking, but applying only to a single class of the French, the peasants. Yes, undoubtedly these Frenchmen can prefer the present government, without

44. See Gargan, *Alexis de Tocqueville*, 227–234.
45. Letter of Tocqueville to R. Monckton Milnes, Feb. 9, 1852 (Milnes Mss, Trinity College Library, Cambridge, Eng.). See also *Oeuvres* (M): *Correspondance Tocqueville-Beaumont*, II, 252, and III, 19. Louis Napoleon's plebiscitary legitimation left a legacy of suspicion among the liberal notables. See Letter of Beaumont to John Murray Forbes, Aug. 17, 1865 (*Letters of John Murray Forbes*, II). As the disillusionment of the coup became more remote, some of Tocqueville's old sympathetic feeling returned, and the peasantry were again "perhaps the most original, and French of us all" (Tocqueville to William Gladstone, July 13, 1858, Gladstone Papers, British Museum, Additional Ms 44390, fol. 54). On the ebb and flow of Tocqueville's perception of class see note 6 above.

it being possible to note any sign of degradation in them. They bear its yoke without feeling it. They think that the present government is a kind of victory for their class. They are often proud of those who control them; they have the latter's prejudices but not their baseness. The education that they have received, the poor behavior of the upper and middle classes toward them while free institutions existed, did not really allow them to form an ideal of government beyond what we observe. It is not they whom I despise but those bourgeois who found constitutional liberty scarcely endurable, and who fell to their knees before a despotic violator of liberty and law with full knowledge of the value of these words, and who submit with delight to a form of government that they condemn because there are money and appointments to be had. The ones we must despise are those *plats pieds de prêtres*, who, after having demanded freedom for eighteen years [the July Monarchy] and who cried, "Long live the Republic!" at the top of their lungs, now wear the Master out with their incense. The ones who must be despised most are those antique gentlemen who refurbish their *armoires* by adorning them with portraits of their ancestors, and who rediscover or invent noble titles ... without conserving in their whole beings an atom of the proud and independent spirit which alone glorified their forefathers, they, who accumulate parchments and trample on the true nobility of their ancestors, which lay in their hearts. These men can indeed be very assiduous Christians, very upright people, very good family men—quite worthy of an epitaph. But I say that they are bastardized beings, who have degenerated from nobles to serfs, and out of whom there will never come anything but a race of gilded pygmies, fully worthy of the scorn of their contempories and of their posterity. Male or female, I exempt none of them.[46]

46. Yale Mss C.I.b.2: one of "Three undated documents." This respondent was addressed in the familiar *(tu)* form and the letter was certainly written after the coup of Dec. 1851. The recipient, if not a member of Tocqueville's immediate family, may have been Louis de Kergorlay, a childhood friend and one of the few whom

It is no wonder that his *Ancien Régime* assailed every class in France for its political servility and described the separation of classes as the ultimate crime of the French monarchy and the ultimate disease of the old regime. The *Ancien Régime* recognized that there were individuals who fought against the alienation of classes, but he would speak only of the behavior of classes as a whole—"they alone are the concern of history."[47]

Tocqueville addressed in the familiar. Another letter (C.I.b.3), probably in response to a defense of the clergy after the coup, declared: *"You are perhaps right in saying that I attach too much importance, as far as faith is concerned, to the incidental conduct of the clergy.* You must allow something for the grief—I might almost say for the despair felt at what is happening before the eyes of a man as convinced as I am that the true greatness of man is only in the linkage of liberal sentiment and religious sentiment working together to vitalize and to restrain souls, someone whose one political "passion" for thirty years had been to further this linkage. . . . I have no doubt that the populace is edified by the sight of the clergy blessing soldiers who return from the violent overthrow of their country's law, while in turn, these same soldiers follow the religious processions. I know that the majority would pay less respect to a poor and neglected clergy than a clergy which can rely on the *gendarmes* and who are endowed with confiscated properties.

"As for me, I confess to you that this whole fusion of what I most prize and most despise fills me with disgust and horror. I confess that such a spectacle hurls my spirit into much deeper and more miserable turmoil than ever resulted from reading the complete works of Voltaire and of Rousseau, plus all the theses and other similar philosophical *canailles* produced by the howling pack that followed them." (Tocqueville's final allusion may refer to his own youthful discovery of Enlightenment writings and the religious doubts that ensued.)

47. *Oeuvres* (M): *Ancien Régime*, I, 179. One should not make too much of the substantive implications of this statement. What Tocqueville meant was that general behavior patterns were more important than individual exceptions. This was, in essence, little

At a less conscious level, however, the experience of 1848–
1851 had cut even deeper into Tocqueville's social prognosis. In the aftermath of the July Revolution he had
regarded the attempt to establish a *pays légal* society as
an artificial, temporary, and in the long run a dangerous
expedient. Exclusivist pretensions in any class were vani-
ties built of rubble. The great homogenizing revolution
had triumphed and France had entered a new age. The
one-class society he perceived in Jacksonian America was
the harbinger of the future. Since a new science of politics
was needed for a new world, and new cures for new ills,
the world's first new nation was the appropriate object of
study for the new France. After 1848 Tocqueville sought to
understand contemporary French social realities from a
study of the old regime. The feudal remains had indeed
crumbled but they had revealed deeper faults beneath their
foundations, and fissures from which lava still flowed. Class
became not only the unit of analysis for describing the past
but for contemplating the present and the future as well.

Richard Herr, in his study of *Tocqueville and the Old
Regime*, comments on the fact that, strangely, the word
"democracy" appears infrequently in the text of the *Ancien
Régime*, and surmises that Tocqueville was clearer about
his basic thesis of the centrality of the democratic process
in his article on the same subject in 1836.[48] In 1856 the

---

different from the similar statement in the *Penitentiary System* that
what affected the many was more important than what concerned
individuals. But it should be noted that where Beaumont and
Tocqueville used "majority" or "mass" in earlier works, "class" came
more naturally in the *Ancien Régime*.

48. Herr's discussion is in his *Tocqueville and the Old Regime*,
42–43. Tocqueville's essay of 1836 was published in English as "Po-

"uninitiated reader can hardly suspect that the subject of democracy still concerns its author." Herr adds that the notes and foreword of the *Ancien Régime*, which were "largely written . . . after the book was in press, when he was letting his innermost thoughts come out most clearly—refer pointedly to aristocracy and democracy." But why, one must ask, should a lucid and outspoken writer, who took extraordinary pains to make his main points clear beyond doubt, have concealed his innermost thoughts? The very question should be posed differently. Why should the terms "democracy" and "democratic" not have flowed naturally from the pen of a man who, more than any other writer in history, had built his reputation on the elaboration of their social implications? He experienced no such reticence in maintaining the continuity of his terminology on centralization, on individualism, on despotism, and a host of subordinate concepts. One might well question the continuity of Tocqueville's thought on the process of social democratization in France. Did his references to democracy in the foreword and the notes reveal his innermost thoughts or his afterthoughts? Were they produced, like his affirmation of devotion to liberty in the foreword, out of a sense of uneasiness at the implications of the textual analysis? The 1836 essay on the social condition of France was shot through with references to democracy, and the word was applied incessantly even to *pre*-Revolutionary France.

---

litical and Social Condition of France, First Article," translated by John Stuart Mill and published in the April 1836 issue of *London and Westminster Review*, III and XXV, 137–169. The original French version is published in Tocqueville's *Oeuvres* (M): *Ancien Régime*, I, 31–66, with the title "Etat social et politique de la France avant et depuis 1789."

There was no need for a foreword or notes to bring out the frame of reference.[49]

49. Even including the notes and foreword, the use of "democracy" and "democratic" is almost insignificant when compared with the essay of 1836. Even allowing for the political reasons that might have caused Tocqueville to restrict their applicability to the old regime in 1856 (see Drescher, *Tocqueville and England*, 215), the use of the words to either eighteenth- or nineteenth-century French social structure in the *Ancien Régime* is still more restricted than a comparative word count would indicate. Out of eleven references to "democracy" or "democratic" I have counted in the text of the *Ancien Régime*, two refer to democracy in general (84, 213), three to medieval local government (115, 119), one to America (148), two to hostility to inequality (210, 244), one to the use of democracy as a façade (121), two to the nature of the French Revolution in terms of institutional innovations (129, 247). There is *one* reference to contemporary France as a democracy, which is rather ambiguous (148). In the foreword and notes there are seven separate uses of the word, including one double reference: one is to democratic society in general (266); one is to the French and British colonies in North America (287); one is to democracy used as a façade (Frederick the Great's Code) (269); one is to democratic political institutions (72); and two to democratizing political agencies (266, 283). Two references clearly relate to France as a democracy (269, 310); and there is one implied though obvious reference to the same (75). The one *textual* use of the word as applied to contemporary France is strangely negative in its implications. It comes in the context of a discussion of the relative *lack* of social exclusiveness in England compared with France. "If you want to know whether caste, and the ideas, habits, and barriers it has produced among a people are definitely abolished, just look at their marriages. There you will find the necessary and decisive symptom. Even now, in France, after sixty years of democracy, you often look for it in vain. Old and new families who seem intermingled in all things, all the more that they can do so, avoid intermarriage" (*Ancien Régime*, I, 148). Note that Tocqueville was contrasting the elite in "democratic" France and aristocratic England. His marriage criterion in the *Ancien Régime* is interestingly cited by Daumard for analyzing the Parisian bourgeoisie of the nineteenth century (see *La Bourgeoisie parisienne*, 379). Tocqueville's most important criterion of a class was self-definition and concerted action by a relatively

This is not to say that Tocqueville was giving up his original model of the general process of democratization. History as the evolution of society toward equality was still a
fundamental theme. His real difficulty over using his old
model of democracy was integrating the novel theme of
class hostility[50] into his model of the classless society. It was
the difficulty of fitting his vivid personal experience of the
depth and durability of this hostility into an historical
framework which had assumed in 1836 that the old regime
had only two important classes, aristocrats and others, and
that historical sociology could be safely confined to the
decline of the French nobility in relation to the bourgeoisie.
From the lack of reference in the *Ancien Régime* to
democratization in France I would ascribe one basic change
of emphasis.

France was not as close to mass society as Tocqueville had
implied in the *Democracy*, nor to the end of her democratic
revolution. He was not, as he had believed in 1840, writing
in a country where the struggle was finished.[51] In the *Ancien*

---

permanent group in terms of a negative reference group. In *Democracy in America* he could assume that because all democratic social relationships were embedded within a structureless society and an egalitarian ideology, no tendencies toward "class" attitudes could result in the formation of classes "properly speaking." But he declared in the *Ancien Régime*: "Indeed, even today, though class distinctions are no more, the jealousies and antipathies they caused have not died out." Both class ideology and class behavior could outlast the juridical abolition of separate classes in 1789, if one could conceive of classes "improperly speaking" generations after the disappearance of classes "properly speaking"—not to mention the possibility of the formation of new classes.

50. See Herr, *Tocqueville and the Old Regime*, 78.

51. Letter of Tocqueville to Reeve, Nov. 15, 1839 (*Oeuvres* (M): *Correspondance anglaise*).

Régime there was a chapter headed "That France was the country where men had become most similar to each other." It was a statement that in effect summarized the major conclusion of his *Westminster Review* essay of 1836. If the words "in Europe" were added it could have appeared in the *Democracy* as well. But in the *Ancien Régime* this chapter was followed by another chapter whose heading had no counterpart in the writings of twenty years before: "How these men, so alike, were more separated than they had *ever* been into small groups, alien and indifferent to each other." It was a concept far removed in conception from the fluid and, socially speaking, thoroughly artificial, accidental and voluntary "small private circles" described in *Democracy in America* as the rule in America, and natural to democratic societies.[52] In the *Ancien Régime*, France was torn by an inverse "non-mass" tendency toward status differentiation unparalleled in America or even England. Although the elite classes were prepared by their growing similarity to place themselves ideologically, fiscally, and juridically on a footing of equality in the cahiers of 1789, and to take their life chances as civic equals, they were far from ready, as Tocqueville maintained in the face of his own evidence, to immerse themselves "in the same mass provided that no one had anything more than the

52. Compare Tocqueville's "Etat social" (*Ancien Régime*, I, 53, 65) with the *Ancien Régime*, I, 143, 147; *Democracy in America*, 580–581. It seems to me that the *idée mère* of Tocqueville's description of classes in the *Ancien Régime* can be found nowhere in the essay of twenty years before: "Inequality growing in institutions and *moeurs* in proportion as it decreased in [political, economic, intellectual] facts" (title of a note published in *Oeuvres* (M): *Ancien Régime*, II, 360).

others and did not rise beyond the common level."[53] On the contrary, "it was easier to divide men under the old regime than reunite them after sixty years of the new." Twenty years before the *Ancien Régime,* Tocqueville had been so imbued with the idea that equality was the "soul of France" that he had read democracy back into the old regime. France, before the Revolution, was already the most homogeneous society in Europe. In 1856 the weight of history hung so heavily that he could scarcely think of his own nation as part of the classless future he had once seen embodied in America. The spatial analogue was effaced by the historical analogue. The age of the masses slipped into the footnotes of the *Ancien Régime,* and the remote horizon of Europe's future. Despite the pulverization produced by the Revolution, the *moeurs* of class, like those of centralization, had been reconstructed from the debris of the old regime. They formed the mold of the process of industrialization.

Under such intellectual pressures the whole problem of the role of violence and revolution was seen in a different light by Tocqueville in 1856 than it had been in 1835–1840. There was a new perception of the durability of the revolutionary mentality in modern society. It has been often remarked that Tocqueville twice began a study of the French Revolution and twice stopped short of a description of the impact of the violence itself on social development. At the outset of his career he wanted to draw a clear distinction between revolutionary and stable societies as distinct historical stages, thereby reducing revolutions to the role of transitional catalysts. In 1840 he had already broken down

53. *Oeuvres (M): Ancien Régime,* I, 158.

this historical distinction with the concession that, at least insofar as the growth of the state was concerned, revolutionary habits could become permanently embedded and even eternalized in a stable democratic society. At that point, however, Tocqueville was still speaking of those results of the revolutionary process that enhanced the administrative power and stability of the state rather than those elements which undermined governments. In 1856 he took a further step in breaking down the dichotomy between revolutionary and democratic stages. Under the impact of 1848, he saw France faced with a revolution without a foreseeable end, and he acknowledged total confusion as to what the long-range outcome would be. The whole idea of stable democracy in France was set aside for a new set of questions concerning revolution. Why does a revolution occur, and what does it leave in its wake? Tocqueville felt that he had resolved the first question in his *Ancien Régime*. The second remained totally unanswered, even in outline, at his death.

After he had completed the *Ancien Régime* he had still not come to grips with the problem of the long-range *effects* of violent social change in France. Groping for a proper analogue, he referred to the revolutionary "spirit" as "a new and unknown virus," an analogy that left open the question of whether the disease would ultimately be diagnosed as acute or chronic, and what were the conditions of relapse or cure. One of the reasons he found it so difficult to integrate the continuing revolution into his general theory of social developments was his lingering general commitment to the idea that, once a country had abolished juridical inequalities and corporate privileges, its democratic revolution should essentially be over. He was satisfied from first to last that the end of the old regime was explicable in terms of the tension between a parasitic hierarchical structure and the demands of a modernizing state and society. In terms of this tension and the continuously shifting balance of power between the two segments, the demise of the old was inevitable. But once the essential changes in Tocqueville's terms had been brought about through the abolition of special corporate juridical status, residual claims on property or office, the rationalization of administration, and the adoption of popular sovereignty as the ultimate source of political legitimation, why should revolutions and revolutionaries persist?

One answer was that the egalitarian process as defined originally by Tocqueville was still incomplete. But this also implied that all societies without absolute equality of wealth and social benefits, and without selection by lot for every position in society, were continuous prey to revolution, and that the closer one got to this condition, the less susceptible the society was to further revolution. Tocqueville had in part adopted this idea in 1835–1840, but for him, "a state of perfect equality [was] a dream," not the probable terminal point of human history.[54] In the *Ancien Régime* he contrasted modern France not with democratic America, but with aristocratic England. Revolution had come to a society already more equalized than that of England and persisted in the same contrasting situation. Ana-

54. Yale Mss C.V.K: draft of his preface to the second part of *Democracy in America*, Feb. 5, 1838, paq. 7, cahier 1.

lytically, the cause of *violence* in Tocqueville's *Ancien Régime* lay not in the existence or persistence of inequalities per se, but in the inability of the political and social network to cope with the internal and external demands made on it. Here the crucial role of the political rather than the social structure became significant. The last great social problem that he posed for himself—under what circumstances does a revolutionary cycle come to an end?—eluded him to the end.

Implicit in Tocqueville's *Ancien Régime* was a theory that what had occurred in France was a gigantic breakdown of the usually highly adaptive information system that constitutes the means by which an evolving society continually recognizes and adapts to or controls social change. Long-range breakdown occurred not at the center of the system but in the support systems of the local political structure as reliable two-way processing mechanisms. Hence, the shock that was created by the famous cahiers of 1789, which overwhelmed the central government. They revealed both to the Monarchy and to the public the extent of the demands for overhauling the social and political system. "Liberty" was not just part of Tocqueville's value system, but denoted the variable which most clearly defined whether social change could occur without an internal revolution. According to Tocqueville, the absence of an adequate and comprehensive system of political communication (liberty) created an inevitable revolutionary situation when rapid social change was occurring because the effects of change could only be registered cumulatively at relatively infrequent moments of governmental weakness. The development of intermediate networks of organization (association) throughout a society could effectively increase the adaptability of the political system to pressures at any point in the society and reduce the chances of internal revolution.

Tocqueville, however, did not remind his readers in the *Ancien Régime* what was clear to him after 1848, that formal liberty (in the form of constitutional devices) had failed either to prevent or to overcome attempts at violent revolution. Since he wanted to contrast French, as well as English, political liberty with centralized despotism, he did not reintroduce into the *Ancien Régime* his thesis that the July Monarchy fell violently for the same reason as the old regime, the inability by the governing elite to create an information-gathering and decision-making system that correctly measured the cumulative demands of the various classes of France. Both local government and association continued to be undeveloped in the France of 1840 as in the France of 1780 compared with the English or American social systems. Despite the relative social stability of France as a whole in 1830, 1848, or 1851, as compared with 1789, the system continued to rely more heavily on the insulated centralized support systems (police and administrative agencies) rather than maintaining or mobilizing autonomous, public, or private intermediate social organizations. France still lacked the level of organization that could assure relatively integrated non-authoritarian development.[55] By the

55. An unanswered question in Tocqueville's analysis was the extent to which political equivalents of associational support systems could be developed in authoritarian political systems. There was no empirical way that Tocqueville could have anticipated that "association" was not necessarily an exclusively libertarian mechan-

1850's it was clear to Tocqueville that France had not achieved a stable state, but the *moeurs* of violence seemed to have become an enduring, if not eternal social fact.

---

ism; there were alternative means of social mobilization to the centralized-bureaucratic-quietistic, and the voluntary-associational-participatory societies. Revolution could be as effectively prevented by increasing the associational network in an authoritarian as in a pluralistic framework.

VIII

Social Structure and Democratization

"THE gradual progress of equality is a providential fact. It has the necessary characteristics: it is universal, it is enduring, it continually eludes human control; all events, like all men, have contributed to its development." So Tocqueville wrote in 1835, and so he reaffirmed at every significant intellectual opportunity: in 1840, 1848, and 1856. No perceived development caused him to alter this long-range prognosis.

Although his generic statement on the fate of modern societies remained crystal clear, the specific meaning of the statement, as applied to different societies and to a whole range of social problems, shifted like the shadows in the cave of Plato's republic. The light of Tocqueville's vision was brilliant and penetrating. As each object of investigation passed before the light it seemed to him and to his readers a durable component of that vision. On all sides, however, there flitted a host of substantial shades that distorted the image presented to the mind's eye. And often when Tocqueville shifted his light to illumine the periphery, the center of his vision seemed out of focus. Since the entire range of observation was never presented under the same intensity of light, the most sensitive and sympathetic of his contemporaries were often thrown off balance in their attempts to give due proportion to his conclusions. Symptomatically, the more one concentrates on a single work, or a single part of a work, the easier it is to arrive at a sharply defined portrait of social reality. Tocqueville's works could be quoted as authority by men who stood for, or thought they stood for, opposing political or intellectual alternatives.

The contradictory conclusions drawn from Tocqueville's works were not always due to political passions or limited vision. There were even those who with a clear intellectual conscience were convinced that the sheer reliability of Tocqueville's vision, even despite himself, had verified their own fundamental intellectual or moral premises rather than those of their author.

I have resorted to metaphor at this point in order to render my feeling of how Tocqueville was at once analytically lucid and systematically ambiguous. He wrote to achieve clarity, not to settle for a series of brilliant shifting images. His intention was to achieve the coherent image of an anatomist, not impressionistic effects. His stylistic taste was for Pascal and Voltaire, not his romantic contemporaries. To someone who complimented him on the beauty of his *phrases* he replied, "Madame, I have never made a phrase in my life." Yet the reflex of posterity has been to quote individual morsels of his thought. In his classic work he could not sustain a brilliant core model throughout.

By looking consistently at the periphery of Tocqueville's investigation, one clearly sees the uncertain position of even his fundamental thesis over time, both in terms of his own perceptions and that of other "tendencies" of modern societies, which he either ignored or thrust uncomfortably to one side.

The implicit confession of despair about the integration of the urban worker and the persistence of class hostility was not the first time that Tocqueville had diluted the providentiality of democracy or reduced it to possibility or even improbability. *Democracy in America* had specifically excluded all racial relations from the realm of equality. Considering the geographical extent of mixed racial areas, the scope of "democracy" was indeed confined to begin with. Wherever racially heterogenous populations existed, a relationship of permanent domination was the probable social condition. Europe's providential expansion, in fact, promised a widening rather than a contracting of this phenomenon of domination, and Tocqueville enthusiastically supported it without second thoughts. He assumed the superiority of European Christian civilization for the foreseeable future. In this sense democracy was already a parochial phenomenon in 1840. Even within the confines of Western European society and its racially homogenous offshoots, certain social spheres of existence were handed over wholesale to permanent and progressive inequality.

Tocqueville of course thought that an aristocracy, and a servile class, might be created by manufacturing. Although he seems to have regarded this as a restricted fact relative to the more providential fact of democracy (his usual tactic), he left open a very pertinent question about how one was to determine the relation of providential equality to permanent inequality. Why, in fact, should one assume that equality was the wave of the future when inequality rode so imposing a crest as industrial growth?

But the question cut deeper. Inequality was not just a sport within the family of modern political institutions and social structures. Tocqueville, at least as early as the composition of the *Democracy* of 1840, had begun to perceive that inequality was a co-variant of modernization. If the division of labor resulted in functional inequalities in *manufacturing*, why would it not do so elsewhere? In *Democracy in America*, for example, administrative structure was considered primarily from the point of view of its relative power as an institutional unit of the state vis-à-vis society. But there is a curious footnote that referred to administrators as a quasi-aristocracy: "In proportion as the functions of the central power increase, the number of functionaries who represent it grows as well. They form a nation within each nation [one of Tocqueville's traits of aristocracies]; and as they share the stability of the government, they increasingly take the aristocracy's place."[1] This "aristocracy" was perhaps no more, but certainly no less, than the manufacturing one, a corporate body with coherent interests and *moeurs*. It was also a providential, or at least a central historical fact. It was, like democracy, at

1. Tocqueville, *Oeuvres* (M): *Démocratie*, 312n.

once "the past and future" of man's history. It was "universal, durable, eluding all human interference," and all regimes, according to Tocqueville, contributed to its progress. The administrative class, moreover, was no monster, no exception, like Tocqueville's manufacturers. It increased with every expansion of the role of the public sector in society. Thus in an isolated chapter on industrialists and in an isolated footnote on public administrators one was presented with two growing aristocracies with enormous growth prospects in Tocqueville's own terms. But the roster of inequality was still far from complete. Although Tocqueville more than glimpsed this other possibility, he did not elaborate on it in the *Democracy*. But his notes for the *Democracy* contain the same fears of a new aristocracy arising out of the only other large-scale mass association to which he turned his attention—the military.[2] Looking at France and Continental Europe, he saw every likelihood that mass armies and officer corps were also universal and durable facts for the foreseeable future.

The result of these insights, had Tocqueville gathered them into one generalized portrait, would have been a prediction of a new aristocratic system resting on three formidable pillars: the industrial, the public, and the military

2. Tocqueville was somewhat alarmed by Louis Napoleon's attempted coup at Strasbourg in 1836, but was even more alarmed by conversations with Thiers and one of his supporters in 1837 who showed very little concern about the threats to constitutional government posed by military establishments and wars (see Yale Mss C.V.a, paq.h., pp. 46–47, 50, and C.V.c, pp. 15–24, and especially p. 26 on the possibility of a military aristocracy). Tocqueville at one point in his notes was willing to admit to an error about his prediction that the creation of a new aristocracy was impossible (C.V.e, p. 26) and the soldier and bureaucrat were recognized as men of the future.

sectors of society. These were not of course hereditary aristocracies in the old regime's sense of the term. The fact that Tocqueville found no better term to describe them than as "kinds of aristocracies" and not aristocracies "of a new kind," as he described varieties of democratic regimes, shows that the idea of functional elites as a general phenomenon of modernity had not clearly crystallized in his thought.

At every turn Tocqueville instinctively recognized a problem in dealing with large-scale organization and its relation to democracy, but he never attempted to work out that relation. The vision of a socially atomized society without hierarchy derived from Jacksonian America and Orleanist France remained the normative social condition of modernity. Tocqueville's conception of modern society as essentially undifferentiated enabled him to conceive of it in terms of a single psychological unit of "social" character. It was thus capable of personification through analogical categories derived from the psychology of socially undifferentiated individuals. In this way the *moeurs* of a democratic or essentially classless society, unlike an aristocratic hierarchical society, could be analyzed in terms of the ideas, feelings, and manners of democratic man in *Democracy in America* (1840) as contrasted with the explicit class analysis of the *Ancien Régime*. Since democratic society was essentially no more than an endless series of interchangeable individuals, the idea of social mobility was logically restricted to individual, not group movement. The socioeconomic ladder of wealth and power was so easy of access as to prevent the formation of relatively stable classes or class consciousness. Social mobility in effect was merely the sum total of individual mobilities. With this "mass" conception of social structure, all functional or economic elites could and did strike Tocqueville as either benign vestiges of the old regime or as malignant symptoms of a new aristocracy. The industrial, military, and administrative elites seemed less like correlates of modernization than inflexible threats to democracy.

Since his image was of an unstratified society based on the providential and progressive tendency toward equalization, functional stratifications threatened reversions or perversions to a premodern social condition just as centralization threatened a reversion to a premodern political condition. Tocqueville was aware that these "aristocracies" were not as stable or durable as the older landed aristocracy in terms of wealth, status, and power preserved through heredity. But he treated each of them as distinct pathologies arising out of the social mass that could lead to something akin to a new hierarchical order. He did not consider that functional hierarchies other than those of public administration might be symbiotically related to democratization, or that these hierarchies constituted particular examples of a single social fact as providential as democratization—the division of labor. Authority and power differentiation as a general rather than as an exceptional fact struck both Tocqueville and his readers at the end of the *Democracy* as a nightmare of a new kind. By dealing with isolated symptoms rather than with the general social phenomena, his analysis proceeded by fits and starts. That democracy and not the division of economic functions was the primordial social fact was simply a projection of the image he had formed from his view of certain aspects of America and

France as the dominant social structure of the future. In a world where undifferentiated, independent individuals were declared normative, large-scale organization, professionalization and elites were inherent threats to the social system of independence, and they were treated as such wherever found.

Tocqueville could and did prove capable of recognizing the compatibility of both large-scale organization and inequality in certain areas of modern societies. Early in his career Tocqueville had assumed a total incompatibility between large-scale agriculture and democratization. His early vision of democracy had included the necessary triumph of small individual property in all areas of economic activity. This had to be the more so in agriculture, since it provided the central socio-economic *moeurs* for his model of democracy. In the *Democracy* of 1835, the structure of landholding was regarded as the key to social analysis, and the division of landed estates as the inevitable co-variant of all democratic revolutions.

Equally fundamental to his early idea of social causality was the axiom that large landed estates could not survive democratization. His certainty was shaken by English economists who insisted that on the basis of productivity and efficiency an acquisitive society might be compatible with large-scale agriculture. The possibility of forms of controlling wealth other than individual proprietorship was not yet raised, but arguments from productivity and efficiency as an alternative goal to equality of ownership made a deep impression on Tocqueville. He had already recognized that modern society was dedicated to material well-being and economic growth as well as equality. Although he never considered consolidation of land as a co-variant of democracy, or even as a desirable condition for otherwise egalitarian societies, he recognized that concentration of holdings could occur in the most advanced and stable industrial societies.

Once again, however, the technological and rationalizing tendencies of modern society seem to have escaped him. He made room for the "accident" of large holdings only on the basis of economic and social facts external to agricultural productivity. His perception of large landholdings was always from the point of view of their legal status as estates rather than units of production. The economic rationalization of agriculture was in any case not linked to the rationalization of social power. Landowners were the sector of modern society most likely to escape the control of the supreme power, and therefore they did not directly contribute to the centralization of public power. The core of his fears was not the concentration of wealth, but the concentration of political power. Tocqueville could conceive of a stable democratic community with large-scale agriculture because the concentration of power remained isolated at the level of the individual proprietor. No open door was provided for higher levels of administrative organization and hierarchy. And the large landowner had the clearest similarity to the dispersed power that had always formed a counterweight to the power of the state.

Tocqueville's conception of scientific productivity was as detached from a general theory of growth as his conception of economic growth was from technological innovation. Scientific discovery was leisured, aristocratic, disinterested, and above all individual. He could not readily perceive that the same processes which were at work to create economic, administrative, and political elites were at work in maintaining a scientific community.[3] The relationship between theoretical science on the one hand and technology and economic growth on the other was narrowly conceived and rigidly separated. Theoretical science was "impractical" thought tied to ages of great passions and pure beauty, therefore socially disfunctional in democracies.[4] That productivity and innovation should be perceived as long-run factors in economic growth and institutionally more important to modern democratic societies than to traditional, if aristocratic, ones was seen as significant only in the last resort—like charity, as a means of maintaining, not increasing, a tolerable material condition. This is further evidence that Tocqueville's perception of the process of large-scale organization as a response to economic, technological, and scientific growth was intermittent and not based on a unified evolutionary conception like those of Auguste Comte or the Saint-Simonians.[5]

3. Tocqueville felt that academic institutions were contrary to the *génie* of democracy (see Yale Mss C.V.a: Tocqueville's notebooks for the *Démocratie*, paq.h., p. 2, and C.V.f, paq. 4, cahier 1, pp. 11–12. In his view of the relationship between science and technology, Tocqueville was harking back to a preindustrial era, in which science and technology were discrete bodies of knowledge embedded in different social classes. This is almost startling in view of the early and prominent role played by France in attempting to institutionalize the fusion of science and technology in the nineteenth century. Napoleonic centralization had, if anything, encouraged it and in 1840 France was still a recognized leader in the process.

4. See Yale Mss C.V.f: notes for the *Démocratie*, paq. 4, pp. 11–12. Tocqueville added, "I assert this idea without proving it."

5. Tocqueville, of course, was unaware of many of the contemporary probings of scientific, economic, and technological development.

The institutionalization of science in Europe was thus conceived of as a fortuitous aristocratic inheritance, and the primary danger to modern society was the loss of its theoretical heritage as had occurred in China. As with land use, his vision was focused on status rather than achievement. It was therefore not the scale of organization but the perceived susceptibility of the particular sphere of human activity to bureaucratic concentration of power

---

Others, like the writings of the Saint-Simonians, he dismissed as aberrations. Yet even as early as the completion of *Democracy in America* he was confronted by a challenge to the sufficiency of his causal analysis by a reviewer whose opinions he valued as highly as those of any contemporary. John Stuart Mill in his otherwise laudatory review of *Democracy in America* in 1840 commented that Tocqueville had confused democracy with what Mill called "Civilization": "He has bound up in one abstract idea the whole of the tendencies of modern commercial society, and given them one name— Democracy. . . . But this growing equality is only one of the features of . . . the incidental effects of the progress of industry and wealth: a most important effect, . . . but not therefore to be confounded with the cause." Much of what Mill diagnosed by the term "civilization" could readily be included in what we mean by the more (though by no means completely) neutral terms "modernization." While Tocqueville never responded directly to Mill's criticism, his work was part of the general discussion of modernization from the moment it appeared. Tocqueville made one early attempt to analyze his theory of democratization in terms of a larger process of "civilization," including the process of industrialization, in his *Memoir on Pauperism* (see *Tocqueville and Beaumont on Social Reform*, ed. Drescher, 3–9). But he arrived only at a fundamental, providential, and eternal dualism between the victims of industrialization and the beneficiaries of civilization that left no opening for their future integration. His dichotomous model of civilization was later put in more problematic terms, but never revoked (see also *ibid.,* 200). It was almost made to order for working-class visions of an apocalyptic reversal of proprietary civilization and a condition of permanent insurrection.

which was the determinant of Tocqueville's attitude. It is also clear in this perspective why he viewed with suspicion any socialization or consolidation of the means of production whatsoever. It almost automatically entailed increases in the scale of economic organization of the juridical complexity of economic activity, and increases in the need for public sanctions and controls of formerly extra-political spheres of society. The only solution that Tocqueville could envision for this threat of industrialization while working on *Democracy in America* was to stress the need to "discover a means (associations or otherwise) that could do business without agglomerating so much capital."[6] The first developments which aroused his anxiety were not the Saint-Simonian and Fourierist conventicles but the large-scale corporations and investment operations of the July Monarchy and the demands for public sanction to encourage further development. When one fearfully viewed all state organization of public welfare, banks, corporations, the public debt, and rapid growth itself, as signs of critically dangerous overcentralization of social power, socialism presented itself in more reflective moments less as a revolutionary economic system than as a logical stage in public administration.

This, it seems to me, was the framework in which Tocqueville voted against both the systematic subsidizing of the railroad system in the July Monarchy, and the right to work in the Second Republic. He conceived of ideal economic, like social and political, organization primarily in terms of association, in terms of the direct participation of unspecialized equals in unspecialized structures. The

6. Yale Mss C.V.g: notes for the *Démocratie*, paq. 9, cahier 1, p. 4.

individualism embodied in the *Code Napoléon* was sufficient to form the public framework for human relations. It is clear that Tocqueville considered economic growth as something tolerable but hardly worth his talent. An ant-hill egalitarian socialism, redistributing claims on national wealth, became part of the range, if not of the logic, of imagined possibilities. A truly libertarian society institutionally and ideologically geared to planned accelerated productivity was simply unimaginable.

The most important effect of Tocqueville's failure to seize on the division of labor as a decisive historical tendency was not that he did not collect his data into a "tendency." Rather, he vaguely sensed a multitude of dangers to both social equality and liberty and responded with anguish to each inegalitarian warp in the emerging society. Perhaps the greatest casualty of this reaction was simply that he felt no need to pursue its possibilities, or, as Tocqueville would have had it, its tendencies. Tocqueville was never willing to place centralization in the same neutral analytical position as political democracy or equality. He was willing to educate himself and his generation to accept democratization as inevitable, because it was only through understanding all its potentials could one overcome potential threats to the things he prized. Only through democratic institutions could the problems incurred by democracy be resolved. But he indicated no such multiple potential in large-scale organization. If, unlike democracy, liberty and centralization were a priori antagonists, nothing was to be gained for liberty by studying different potential models of centralized administration. There is nothing in Tocqueville's writings to indicate that there was more than one possible "bureaucratic behavior."

Tocqueville, in fact, became progressively more anti-bureaucratic in each of his works. The sense of balance in his evaluation of centralized administration in the *Democracy* of 1835 was already gone in 1840. By 1856 Tocqueville's tone had become positively bitter. The *Ancien Régime* dropped its spare and anecdoteless argument to comment on the lifeless mediocrity of bureaucratic thinking and writing. It not only disparaged centralization as politically pernicious and administratively ineffective, but its agents were characterized as apolitical and illiberal by temperament. Their colorless, monotonous, apolitical statistic-gathering propensities were an occupational disease and an intellectual debasement.

The only alternative to administrative centralization was administrative decentralization, the only antidote to bureaucratized populations was voluntary association. Where bureaucracy increased, association decreased; where administrations regulated, liberty diminished; where large-scale institutional loyalties increased, small-scale loyalties disappeared. While later observers could inquire if authority and association could constitute interdependent but autonomous spheres of thought and action in all societies, Tocqueville's analysis related them as mutually exclusive conditions.

This rigidity toward large-scale institutions was also expressed in a persistent suspicion of the process of urbanization. Demographic agglomeration, with its concomitant organization and specialization, was the co-variant of institutional agglomeration. The fact that the rootless, unstable, violent, urban poor were also the preponderant element in the urban environment tended to make Tocqueville think of the city as another negative, exceptional, and monolithic element in modern society. This perspective may have been especially sharp after 1848,[7] but it was a long-term sociological assumption. Concerning his own country Tocqueville had noted in preparing *Democracy in America* that "the barbarians of the fourth century are in our cities."[8] Urbanization was therefore a footnote to Tocqueville's social outline of both Europe and America. But it was an insidious presence. It made many of his conclusions problematic because it again ran directly counter to his providential egalitarian fact. Tocqueville specifically placed the city outside his analysis of democracy in America along with the poor, the Negro, and the Indian. The American city in 1835 was considered to be even more violent and alienated than its European counterpart, and Tocqueville forecast the formation of a large armed force specifically to restrain it. Cities were durable expanding sources of permanent inequality. The democratic republics of America would soon be threatened by the size and above all the nature of their urban populations.[9]

European cities also were breeding places of violence. Their urban industrial environment was conceived to be

7. In the quiescent 1840's Tocqueville spoke against the fortification of Paris on the grounds that it would disfigure the image of the city as the libertarian capital of Europe.

8. Yale Mss, C.V.b, paq. 13, cahier 1, pp. 28–29.

9. *Democracy in America*, 256. While still in America Tocqueville had written, "unlimited democracy particularly dangerous in the big cities" (Yale Mss B.II.b: general notes for the *Démocratie*). But the nature of Tocqueville's analysis and its appearance in a footnote lead me to believe that Tocqueville's remarks on American cities were occasioned by the same New York race riot of July 1, 1834, that was the basis of one of the central chapters of Beaumont's *Marie* (Chapter 13, "The Riot"). The incident caused widespread discussion in Europe over the threat to America posed by urban riots.

totally inegalitarian. "From this foul drain," Tocqueville wrote of Manchester, "the greatest stream of human industry flows out to fertilize the world. Here humanity attains its most complete development and its most brutish; here civilization works its miracles, and civilized man is turned back almost into a savage."[10] Tocqueville also relegated this industrial city to the realm of exceptions. But again the cost to his analysis of the future was paid as much in his assessment of the relative importance of urban to rural environment in industrial society, or of urbanization to democratization, as in his understanding of the potentialities of cities. Where even less sensitive eyes could glimpse cities of parks, boulevards, and vistas, Tocqueville could see only the reinforcements of the proletarian army. Urbanization was less a process, with exciting possibilities for humanity, than it was a vast sewer of poverty, inequality, and violence, the sewer of civilization's discontents. Tocqueville assumed that the proletarians could only be neutralized through provincial majorities or controlled by the threat of an army. Violence might be avoided but not degradation and alienation. Given this psychological outlook, socialism could seem nothing less than a marriage of proletarian hostility to state centralization, with liberty as the nuptial sacrifice.

Beneath Tocqueville's hostility to the processes of the impersonal, rational aspects of modernization was not, I believe, a systematically conceived set of economic and social axioms. He was too tentative and too empirical in his approach to have worked out a systematic view of modern society, much less to base his defense of the present on its

10. Tocqueville, *Journeys to England and Ireland*, 107–108.

efficiency or productivity in terms of other systems. He seems rather to have formed, in the years before he wrote *Democracy in America,* a vision of a small property-owning free market and capitalistic economy as the assumed society of the future. It was the socio-economic counterpart to the individualist social equality that he observed in America and France, characterized by two normative traits, small-scale entrepreneurship and unspecialized labor. It is no wonder that Tocqueville and Beaumont had so large a psychological stake in any evidence for the tendency toward equality of scale of enterprise as well as landholding when they wrote their early works. The speculative spirit and rapid economic growth itself was viewed with grave suspicion.[11] If the scale of human organization and voluntary association were mutually exclusive, if every technological, political, and economic development favored concentration, then humanity was destined for servitude in the long run, with or without the abolition or modification of the rules of proprietary ownership. If the supreme social power, on the other hand, could voluntarily maintain, sustain, or even create a network of institutions alongside theoretically supreme authorities, as Tocqueville himself had noted in scattered cases, then bureaucracy and association need not be mutually exclusive.

Just as Tocqueville narrowed the libertarian range and tendencies of large-scale organization in politics, he also narrowed the limits of integration of the nonpossessor into a social order dominated by a democratic value system. At

11. See Tocqueville to Theodore Sedgwick, Aug. 14, 1854, in *Newly Discovered French Letters,* ed. Richmond L. Hawkins (Cambridge, Mass., 1933), 203; conversation, May 17, 1853, *Correspondence and Conversations with Nassau William Senior,* ed. Simpson, II, 37.

the heart of Tocqueville's dilemma about the place of industrialization and poverty in the modern world was his ambiguity concerning the dimensions of the democratic revolution and the ultimate social meaning of equality of conditions. From the outset of his intellectual career Tocqueville had accepted equality as a natural terminal point for social evolution and, all things considered, the only just one for mankind. In *Democracy in America* he posited it as more than natural and just. He called it historically inevitable and providentially established. God and History were called upon not just to reinforce the importance of equality in the eyes of his audience but to place the question beyond the realm of possibilities.

In his original portrait of democracy, at least two positive characteristics seemed assured. They were security of property and its ever more equal distribution. This juridical security and distributive economic equality guaranteed that irremediable poverty and permanent social inequality would both be unknown. Men might become increasingly dependent upon the state but their independence and power vis-à-vis *each other* seemed guaranteed by his very definition of equality. There would be a greater propensity to extend the rights of society in a multitude of things at the expense of the sphere of individual initiative, the right of individual property, the continuous division of private property, and the economic and social independence and mobility implied in this right were safe.

Since the increasing independence of man from man was the propensity, even the disease of modernization, the increasing dependence of man upon the state was *the* social question for Tocqueville. He was to thrust to one side social facts such as inequalities and dependency between social classes which would draw men's attention toward increasing rather than decreasing the role of the state. He tended either to deny any permanent dualism between independent and dependent social classes or to relegate them to inevitable or exceptional spheres of the social order. In periods of crisis or quiescence, any increase in aid to the improverished or dependent minority had to be weighed against the threat to individual independence implied in any general extension of the role of the state. Whatever could not be accomplished through individual or associational action outside the control of the state intensified the threat of democratic despotism.

On the other hand, Tocqueville was never prepared, like many of his contemporaries, to consider that some permanent stage between social dependence and independence was possible in a democratic society. The new conception of dignity based on equality affected all relationships involving authority and obedience. General dependency relationships were henceforth equated not only with degradation, but self-imposed degradation. Tocqueville illustrated this idea through examples drawn from the relationship between individuals and public authority, but it was equally applicable to all social relations: "From the moment when this notion of liberty has penetrated deeply into the minds of a people, and has solidly established itself there, absolute and arbitrary power is no longer anything but a material fact, a fortuitous situation. Each person embodying an absolute right unto himself, it follows that the sovereign will can rightfully emanate only from the union of all wills. At this stage obedience has lost its moral character, and there is no longer a middle term between the proud and manly virtues of the citizen and the base compliances of the slave."[12]

Authority that was not based on reciprocity and temporary contractual obligation was henceforth inherently degrading. Dependency clearly continued to exist in human relationships. The real social question of 1848 in France concerned groups who were neither physically dependent, like children or the invalid poor, nor psychologically dependent, like the traditional contented domestic. It involved those who were already psychologically independent, hostile "clients" who regarded charity as degrading and who were capable, above all, of varying degrees of violent opposition to their condition.

The conditions of the poor were never articulated with the care that the analyst of equality of conditions bestowed on the elites. At critical moments Tocqueville recognized that the pauper-worker-criminal-revolutionary continuum was not an accurate description of the nether world. As this or that manifestation of behavior and attitudes among the poor swung into Tocqueville's focus, his denotation of their characteristics altered. At times he considered them as part of an acquiescent culture of impoverished dependency, at other times as a culture of criminal activity, and at still others a culture of revolutionary hostility. The result was not delineation and comparative analysis on the basis of two or three subcultures but a kind of fluid portraiture. Where there was no diagnosis there could be no prognosis.

Even granted that Tocqueville could foresee no stable society that was not founded on the institution of private

12. Tocqueville, *Oeuvres* (M): *Ancien Régime*, I.

property and individual appropriation of wealth, what was to be the future relation between the organized rich and the organized poor? Tocqueville was prepared to offer solutions to social alienation based on personal and voluntary networks when the vocal portion of the urban working class was increasingly demanding institutional support. In the crucial question of the function of the state, the chosen instrument for the transition from slavery to freedom was judged illegitimate within the context of metropolitan France. In 1848 the mobilized working classes did request the sacrifice of both money and pride, and the legislature refused both. But they asked it in a novel way, through the progressive income tax and the right to work. They sought to use the agency of the state as a mechanism of redistribution of accumulated wealth, and as a regulator of the economy so as to guarantee their status as producers regardless of fluctuations in the economy. It was a different form of sacrifice of pride than Tocqueville had envisioned, since it implied that wealth was created and guaranteed by the society as a whole and should be responsive to temporary social and economic imbalances. It was an attack on the very pride of independence from the state as Tocqueville had conceived it in 1840. Those who possessed were asked to conceive of the existing distribution of wealth as simply part of a social balance sheet.

Within Tocqueville's definition of democracy the principle of equality was the inevitable foundation of modern societies. Tocqueville spoke of a variety of political structures that were compatible with a democratic social structure. A liberal or despotic political order was equally part of democracy's logic of possibilities. A single economic structure on the other hand was built into the assumptions of his sociology before 1848; when he realized that a democratic social structure might permit a variety of economic as well as political structures, his response was different. The values of political democracy, of individualist ethics, and of classical economics had been studied to see whether they could be made safe for liberty. But the unprivileged classes remained at the end of Tocqueville's intellectual development what they had been at the beginning—a penumbra of beings, neither free nor enslaved, neither dependent nor independent, neither equal nor unequal. Yet, unless a whole sector of the economy could be eliminated from industrial society or until the society made the required adjustments to integrate this element into the community on the basis of a mutually accepted principle of claims and rights, the democratic revolution would continue. Tocqueville's own vision of a final democratic social structure not yet come into being depended on this integration.

In a sense the fate of Tocqueville's prophetic reputation in the course of the past century and a half is proof of the dependency of his prognosis on the fate of this question. Despite hagiographers' claims that Tocqueville was being misunderstood, it was less the short-sightedness of later generations than the diminished relevance of his concerns to theirs which caused Tocqueville's influence to decline toward the end of the nineteenth century. His influence as a prophet of the mass age probably never stood higher than in the decade following his death, when Europe was accommodating itself to the introduction of universal manhood suffrage. In England, where the introduction of the franchise to the lower classes was the result of a long public debate, Tocqueville came as close to being recognized as the universal authority on the nature and future of democratic societies as any single writer. Yet, by the time of the reform bill debates of 1884, Tocqueville's name had almost disappeared from political discussion. His fate elsewhere in Europe and America was similar to that in England. His reputation as a pioneer in the study of American society and of the French Revolution was recognized, but the general consensus of the world of 1900 was that he no longer spoke as a contemporary.

The basic reason for the increasing irrelevance of Tocqueville's prognosis was essentially his vision of the arrival of the classless, atomized society. Succeeding generations saw that the extension of universal suffrage did not bring an age of "masses." Under the impact of industrialization, wealth was not radically redistributed, and social positions as defined by birth, religion, or occupation seemed a more empirically significant fact than the rhetoric of equality and of social mobility. The omniscience of the democratic principle seemed belied by the facts. Historians of contemporary Europe continued to write of classes. Tocqueville had overdramatized the social and moral power of the process of democratization. Political democracy and political bureaucracy were not accompanied by economic equality and diminution of political or associational life. Taking Europe as a whole, Tocqueville had also vastly underestimated the staying power of traditional hierarchies and the growing power of new ones even in the midst of plebiscitary regimes. Moreover, he had underestimated new social facts, which ran counter to his providential fact: revolutions were not frequent in pre-1914 Europe, but the social facts of inequality and alienation were strong enough to sustain the ideology of a social apocalypse among political parties and social movements throughout Europe. Only among a small remnant of pessimistic literary conservatives concerned with the intellectual and social decadence of modern man did Tocqueville's vision of the mass society seem to retain its cogency as a prognosis of cultural decline.

Tocqueville was a victim not of misconception or misunderstanding, but of a general consensus about social reality. Edward Bernstein's famous critique of Marx's prognosis might have been paraphrased by a Tocquevillian "revisionist" prior to World War I, had such a species existed: classes did not tend to disappear, great distinctions of wealth did not tend to disappear, intermediary associations between the individual and the state increased, ethnic and religious identities intensified, intellectual creativity expanded, the arts flourished luxuriously and creatively, and messianic ambitions abounded. Even the bedrock assumptions of *Democracy in America*, aside from security of property, were highly questionable at the beginning of the century. The divisive ties of race and nation were not disappearing into the great bond of humanity. Rather, the articulation of ethnic and racial hostility grew in most of the European continent. The education of the masses in Europe and the creation of a national consciousness was often predicated on an historic or racial struggle against a variety of historical enemies, both oppressors and subordinates.

Another of Tocqueville's footnotes became the theme of a central drama. Speaking of the tendency of democratic customs toward mildness, in *Democracy in America* he had concluded that as nations became more like each other they became more compassionate. But if a democratic people placed another outside the pale of reciprocity the most frightful cruelties might be inflicted without arousing their feelings. In 1840 this kind of human inequality seemed confined to the periphery of the European world and doomed to extinction. The indifference to Gobineau's doctrines in France a decade later offered little room for reconsidering that conclusion. By 1900 the doctrine of the radical inequality of races gained increasing respectability in Europe, while outside Europe inequality seemed to be enshrined in the increasing tempo of imperialism after 1880. By the end of the nineteenth century it would have been difficult to decide on the basis of available evidence whether increasing equality or subordination were more providential.

None of these counter-egalitarian manifestations in social development were completely hidden beneath the surface in Tocqueville's own lifetime. He had in fact illuminated their existence and persistence in every society that he had studied, and at every phase of his intellectual development. From his arrival in America through the last note written for the study of the French Revolution he had not only acknowledged the persistence of social inequalities but had often accepted it almost fatalistically, exhibiting the very quality he abhorred most in intellectual analysis. If Tocqueville regarded the Negroes as a permanently unassimilable race in America, this was only a specific example of a more general tension in his perception of social change. Despite the fact that his general model of human relationships asserted a tendency toward identity, mobility, and interchangeability, his descriptions of specific human groups time and again implied the existence of relatively unchanging social relationships. The most striking example of this was his discussion of race relations in America. But the unassimilability of Negroes and Indians in a white society was only a specific example of a much more inclusive intellectual reflex. Even groups with no difference of skin color were regarded as inherently dangerous to any culture if they reached a given, though unstated, proportion of the dominant culture. They were in this condition not only dangerous, but relatively alien and disruptive of the major culture. If Tocqueville threw out Gobineau's theory of biological determinism for group behavior, he accepted long-run tendencies of the same phenomenon without ever describing the conditions in which these characteristics would tend to remain or to disappear. And the lower such a group ranked in his value system the less susceptible of integration they appeared to him. Thus, while Tocqueville rejected the biological monocausality of Gobineau's racism, he was willing to accept the term as applying to ethnic or linguistic groups, with all of the connotations of permanence implied by the term. "I believe absolutely none of it," he commented to Beaumont on Gobineau's theory, "and yet I believe that in each nation, whether it comes from the race or rather the education of centuries, there is something very tenacious, perhaps permanent, which ties into all the events of its destiny and can be observed throughout every turn of fortune, in every epoch of its history."[13]

He would not allow Gobineau to predict the decadence of peoples who were carriers of his own political values or

13. Letter of Tocqueville to Beaumont, Nov. 3, 1853 (*Oeuvres* (M): *Correspondance Tocqueville-Beaumont*, III, 164).

those whose political values he wanted to affect. But other human groups did not fare as well. At one point or another this durability thesis was applied to the Irish, Russians, and Germans. American democratic culture, for example, was not only white, but Anglo-American. In the 1830's Tocqueville saw the Irish as a disruptive and degenerating force in American life, a permanent source of crime and voluntary pauperism that threatened to undermine the society embodied in the culture of the puritan founding fathers. Twenty years later he was even more shocked by the spectacle of hundreds of thousands of Germans flocking across the Atlantic and retaining their language and social cohesion. It reinforced his earlier conviction that the rapid introduction of nonmembers of the English "race" was the *greatest* problem faced by America. It was the one which, more than the problem of color, made the success of her democracy problematic, since new races were creating a new and divided people unlike the one that had been united at the end of the eighteenth century.[14]

Even in America, then, the problem of "massification" seemed threatened by the durability of social character. If one adds the unassimilability of the racial and national nether world to the unassimilability of urban industrial groups and the unassimilability of activities in society demanding functional hierarchies, democracy as defined

14. See *Du système pénitentiaire*, appendix on pauperism; *Democracy in America*, 256n; Tocqueville to Beaumont, Bonn, Aug. 6, 1854, in Yale Mss D.I.c and *Oeuvres* (M): *Correspondance*, III, 229; Tocqueville to Sedgwick, Aug. 14, 1854, Aug. 29, 1856, and Oct. 14, 1856, *Newly Discovered Letters*, ed. Hawkins, 202–203, 220, 222. Nonwhites were considered too far outside Anglo-American society to be agents of internal decomposition.

by Tocqueville was faced with more than a dilemma. It threatened to be engulfed in a sea of social differentiation. The historical basis for this dilemma seems clear. Tocqueville, as was analytically imperative, chose two societies as his basis for generalization about democracy, America and France. Within these societies he chose to use the independent middle class as his ideal type and to systematically exclude or quarantine all dissonant data. Starting with the cultural, linguistic, juridical, and economic homogeneity and convergence within both these groups he could build a model of social reality expressed as a general tendency of all societies. But the step from elaborating the internal logic of a social process to describing the probable future of society was a psychological imperative for the political man in Tocqueville. Democracy was not simply an historical process, it was the key to understanding *the* historical process—or, in Tocqueville's terms, the will of providence. This was a bold and dramatic step, but valor precluded discretion. Is it any wonder that the negative data of races, classes, and inequality, banished to irrelevancy by analytical choice, came rushing back like furies into history? If Tocqueville had really intended to describe the process of modern development, he required what he did not reveal: a systematic theory of social change. To describe the demise of inequality as providential or to describe its persistence as permanent, both of which Tocqueville did, although on different occasions and in different proportions, were avowals of defeat. They were confessions of defeat not because they contradicted each other, but because each, even taken separately, led away from the problem of social change. They could not supply any explanation as to why a particular relationship of inequality disappeared, persisted, or developed, why any relationship of equality did the same, or what were the probabilities of integration in a social system.

It should be evident that Tocqueville's description of social development has seemed truly pertinent only to a limited area within certain societies in a small part of the globe, and for a few decades of human existence as yet. He presumed the universal acceptance of the principle of equality as a regulating principle of social action. He presumed the nation-state in which one had already arrived at an egalitarian community, the formation of a national culture, the breakdown of institutions based on blood relationships and permanent social distinctions, the formulation of a universal law and impersonal administration. Tocqueville's thought blossomed in societies with high employment rates, extended welfare programs, reduced ideological politics, and diminished cultural or ethnic conflict. In this context his warnings against the subtle destruction of social independence and associational life find echoes among commentators on contemporary society. And against his portrait of the mass age, most contemporary prophecies seem narrow and naïve by comparison.

Bibliographical Note

I

THE various references to manuscript materials, printed works, and background literature mentioned in this book[1] may be supplemented by the extensive bibliographies and descriptions of manuscripts in the studies of Pierson (see also the 1959 abridged paperback edition, published by Doubleday), Gargan, and Drescher cited in the introductory chapter of this book, in both the Bradley and Mayer editions of *Democracy in America*, and in Bernhard Fabian's *Alexis de Tocquevilles Amerikbild* (Heidelberg, 1957).

On the printed works of Tocqueville, the major collection is the *Oeuvres complètes*, edited under the direction of J.-P.

---

1. This note, slightly altered, is taken from *Tocqueville and Beaumont on Social Reform*, 218–222. All books referred to here by name of the author alone may be located in the index under the author's name along with the page on which the full title appears.

Mayer (Paris, 1951–   ). Its scheme of publication is described by Charles Pouthas in *Alexis de Tocqueville: Livre du centenaire 1859–1959* (Paris, 1960), pp. 35–43, and in the Mayer and Lerner edition of *Democracy in America*, p. 776. A list of the volumes published to date is included at the end of the bibliographical note. The Beaumont edition of Tocqueville's *Oeuvres* still remains useful for sections of Tocqueville's works not yet covered by the new edition.

Recent English translations are now available for almost all of Tocqueville's major works and most are both reliable and readable. In addition to the Mayer and Lerner edition of *Democracy in America* (1966), there are Tocqueville's *Journey to America* (New Haven, Conn., 1960), and his *Journeys to England and Ireland* (New Haven, Conn., and London, 1960), both edited by Mayer and translated by George Lawrence. On *The Old Regime and the Revolution* there is the translation by Stuart Gilbert (New York, 1955), which could be checked against the older translations of Reeve and Bonner. John Lukacs has translated large parts of Tocqueville's unfinished sequel to the *Old Regime*, as well as Tocqueville's correspondence with Arthur de Gobineau, in *The European Revolution and Correspondence with Gobineau* (New York, 1959). Mayer has also edited a translation of *The Recollections of Alexis de Tocqueville* (New York, 1949). Only Tocqueville's correspondence remains to be fully translated. Many of the Beaumont edition letters were published in 1862 in *Memoir, Letters, and Remains of Alexis de Tocqueville*. The *Correspondence and Conversations of Alexis de Tocqueville with Nassau William Senior*, ed. M. C. M. Simpson (London, 1872), is being re-edited for publication in the *Oeuvres complètes* as volume 2, or volumes 2 and 3, of Tome VI, *Correspondance Anglaise* (texte etabli par J.-P. Mayer et Hugh Brogan; introduction et annotation par Hugh Brogan).

A full-length critical study of Tocqueville's life is long overdue, but one may profitably consult R.-P. Marcel, *Essai politique sur Alexis de Tocqueville* (Paris, 1910), and A. Redier's *Comme disait M. de Tocqueville . . .* (Paris, 1925), or, in English, Mayer's *Alexis de Tocqueville* (the up-dated Harper Torchbook edition of 1960), and the essay by Gargan, *De Tocqueville* (New York, 1965).

On the philosophical affinities and background of Tocqueville's thought one should consult Luis Diez del Corral's *La Mentalidad Politica de Tocqueville con especial referencia a Pascal* (Madrid, 1965). Jack Lively's *The Social and Political Thought of Alexis de Tocqueville* is an indispensable introduction to Tocqueville's thought. It can be supplemented by Marvin Zetterbaum's, *Tocqueville and the Problem of Democracy* (Stanford, Calif., 1967), the unabridged version of Pierson's *Tocqueville and Beaumont in America*, Thorsten Sellin's introduction to the new edition of *On the Penitentiary System in the United States*, the works of Gargan, Lawlor, and Drescher, and the numerous articles cited in the notes.

Because Tocqueville scholarship is so lately revived, one can only begin to point to a corpus of sustained critical literature on his thought. Until now the main task has seemed to be descriptive, a perspective reinforced by the fact that so vast a portion of Tocqueville's papers has just begun to see the light of day. The recent balanced studies by Lively, Herr, and Richter give evidence that the need to champion an unrecognized genius is no longer in tune with reality.

At least as important as the growth of Tocqueville studies themselves has been the use of Tocqueville's insights by a host of writers in the most diverse fields. Many of these authors are cited in the recent bibliography of *Democracy in America* (Mayer and Lerner), and the list continues to expand rapidly.

Further discussions of previous scholarship and contemporary research problems not mentioned in the notes include: Gargan, "Some Problems in Tocqueville Scholarship," *Mid-America* (January 1959), Jurgen von Stackelberg, "Bemerkungen zur Sekundarliteratur über Alexis de Tocqueville," *Romantisches Jahrbuch*, VI (Hamburg, 1956), 183–190, Drescher, "Tocqueville's Two *Démocraties*," *Journal of the History of Ideas* (April–June 1964); Bernhard Fabian, "Die sogenannte definitive Ausgabe von Alexis de Tocqueville's *Démocratie en*

Amérique," Archiv für Kultur-geschichte (1955), 37:358–63; F. Pergolesi, "Appunti sulla storiografia politica di Alexis de Tocqueville," *Sociologia* (Milan) (October–December 1959), 4 (4): 547–609.

On particular facets of Tocqueville's thought and influence see *Alexis de Tocqueville: Livre du centenaire*, with essays by M. Allix, C. Pouthas, P. Bastid, Luis Diez del Corral, G. W. Pierson, M. Beloff, L. Monnier, F. van Kalken, H. Baudet, P. Moreau, P. Renouvin, M. Degros, M. Reinhard, and R. Rémond; the articles by H. G. Nicholas and J. F. Sutter in the *Revue International de Philosophie* (1959), XIII, 49; Mayer's introduction to *Democracy in America* (1966).

The remaining entries are listed alphabetically. R. E. Angell, "Tocqueville's Sociological Theory," *Sociology and Social Research* (1941–42), 26: 323–33; R. Aron, "La definition libérale de la liberté II, Alexis de Tocqueville et Karl Marx," *European Journal of Sociology (Archives de sociologie Européen)* (1964), 5: 159–89; D. Bagge, "Tocqueville et le renouvellement de la science politique," *Politique* (April–June 1961), 14: 5–22; N. P. Barth, *Die Idee der Freiheit und der Demokratie bei Alexis de Tocqueville* (Zurich, 1953); L. Bergsträsser, "A. de Tocqueville, Kritiker und Verteidiger des Demokratie," *Der Monat* (March, 1950), II (18): 608–20; P. de Boisdettre, "Tocqueville et Gobineau," *Revue de Paris*, A. 66 (1959), 10: 96–106; T. Brunius, *Alexis de Tocqueville, The Sociological Aesthetician* (Upsala, 1960); C. Burckhardt, "Alexis de Tocqueville," in *Bildnisse* Frankfurt, 1959); *Catalogue de l'Exposition. Hommage à Alexis de Tocqueville, 1805–1859, organisée à la Bibliothèque nationale, 1959* (Paris, 1959); J.-J. Chevallier, *Les grandes oeuvres politiques, de Machiavel à nos jours* (Paris, 1949); E. Chichiarelli, "Alexis de Tocqueville e Arthur de Gobineau . . . ," *Nuova Revista Storica* (1941), 25: 312–22; M. Einaudi, "Epilogue," *The Roosevelt Revolution* (New York, 1959); D. S. Goldstein, "Alexis de Tocqueville's Concept of Citizenship," *Proceedings of the American Philosophical Society*, Vol. 108 (1) (February 1964), 39–53; M. Horwitz, "Tocqueville and the Tyranny of the Majority," *Review of Politics* (July 1966), 28:

293–307; A. Jardin, "Tocqueville et l'Algérie," *Revue des travaux de l'Académie des Sciences morales et politiques,* 115 A. (1962), 61–74; Jardin, "Tocqueville et la décentralisation," *La Decentralisation,* VIᵉ colloque d'histoire, Aix-en-Provence, les 1ᵉʳ et 2ᵉ décembre, 1961. Publications des Annales de la Faculté des Lettres, Aix-en-Provence; H. L. Lang, "Tocquevilles Entwurf der amerikanischen Literatur—Ein Problem der vergleichenden Literatur-geschichte," *Libris et Litteris, Festschrift fur Hermann Tieman* (1959); M. Lerner, "Tocqueville's *Democracy in America:* Politics, Law and the Elites," *Antioch Review* (Winter 1965–66), 25: 543–63; A. Martel, "Tocqueville et les problèmes coloniaux de la Monarchie de Juillet," *Revue d'histoire economique et sociale* (April 1954), 32: 367–88; P. Martelli, "A. de Tocqueville e il liberalismo della Restaurazione," *Humanitas* (March 1958), 13: 219–22; J.-P. Mayer, *Les voyages de Tocqueville et la genèse de sa sociologie politique* (Paris, 1957); M. Meyer, *Der Begriff der Freiheit im Denken Alexis de Tocquevilles,* Diss. phil. (Zurich, 1955); M. Meyers, "Venturous Conservative: On Tocqueville's Image of the Democrat," in *The Jacksonian Persuasion* (Stanford, Calif., 1957); C. Pouthas, "Le Corps électoral de l'arrondissement de Valognes au temps de Tocqueville," *Mémoires de la société nationale académique de Cherbourg* (1961); L. Monnier, "Alexis de Tocqueville et Auguste de la Rive à travers leur correspondance," in *Mélanges offerts à M. Paul-E. Martin* (Geneva, 1961); H. O. Pappé, "Mill and Tocqueville" *Journal of the History of Ideas* (April–June, 1964); T. H. Qualter, "John Stuart Mill, Disciple of Tocqueville," *Western Political Quarterly* (December 1960), 13 (4): 880–89; H. Read, "De Tocqueville on Art in America" *The Adelphi* (October–December 1946), 9–13; R. Rémond, *Les Etats-Unis devant l'opinion française, 1815–1852,* 2 vols. (Paris, 1962); R. Resh, "Alexis de Tocqueville and the Negro: *Democracy in America* Reconsidered," *Journal of Negro History* (1963), 48: 251–59; M. Richter, "Tocqueville on Algeria," *Review of Politics* (July 1963), 25: 362–98; M. Richter, "Debate on Race: Tocqueville–Gobineau Correspondence," *Commentary,* (February 1958), 25: 151–60; R. Ruland,

"Tocqueville's *De la Démocratie en Amérique* and *The Education of Henry Adams*," *Comparative Literature Studies*, XI (3) (1965); A. Salomon, "Tocqueville 1959," *Social Research* (Winter 1959), 26 (4): 449–70, reprinted in *In Praise of Enlightenment* (New York, 1963); J. Sirol, "Tres profetas politicos franceses, Bodin, Tocqueville, Saint-Simon," *Revista de la Facultad de Derecho de Mexico* (October–December 1963), 13 (52): 981–1009; F. R. Sylvain, "Relations d'Alexis de Tocqueville avec les Catholiques américains," *Revue de l'Université de Laval* (1957), II (6): 471–86; A.J.P. Taylor, "De Tocqueville in 1848" in *From Napoleon to Stalin* (London, 1950), pp. 61–66; R. Virtanen, "Tocqueville and the Romantics," *Symposium* (Spring, 1959), pp. 167–85; Virtanen, "Tocqueville on a Democratic Literature," *The French Review* (1941–42), 23: 214–22; P. West, "Literature and Politics II: Tocqueville on the Literature of Democracies," *Essays in Criticism* (1962), 12 (3); A. Zanfarino, "Alexis de Tocqueville politico e moralista," *Studii politici* (January–March 1958), 5 (1): 3–44; M. Zetterbaum, "Tocqueville: Neutrality and the Use of History," *American Political Science Review* (1964), 58: 611–21.

II

TOCQUEVILLE'S COMPLETE WORKS
(Gallimard edition)

Alexis de Tocqueville: Oeuvres complètes. Edition définitive publiée sous la direction de J.-P. Mayer, sous le patronage de la Commission Nationale pour l'édition des oeuvres de Tocqueville (Paris: Gallimard, 1951–   ). This definitive edition, now in the process of publication, has been published so far in the following tomes and volumes, which are cited in the notes as *Oeuvres* (M) followed by a distinguishing part of the title.

Tome I.   *De la démocratie en Amérique*, 2 vols. (1951). Introduction par Harold J. Laski.

Tome II.	*L'Ancien Regime et la Révolution*, 2 vols. (1953). Introduction par Georges Lefebvre. Volume II is subtitled *Fragments et notes inédites sur la Révolution*. Texte établi et annoté par André Jardin.
Tome III.	Vol. I. *Ecrits et discours politiques* (1962). Texte établi et annoté par André Jardin. Introduction par J.-J. Chevallier et André Jardin.
Tome V.	Vol. I. *Voyages en Sicile et aux Etats-Unis* (1957). Texte établi, annoté et préfacé par J.-P. Mayer. Vol. II. *Voyages en Angleterre, Irlande, Suisse, et Algérie* (1958). Texte établi et annoté par J.-P. Mayer et André Jardin.
Tome VI.	Vol. I. *Correspondance anglaise: Correspondance d'Alexis de Tocqueville avec Henry Reeve et John Stuart Mill* (1954). Texte établi et annoté par J.-P. Mayer et Gustave Rudler. Introduction par J.-P. Mayer. Vol. II. (To be republished as part of the *Oeuvres*). *The Correspondence and Conversations of Alexis de Tocqueville with Nassau William Senior*. Texte établi par J.-P. Mayer et Hugh Brogan; introduction et annotation par Hugh Brogan.
Tome VIII.	*Correspondance d'Alexis de Tocqueville et de Gustave de Beaumont*, 3 vols. (1967). Texte établi, annoté et préfacé par André Jardin.
Tome IX.	*Correspondance d'Alexis de Tocqueville et d'Arthur de Gobineau* (1959). Texte établi et annoté par M. Degros. Introduction par J.-J. Chevallier.
Tome XII.	*Souvenirs*. Texte établi, annoté, et préfacé par Luc Monnier (1964).

Translations from the French are the author's unless otherwise indicated.

Index